Praise For Self Publishing: Writing A Book And Publishing Books and eBooks For Yourself And Others

From the days of Guttenberg's invention of movable type down to the present time it has never been easier to turn a manuscript into a book. Among the growing library of 'how to' books for the aspiring self-published author, one of the newest is also one of the best: "Self Publishing: by entrepreneur and author A. William Benitez is a 200-page compendium of thoroughly 'user friendly' instructions that are based upon Benitez personal experience and expertise as a self-publishing author with both print editions and ebook titles to his credit. Beginning with reasons for writing and self-publishing a book, Benitez' "Self Publishing" manual offers step-by-step instructions and experience-based commentary on how to plan the book; the value of and tools for backing up your writing; the vital market-based importance of title selection; the reasons and tools for creating and editing drafts as you prepare your manuscript for publication; obtaining an ISBN; creating a competitive book cover; creating your own book marketing web site; and more. Of special note are the chapters on setting up a publishing services company; self publishing options such as CreateSpace; ebook options like Kindle and other options for eBook publishing; and creating effective screen shots. Informed and informative from beginning to end, "Self Publishing" is an ideal and instructive introduction that is especially recommended for novice authors seeking to publish print and/or ebook editions of their work writing books of all genres, topics and subjects in today's highly competitive marketplace.

The Midwest Book Review
http://www.midwestbookreview.com

This workbook is an amazing publishing guide for any author who wants to do it all him or herself.

Patricia Fry, author, speaker, editor
www.patriciafry.com

At last, a clear an comprehensive guide through the self-publishing process, using free and/or inexpensive software.

Barbara Florio Graham, author and publishing consultant,
www.SimonTeakettle.com

Based on his experience, Bill Benitez guides us through twenty organized and mandatory steps towards the successful self publishing of your book.

Self Publishing: covers all the questions we might ask ourselves, starting with 'Why should I write that book?'

The book is abundantly illustrated with screen snapshots of an easy-to-use and inexpensive book formatting software. The author also tells us how to choose the best title for a book, the importance of buying the right ISBN, and much more.

This easy-to-read guide will take your book to its final goal: publish while saving time doing the research and avoiding the pitfalls of self publishing.

C.K. Omillin
www.omillinplanet.com

If you want easy to follow instructions on how to use Page Plus or if you are interested in Print-on-Demand or eBook publishing, this is a great resource! The free tools that Bill recommends are worth the price of the book.

Leslie Korenko author of three Kelleys Island history books
www.KelleysIslandStory.com

Self Publishing:

How To Publish
Your Print Book or eBook
Step by Step

A How-To Workbook From
Positive Imaging, LLC

A. William Benitez

Self Publishing:

How To Publish Your Print Book or eBook Step by Step
Revised Edition

A How-To Workbook From Positive Imaging, LLC

A. William Benitez

Published By
Positive Imaging, LLC
9016 Palace Parkway
Austin, TX 78748

Cover Photos by Erin Molloy Photography

All rights reserved. No part of this book may be reproduced, transmitted or downloaded in any form or by any means, electronic or mechanical, including copying, photocopying, recording or by any information storage and retrieval system without written permission from the author, except for the inclusion of brief quotations in a review.

Copyright   2018   A. William Benitez

ISBN: 9781944071561

Contents

	Preface - Why and How This Book Was Written	9
	Introduction	13
1	**Reasons For Writing A Book**	17
2	**Why Self Publish Your Book**	19
	Traditional Publishers	
	Vanity Publishers	
	Subsidy Publishers	
	POD Publishers	
	Self Publishers	
3	**Planning The Book - The Outline**	23
	The Plan	
	The Outline	
	Your Objective	
	Knowing Your Market	
	The Final Format	
4	**Backup Your Writing**	27
	The Habit of Backing Up	
	Backup Defined	
	Backup Tools	
5	**Choosing The Best Title For Your Book**	31
	Why Are They Advertising	
	Keywords and The Keyword Tool	
	The Book Cover Font	
6	**Creating The First Draft**	33
	Personal Stories	
	Using The Outline	
	Don't Edit While Writing	

7	**Tools To Use For Writing Your Book**	35
8	**The Discipline of Writing**	37
9	**Editing Your First Draft**	39
	A Great Editing Tool	
10	**Layout, Formatting, and Typesetting**	43
	About PagePlus X4	
	All In One Desktop Publishing Studio	
	Quality Publishing	
11	**Using PagePlus X4 For The Print Ready File**	47
	Master Pages	
	Built In Applications To Help With Layout and Formatting	
	Ready To Begin Formatting and Layout	
	Creating The BookPlus File	
	Beginning The First File - Chapter, Section, or Part	
	Formatting Paragraphs	
	Reviewing The Transfer of Text Content To PagePlus X4	
	When Not To Use WritePlus	
	Using PagePlus X4 To Format Books For Others	
	Creating A Table Of Contents	
12	**The Free Options**	81
	OpenOffice Suite	
	Scribus	
	GIMP	
	Photoscape	
	Inkscape	
	NVU	
	About Free Software Applications	
13	**Getting Your Own ISBN**	87
	Bowker, The Official Source in the USA	
	Save With Ten or More	
14	**Publishing With Createspace**	91
	Creating The Cover For Your Book	

15	**Creating and Publishing For The Kindle**	103
	Creating A Kindle eBook	
	For Open Office Users	
16	**Creating and Publishing eBooks For Smashwords**	109
17	**Creating and Publishing eBooks - Other Options**	113
	Your Own eStore	
18	**Creating a Cover For Your Book**	117
	The Book Size	
	Creating Text For The Spine	
	Using The Createspace Cover Creator	
19	**Creating a Web Site To Market Your Book**	145
	WebPlus X4 and X5	
	NVU and Kompozer	
	Website Tonight	
	Yahoo Small Business	
	Using Web Sites and Blogs For Free Content	
	Web Site Hosting	
20	**Creating Sharp and Clear Screen Shots**	161
21	**Final Notes**	165
	Doing It All Yourself	
	Using Createspace As A POD Printer	
	Createspace Professional Services	
	PagePlus X4	
	Book, Ebook, or Both	
	Marketing Your Book or Ebook	
	Changes From Screen Shots	
	Another Benefit of POD	
	Publishing Services Company Caution	
	Glossary	169
	About A. William Benitez	179
	Disclaimer	181
	Other Books From Positive Imaging, LLC	183

Preface

Why and How This Book Was Created

As a self publisher and the owner/operator of a small publishing company, I am constantly reading about writing and publishing. This is essential because operating a one-person publishing services business requires knowledge and a significant variety of skills. Gaining professional level skills demands extensive reading, training, and practice.

To some that means attending classes, seminars, or even webinars. Unfortunately, I have never been a good student and find the entire classroom or group learning idea problematic and, since I lack patience, sometimes frustrating. I usually learn on my own time by reading, watching video tutorials, listening, and most importantly, examining the work of others.

Even while getting my MCSE (Microsoft Certified Systems Engineer) certification for network administration, I managed it using only home study. I can't imagine doing self publishing any other way. To glean as much knowledge as possible, I have collected a nice size library of books on the subject and many of them were quite helpful as I worked on establishing my own methods.

Not every writing and self publishing book I purchased was useful, some approached worthlessness but even those had some tidbit of value. On the other hand, some of these books were extraordinary and I learned a great deal from them. Some of them I read cover to cover while others I just went through reading the parts of interest to me.

The better books sometimes provided too many choices. Probably most people would find that a benefit but I prefer to learn one good method that works and then use that knowledge to improve upon what I have learned.

I also visit a variety of blogs and join writing and self publishing groups to gain even more information and learn what other writers and self publishers are doing. Like the books, some blogs are invaluable while others not so much. You have to read and evaluate the ones that are of real help and drop the others. As they say, you have to kiss a lot of frogs before finding a prince.

It may sound odd to complain about too many choices but I believe that instead of several ways to do things, a person starting out needs one proven method that works consistently. And, that method must be described in careful detail so the instructions can be followed by anyone regardless of their level of experience. Details on alternative methods may be interesting and even useful, but can also be confusing.

While working on my first couple of books I learned valuable lessons which helped me develop the method I now use to write and publish books. This book is based entirely on that method and includes detailed descriptions of the software tools I use to create the final draft, the print-ready file, and the companies I deal with during the process. Every step for successfully creating a quality book using this method is covered.

To ensure consistent quality, I stick to what I know works every time and in this book I pass that along to you. You can follow in my steps as I create and publish this book. You will see each step and know exactly what I am doing and what application I use to write the content, edit the book, layout and typeset, and process the file for final printing and marketing preparation. Since I do my own editing, I also describe my editing methods in detail.

Once the editing is complete you will follow the layout or typesetting process. For this I recommend a specific tool, not because it is the best or the only one available, but because it is easy to use, works well, and most importantly it is inexpensive. Even though this application comes with a comprehensive user guide covering all its potential functions, this book will take you through the steps related directly to the creation of an excellent print-ready file.

My method is not the only one and some writer/publishers prefer other methods and tools. Those methods may work just as well and I'm not implying that my method is best, but I can guarantee that if you follow my instructions carefully you will end up with a quality book. I know it works because I created almost a dozen books using exactly these methods and tools.

My method can be hard work and requires a serious effort to learn the steps and do the work. Not everyone is willing to make the effort. A common problem I notice in blog comments is the lack of interest in learning how to work with the necessary tools. Some would-be self publishers seem to be looking for someone to simply answer all their questions with little effort or investment on their part and won't take the time to learn.

It does take time and effort to learn but there are books and tutorials available for almost any software product you use to prepare your book. The companies that print the books have excellent tutorials to take you through every step. In addition to this book, make use of all the information you can find and learn how to use these products. It is an essential part of becoming a successful self publisher.

I still remember when I started using Photoshop. It was a nightmare and I had no idea how to proceed and no concept of layers. Now I produce my own covers and improve the covers produced by others using Photoshop. It didn't happen overnight but it did happen by reading instructions, watching tutorials, reading books, and practicing with the software. If you really want to self publish without paying others hundreds or even thousands to do work that you can do yourself, take the time to learn.

NOTE: I mentioned making covers with Photoshop because I have made several covers using this great application. I did not use it for the cover of this book nor do I discuss how to use it to make a cover because I have tried to work with inexpensive or free tools that will do the job. Both PhotoPlus X4, the application I used to create the cover of this book, and PagePlus X4, the desktop publishing software that I used to layout and format this book, are priced under $20.00 each as a download from Amazon.com. The two applications together comprise only a fraction of the cost of Photoshop.

Since the original edition of this book it's now possible to lease Photoshop for only $9.95 a month and always have the latest version. That's what I do now and suggest the same to others.

Notes and Ideas

Introduction

Seeing the title of this book, your first thought was probably, "Wow, just what we need, another book on self publishing." There are already so many books on the topic that one could easily get discouraged about writing another one. But, for someone who regularly lurks and sometimes contributes to self publishing blogs, it quickly becomes apparent that there still are many unanswered questions. Perhaps it is better to say that there are an adequate number of answers but sometimes they are clear only to someone with experience but little help to those lacking basic knowledge and skills.

No single book can answer all the questions about self publishing and this one doesn't either. What you will find in this book is a straight-forward, proven method, to write and self publish your book. All the answers you'll find here are based entirely on my first-hand experience, not on research, surveys, or interviews with anyone else. I'm not implying that those are not valid methods. I'm simply stating that this book is not based on them. I believe that first-hand experience conveys assurance based on the direct knowledge of the author and therefore a certainty that the methods described have been tested. The reader is then assured that he or she will experience a successful outcome by following the instructions.

Every step involved in successfully self publishing books is covered in detail beginning with the idea, creating the outline, the draft, the final manuscript, the print ready file, proofs, and the book. With a little effort and study you should be able to design and format the interior of your book, and even create several ebook versions. Those who have some graphic software skills, or are willing to learn them, should be able to create an attractive book cover.

The first chapter covers the reasons for writing the book which vary significantly among writers. There is no single reason for writing a book, nor any wrong reasons. Wanting to do it is reason enough.

Chapter two defines self publishing and describes the many benefits gained by publishing your own books.

Chapter Three helps you to plan your book from original idea through a detailed outline to help you organize and then write your book in a professional and logical way that readers will find easy to read and understand.

Chapter Four is about what I consider one of the most critical aspects of any kind of writing today—data backup. How many horror stories have you heard of people who have typed an entire book into a computer and then lost it all when the computer crashed or the flash drive they were using was lost or damaged? Unfortunately, it is a common occurrence and this chapter will help you avoid that misfortune.

Chapter Five explains the importance of creating a good title for your book. It covers how to use strong, searchable keywords so your title ensures online sales. This chapter also helps you make certain the title tells prospective buyers exactly what the book includes and how it could benefit them.

Chapter Six describes how to make use of your outline as a detailed framework for creating a first draft that covers every topic in your book in sufficient detail and provides an excellent basis for your final draft leading to an accurate final manuscript.

Chapter Seven covers the difference between office productivity software applications and publishing software and how to best use each of them. Word processors and text editors are the perfect tools for creating both drafts and final manuscripts but I believe they fall short when used for formatting or typesetting a book. In this book you find complete details about excellent, inexpensive, and highly effective software for publishing.

Chapter Eight includes many ways to discipline yourself to write regularly so your book or books can be finished quickly. It covers several ways used by writers to make certain they write everyday.

Chapter Nine is all about editing your book. While working with an editor is a good idea, it is possible to edit the book yourself following the tips in this chapter. Self editing can be difficult especially if you find it hard to part with redundancy, but it can be done with patience and the tools suggested in this chapter.

Chapter Ten moves into the art of layout, formatting, and typesetting. It describes the potential disadvantages of using office productivity tools for creating print ready files and introduces you to PagePlus X4, an inexpensive, quality publishing application that makes the job easier.

In Chapter Eleven you learn how to use this highly effective publishing software, to create your print ready file from your final manuscript. This chapter is detailed with an extensive number of clear screen shots directly from PagePlus X4 files for this book and describes every step involved in this process.

Chapter Twelve introduces you to the a variety of free yet high quality software products that are safe to download. It describes the capabilities of the best of them and includes great advice for ensuring any free software you download will be safe, not contaminated with viruses or spam.

Chapter Thirteen explains the value of an ISBN, how critical it is to have your own for any book you publish, the various parts of the ISBN, and includes instructions on how to get your own ISBN. For those planning to publish more than one book, there is information on saving money by purchasing multiple ISBNs.

I believe Createspace is the best and easiest to use POD printer online today, especially for inexperienced self publishers. Chapter Fourteen is devoted entirely to using Createspace to successfully publish and market your books.

Kindle may not have been the first ebook but it did stoke the market for them. Kindle ebooks sell by the hundreds of thousands and in Chapter Fifteen I cover exactly how to create and publish an ebook for the Kindle.

Kindle is definitely not the only good ebook publisher. Smashwords is also an excellent place to publish ebooks and in Chapter Sixteen shows you exactly how to create ebooks for the extensive Smashwords market.

Chapter Seventeen covers other ways to publish ebooks. Clickbank is an effective and efficient method but you can also create and market ebooks yourself and this chapter teaches you how.

If you don't believe you can create your own book cover, Chapter Eighteen may dispel that belief. This chapter contains two excellent methods to create your own quality book covers and explains every step in detail.

A web site is an important tool for selling books and Chapter Nineteen includes a number of web sites that are easy to create and introduces free and inexpensive tools to build them.

This book is filled with concise screen shots that help me explain every step of the writing, editing, and publishing process. It's difficult to capture clear, sharp, screen shots for a printed book so in Chapter Twenty I show you exactly how you can capture high quality screen shots for your books.

As a book of this kind progresses a writer learns more and makes changes to the content to improve the book. Some of those changes come at the last minute when the book is ready for printing. For that reason most of the books I write have a section of Final Notes and Chapter Twenty-One contains the final notes for this book.

This book does cover preparations for marketing but promoting books is an extensive and critical topic and really merits an entire book. Many books deal directly with ways to promote and market your book and in Chapter Twenty-One, Final Notes, I name what I consider one of the latest and best of those books. I suggest you use it, or some other book you believe covers marketing well, to help you promote your book successfully.

One

Reasons For Writing A Book

Your reasons for writing a book can set the tone for the entire writing process. It probably isn't possible to list all the reasons why someone would want to write a book. Some write for the sheer joy of it and the potential for making money either doesn't enter into the thinking or isn't an important consideration.

Money or not, most write books because they have something to say or something they would like to teach others. Some write because they wish to entertain others with good stories. Others are simply interested in telling everyone about their life or that of family members. There really are no wrong reasons to write. Wanting to write should be enough reason for anyone.

Profit is certainly a good motive for writing a book and writing is a great way to make a living but profit may not be your motivation. If writing a book and publishing it is your dream, then that is exactly what you should do and this book will help you get it done.

> *For me writing has always been about making money. I really enjoy the writing but my goal has always been to profit from what I write. For that reason, I write about my knowledge and experiences and over the years I've managed to teach people about various topics. In spite of the joy it gives me, I have never considered a writing project simply for the joy of it. But that's just me and you may be completely different. That doesn't make your book any less valuable.*

You may have your own idea for a book from which you could profit. Perhaps you have a skill that others wish to learn and your book about it could help them. It may be a hobby that others would enjoy or a small business idea. If you have some basic knowledge that seems popular, what you know could make a good book. It could be a book about a specific niche. This book, for example, is in the self publishing niche.

Like some others, this book is entirely based on first-hand experience. It was written after the work described on the pages was actually performed successfully many times. Some writers use their first-hand experiences to write valuable and informative books that help readers do many things. It quite possible that you have a wealth of valuable knowledge that others would like to read about and comprise great topics for books.

Niche books can also be written based on thorough research. Some writers spend many months and even years learning about a topic and then write about it. This can be the basis for excellent books but simply isn't the way I work.

Only you can decide what method to use. You might even consider associating with someone who has a marketable skill to write a book about those skills and how others can learn them and perhaps even make money from following the instructions in the book.

Any combination of these methods also work. It's not unusual to see a book with more than one author. In these books both writers bring something to the project and together they create an interesting, cohesive, and valuable book. Some hire ghost writers because they have all the knowledge necessary but simply lack the skills to write it down in an organized and comprehensive manner. A ghost writer can use the information to write the book and the individual takes the credit.

Once you have decided to write your book, regardless of the method used, you must determine how to get it published so everyone can read about your skills or knowledge.

Two

Why Self Publish Your Book

For years the most common reason for self publishing was the frustration of rejections from traditional publishers leading some writers to choose self publishing instead of simply giving up.

Writers still receive rejection letters but things have changed over the years. Now even writers who have been published by traditional publishers are turning to self publishing to increase their profits and maintain more control over their books. There are many reasons for this change including writers gaining more knowledge of the publishing business but mostly the advent of an active POD (print-on-demand) market place has negated the need for a major front end investment to publish a book.

Traditional Publishers

There are other reasons including traditional publishers always keeping the lion's share of the profit. They seem to believe since they do the editing, typesetting, printing, warehousing, distribution, and marketing, thereby taking all the risks, they have a right to a much larger share. While there is some truth in that, unless a writer is famous and the traditional publisher is almost guaranteed the sale of hundreds of thousands, even millions of books, they do little to market the books they publish.

In most cases the writer has to venture out to market his or her own books or they simply don't sell. So, while it is true that editing, typesetting, printing, warehousing, and distribution are costly, there is little question that the most important, difficult, and costly aspect of publishing a book is the marketing. Since the marketing is so difficult and costly and the traditional publisher is unwilling to do much of it for your book, it seems only fair that you should get a larger share of the profits to make up for your expenditures and time in marketing the book. Since that isn't the case, self publishing becomes even more attractive.

Don't be confused as to what really constitutes self publishing. Some costly and problematic methods of getting a book published are often confused with self publishing. These methods are best avoided as they are poor substitutes. One of those methods is appropriately named Vanity Publishing.

Vanity Publishers

This dubious business came by its name based on the way they appeal to the vanity of writers who want to have their work published at any cost. These vanity presses contract to publish an author's work at an excessive cost and they do create a book for the writer. However, these companies do nothing to help the writer market the book. They have no concern regarding the sale of the book since they make their profits entirely from fees paid upfront by the writer. Most of these writers wind up with a garage full of books they can't sell. And, if they do sell any books, their profit is miniscule because of the high cost.

Subsidy publishers

This is somewhat different but is still quite costly for the writer. Subsidy publishers create and distribute books under their own imprint and take payment from the writer to print the book. They are more selective than Vanity publishers who accept any book regardless of quality but they still depend heavily on fees from writers for their profits. Unlike vanity publishers, subsidy publishers distribute the book under their own imprint and they keep a portion of the rights to the book and all the copies in their possession. Plus, the writer has little if any control over the production of the book, the editing, or the cover design.

POD Publishers

POD stands for print on demand and calling these companies publishers is a bit of a misnomer since many of them serve as printers for self publishers. They do provide a better service then vanity or subsidy publishers but can still be quite costly if you purchase all of their services to create your book. They do allow you much more involvement and control over the production of your book. You may still be dependent on them if you don't have the skills necessary to create your own print ready and cover files.

Some print on demand publishers offer a free ISBN and while that certainly sounds like a bargain, free ISBN numbers remain the property of the printer/publisher. You will not be able to take your book elsewhere if you decide to change printers for any reason.

The advantages of some print on demand publishers, especially for those with extensive skills, is that in addition to control over the final book, you get immediate access to valuable distribution channels without making a major investment in books. Everything is setup for you as part of the publishing arrangement and that means your book goes to market quickly and all you have to do is market it to increase sales.

Self Publishers

The last and best method is real self publishing. Exactly what is self publishing? If this is something you want to do, it's important to have a good idea of exactly what it is in addition to how best to handle the process. In its most basic definition, self publishing is the publication of any book or other media by the author of the work, without the involvement or investment of a traditional publisher. This is most commonly done at the expense of the writer.

Most people believe that self publishing is a recent phenomenon but actually is it as old as publishing itself. In the early years of publishing most books were self published because they were written, printed, and sold by the owner of the printing press. Over many years the path of writers and printers separated and the publishing industry developed. Until recently those roles were seen as separate and self publishing was considered unusual and to some maintained a stigma that has been largely overcome by many quality self published books.

Even though many still think of it as unusual, many great authors got their start as self publishers. To help you understand how significant self publishing has been over many years, the next paragraph is a long list of writers who got their start as self publishers.

Self published authors include William Blake, Virginia Woolf, William Morris, James Joyce, Stephen Crane, E. E. Cummings, Deepak Chopra, Benjamin Franklin, Zane Grey, Pat Ingoldsby, Rudyard Kipling, D. H. Lawrence, Thomas Paine, Edgar Allan Poe, Ezra Pound, Carl Sandburg, George Bernard Shaw, Upton Sinclair, Gertrude Stein, Henry David Thoreau, Walt Whitman, and Mark Twain. This is definitely an impressive list covering many years and long before the recent popularity of self publishing.

By self publishing your book you may join this long and distinguished list of successful writers. But, even if you don't, you could produce a useful book that will entertain or educate hundreds, perhaps even thousands of people. In the process you will be doing something enjoyable. What more could you ask.

Notes and Ideas

Three

Planning The Book - The Outline

The Plan

Step one for any book, after the basic idea appears, is to create a clear and concise plan. Knowing why you are writing the book is important to developing a viable plan. If you are writing simply for your own enjoyment and to share some knowledge or an experience with anyone who may be interested, with little concern for potential profit, then the first step should be creating an outline for your book.

The Outline

You begin this outline by writing down all the major topics you wish to convey to your readers. Put them all down without attempting to flesh them out or placing them in particular order. At this early stage, spending too much time on individual topics could cause you to lose focus of the main topics. After you have listed them all, organize them in the best possible order so that each topic logically follows the previous one.

Now is the time to flesh them out. Go back to each topic one at a time and add whatever thoughts come to you. There is no certain length for this and don't worry about structure. You are still at the thought development stage to cover as much as you can before actually beginning the writing. As you write down all these thoughts, new topics and ideas will come to you. Don't dismiss them; write them down as they come to you even if they belong elsewhere. You can move them later. The important thing at this stage is not to lose the thought. Read the section on creating and using an outline to see the simplest way to take full advantage of an outline to create your book.

Your Objective

If profit is the main objective of your writing, another method may be more appropriate for you. Once you know the niche or topic of your book, find the market for that particular niche. That is, determine whom will purchase your book and where you can find these prospects.

This is a critical step because if you are unable to locate readers interested in your topic, it may be that a niche doesn't exist or is so small as to make reaching it difficult and unprofitable. Since your intent is to profit from writing your book, this is a good time to revisit your concept and perhaps alter it for better marketability or perhaps abandon the idea and look for a marketable niche.

Knowing Your Market

While this book doesn't deal directly with marketing and promotion, the odds of a book selling are increased considerably if you know your market and write your book to fulfill their needs. This is not possible if you have no idea about those interested in your book and how to reach them.

While it may seem that this knowledge is about marketing and not writing or self publishing, it's just the opposite. This knowledge will help you write the book so it's of real value to your potential buyers and to create a cover that conveys a strong message indicating clearly that the information these book buyers want is in the book. This will make your book marketable and contribute to increased sales before you even publish.

The Final Format

In this early planning stage you must decide on the final format. Is it just going to be available as an ebook? Kindle is really popular but it doesn't work for some books that require a much larger page. There is a larger Kindle available but it is considerably more expensive then the standard model or the Kindle Fire which is the one to which you should aim your ebook. There are other kinds of ebooks that work perfectly well even with letter size books. Learn more about publishing for the Kindle in chapter fourteen.

Is the book going to be available as a paperback? Are you going to come out with both paperback and ebook at the same time? Making these decisions should be part of your planning. All of these various formats and how to take full advantage of them is covered in other chapters.

> When I was going to publish my first POD book, which was a children's book my wife had written, I spent several hours at a large bookstore going through similar books. I must have looked through at least fifty different children's books to find out if there was some standard formatting that I should use for my first attempt at publishing a book. I learned something very interesting that day. There were no two books formatted the same way. There were some similarities but many more differences. The important thing was to make the book look professionally published and there were obviously many ways to do that.

There is an easier way for you to do the same thing using the Amazon.com web site. Just go to the site and search for books in your niche. Most of the books will have the look inside feature and you can take a look at the layout without going to a bookstore. You can even print out pages for closer examination. There are also some excellent books on the subject of book design. However, don't believe that you are stuck with one certain format as right or wrong. Strive to make your book original and professional and there are as many ways to accomplish that as there are publishers.

If you decide to read one or more books on book design or visit book design blogs, remember that the information you are reading is of value but not carved in granite. Your ideas also have value so use the information to learn the things that look obviously wrong but remember to be creative while maintaining professionalism. For an inexperienced self publisher it can be difficult to choose the correct format for a book. That's the reason studying the work of others is so helpful, at least while publishing your first book.

Notes and Ideas

Four

Backup Your Writing

Even though it may not seem directly related to writing or publishing, this could be the most important chapter in this book. If you ever spent hours, days, weeks, or months writing something you consider a masterpiece only to lose it because either your computer crashed or the flash drive you were using was broken, dropped, or simply lost, then you recognize the importance of well planned data backup.

The Habit of Backing Up

Before starting to write your book, develop the habit of backing up every time you sit down to create. The word habit is appropriate because it's critical that backing up your data become second nature. It needs to be as important as your writing. That may sound strange, especially to someone who loves to write, but all it takes to convince you is to lose an important manuscript because you have no backup.

> *Most new computers have methods to set up automatic backups so they take place without thinking about them. There are also various online methods you can setup to back up the data in your computer. These are good solutions to consider but personally I worry about the whole automatic thing. As an IT person responsible for the backup of four servers and a hundred computers, and somewhat of a computer geek, I'm still an old-fashioned guy who knows that "automatic" things sometimes get glitched up and fail to perform as planned. I handle my own backup using a regular schedule as described in this chapter. If you do op for one of those automatic, set it and forget it, methods, I strongly suggest that you monitor it regularly to make certain it is doing the job and have it send you regular email reports to ensure the backup has taken place. Check your backup content once a week but definitely not less than once a month.*

Data backup is critical and that's why it's included in a book on self publishing. In spite of how easy it is today, backup is still either ignored or misunderstood by a large percentage of computer users. Because computers work so well today people become complacent and wrongly assume that nothing can go wrong. This is complete folly because computers have problems no matter who makes them. Hard drives, the repository of all that valuable data, do go bad and destroy data in the process. Even those new netbooks and touch pads, whose hard drives are actually large flash drives, are vulnerable and can lose data. Regular backups can ensure that your writing is always safe.

Backup has been a critical function related to computer use for many years but there is much confusion about the term. To clarify the term and emphasize the importance of backup, let's start with a clear definition.

Backup Defined

A backup of data means to create a copy or copies of the data in question. The word copy means a second identical item. Therefore, backup means having a second and separate copy of data for safekeeping. If you don't have a second copy, you don't have a backup.

That certainly seems obvious but there are many computer users who work from flash drives or other external drives and keep all their files on them believing that they are protected from potential data loss.

Using an external drive is a great way to keep your files portable so you can take them anywhere but it is not a backup until you have created a second copy. To be a real backup, the file in the flash drive must be a copy of the same file in some other location.

> *My basic recommendation for backup involves three steps. The first is setting up the application that I am working on to automatically backup files every 10 minutes. For example, if you are working on Word it can be set to save as often as you choose but the default setting is every ten minutes and this is adequate. This ensures that if there is a glitch and the program stops functioning, I will have a file that is no more than 10 minutes old.*
>
> *The second step involves saving my files to a folder on the hard drive. Normally, I create a folder with part of the book name in the My Documents folder. For example a folder called SelfPublishing for this book. Within that folder I create subfolders for the draft, another one for any related information I want to refer to as I write. Any ideas that just pop into my head related to self publishing every day. After all, most of us are learning all the time. As I write each day I regularly save the file to the SelfPublishingDraft folder.*
>
> *The third step is to save the entire SelfPublishing folder containing all the related files to an external drive that is connected to my laptop with a USB cable. In addition to manually backing up the file I am working on to the external drive, I also use the built-in Windows software to create a full backup of my computer in case the hard drive goes bad. This full backup also goes into the external hard drive.*

Perhaps I am somewhat of a backup geek since I also backup my small external drive to a larger one in my office.

Is that overkill? Perhaps, but I don't think so. In addition to being a writer and publisher, I am a Microsoft Certified Systems Engineer (MCSE) and have run into many unfortunate individuals who lost all their data because they failed to back it up. It is a terrible feeling to lose even one page of writing but losing hundreds of pages is a disaster no one wishes to face. With just a little effort you can make all your writing safe from loss. On more than one occasion I have been quite glad to have good solid backups. I advise everyone to do the same whether it is writing, business, photos, video, or music. If you don't want to lose it, back it up.

Backup Tools

There are a variety of excellent and inexpensive backup tools available now. The best bet is a small external hard drive that connects to your computer either by USB or Firewire. These are quite fast and easy to carry. Flashdrives are popular but I discourage them except to carry a copy of a specific file. They are fine for transport but not safe for everyday work because they are easily left behind, lost, dropped, or stepped on. I have also seen them broken off accidentally while sticking out of a computer. This almost always renders the data inaccessible.

CD and DVD Writers can be used for backups but are not as convenient for everyday backups. On older computers you can still use floppy disks but I would avoid them since most new computers do not have floppy drives and they have fallen out of favor because of their slow speed and limited capacity.

Backing up your data to a secondary hard drive partition is inadequate unless you also backup to an external drive. While it's better than no backup, it is somewhat vulnerable because if the hard drive fails completely your backups will be gone together with the operating system.

Backup software is readily available and often comes with various external drives. However, most operating systems like Windows 7 come with backup software built in and it is quite adequate. The important thing is not what you use to backup but that you make it a habit every time you work on your book.

In addition to the options described above there is a long list of free data backup software programs. As with all free software, it's important to be careful when downloading and installing it. The safest way is to find your choice at the http://download.cnet.com web site. All of their downloads are safe to use.

For backing up files and folders my favorite is Karen's Replicator which is now available from CNET after the creator of this little jewel passed away. It has worked for me without fail for too many years to remember. It is easy to use with multiple backups and allows you to set them up to work automatically or manually and helps you keep track of them.

Notes and Ideas

Five

Choosing The Best Title For Your Book

A good title can contribute significantly to the successful marketing of your book. Take time to create a title that will be clear and easy to understand. Begin by making certain it relates directly to the content of your book. As simple as this sounds, it's often ignored. By simply perusing the title a potential purchaser should learn exactly what your book is about and something about the content. A brief title should be followed by a subtitle adding to the clarity but it shouldn't be essential and definitely not the sole explanation of the book content.

What Are They Advertising?

Ever noticed how, after viewing some TV commercials, you are left wondering what they were advertising? It's definitely not sensible to spend millions on a TV commercial that almost no one understands but it happens often. The same thing can happen to books and the effects are just as negative. Make certain your title is clear and concise and not only tells the reader what to expect but also entices them to look inside.

Even though your book may be sold online instead of in a retail book store, a good cover is still important. Actually, there are even more factors to consider, especially keywords.

Keywords and The Keyword Tool

Your title should contain searchable keywords directly related to your book's niche. Searchable means keywords that are searched for regularly, especially on Google. You can start by deciding what you believe is the best keyword for the niche you have selected. In the case of this book it was Self Publishing. Then you go to the Google Keyword Tool to find related keywords. You can find this tool at:

https://adwords.**google**.com/select/**KeywordTool**External

It's a simple tool that gives you valuable information. The main function is to help those who use Google Adwords ads but you can use it to learn about the popularity of words and phrases on Google search. The first time you use it you are required to enter a captha word to make certain you are a person and not some robot trying to glean information automatically. A captha is the code you must copy accurately to enter various sites. After going through that you need only type in the words or phrases you want to check out. The tool will not only give you information regarding the popularity of your word or phrase but also create a long list of alternatives and their popularity. These alternatives are especially helpful in creating subtitles.

> *To develop the title of this book I used this tool with the word writing and the phrase self publishing. The tool came up with many possibilities but three keyword phrases stood out and I felt they described the content of this book clearly and were also quite popular. The phrases were "self publishing", "writing a book", and "publishing books." I used all three in my title and subtitle and will also use them in the content and search engine listing for the web site for this book.*

In addition to the search popularity, check that the title isn't busy with confusing or difficult to read text. It should be clear at a glance whether on a web site or on a book store shelf. Don't hesitate to change it several times as you progress through the writing of your book and the preparations for publishing. You want a cover that will give you the best potential for a sale no matter where your prospective buyer sees the book.

The Book Cover Font

The title of your book is critically important but it will be of little use online if the font is too small to view clearly. A large font is important because the first view of your book online will be the small cover photo. It is just barely larger than a thumbnail and a title will only be readable if it is large enough. This is why a short title followed by a concise subtitle is so important. The title can be brief and as large as possible so it is easy to read while the subtitle is smaller but still readable, especially after it is clicked on.

> *A prime example of this is my Woodworking Business book. After doing many searches it was clear that the term "Woodworking Business" was searched for a great deal. I could have started my title with words leading in to woodworking business but I decided to use those two words and then clarify them with a good and sufficiently long subtitle. This worked out well because not only does my woodworking buisness book place high on Google and other search engines, it is consistently number one when searching Amazon.com books for "woodworking business" even though it brings up over sixteen hundred listings.*

> *Another important thing about my title is that the words "Woodworking Business" entirely dominate the cover of my book and show up really well even on small pictures on web sites or shopping carts.*

Six

Creating The First Draft

At this point you should have a fully fleshed out outline listing every topic and subtopic you want to cover in your book. If your book requires research, it should be completed by now. If you still need more research, finish that and bring the additional information into your outline so it is well organized before actually sitting down to write. Once you start you want it to flow with as few interruptions as possible. Questions may come up during the writing that require stopping to get answers but try to keep this to an absolute minimum.

That doesn't mean that you stop learning. As your book progresses, keep reading information of interest and maintain a notebook on everything you do relating to the topic. Ideas can appear at any time and from anyone. If new ideas on a topic arise while you are writing and they contribute to the topic, include them in the book.

Personal Stories

Add stories of personal experiences in how to books to help your readers develop a better understanding of specific topics or to emphasize your meaning regarding a specific point. These should be sprinkled throughout the book as they make reading more interesting and readers usually enjoy these experiences, especially if it involves learning from a mistake. Such stories convey your humanity and get readers interested in you.

Using The Outline

Use the outline to write your book. Don't just print it out and use it as a guide. Instead double space after each topic and then write on that specific topic as many paragraphs as it takes. Don't worry about the formatting during the writing. This is just a draft and requires only a normal style without special formatting. You should be thinking only about your topic, not about the final formatting of the book.

Don't Edit While Writing

Don't try to edit as you go along. Write down all your thoughts on a specific topic to make certain you give your readers an in-depth look at all aspects of the topic. Editing will come later but now you want to make certain that nothing is left out. Don't concern yourself about potential redundancies. Later, during the editing, you can eliminate them or even merge them to make one clear sentence or paragraph.

Complete the entire book using this technique. It allows you to go back to each topic and read through it after reviewing the outline of that chapter. Working within the outline helps you remember every detail you wanted to write about and keeps things relatively organized and this will help later with the editing.

Each reading of the outline will stir new thoughts to add to the chapter. Don't limit yourself to the outline. It is intended to help guide you through every topic you want to cover but if you have an idea for a chapter that isn't listed in your outline, put it down right away and continue writing. Then you can come back and flesh it out in full. This will add the thought in your outline to stir even more ideas.

This is your draft so don't hesitate to add anything that contributes to the value of the book. If you read a lot on your topic or perhaps blog about it, new things will come to mind and this will be even more solid information for your readers. Keep this up during the entire time you are writing your draft and it will increase the value and quality of your book.

Keep writing as long as possible at each opportunity. Try to get the entire draft done in the shortest time possible. This helps you get all your thoughts down and provides a solid and partially completed base to work from to create a final first draft.

Seven

Tools To Use For Writing Your Book

Don't get hung up on the idea that you need some fancy, high dollar software to create a good book. It's important to realize that the formatting of the book for publishing is completely different and separate from the writing of the book.

> *As a writer/publisher I like to keep up with what others in the field are doing. To do that I participate in self publishing blogs and email lists. This is a good practice because you can learn a lot from others. Not only have I found invaluable information that I could use in my publishing business but I also realized that some prospective self publishers use more difficult and costly methods to publish books. The most common problems arise when they use the same tool for writing a book and for creating the print ready file. While publishing my first book I experienced difficulties because of this and now I use office productivity tools for writing my books and publishing tools for publishing work, especially on books with complex layouts.*

Writing and formatting (typesetting) are two entirely different jobs and are best handled with different tools. You can use almost any word processor or text editor to write your book. The simplest thing is to use whatever word processor you already own.

Many of you have some version of Microsoft Word and that works fine for writing your book. If you have an older version, don't invest in the latest version because you believe it's necessary for your writing. For the preparation of files for ebooks, the older versions work better.

Purchasing the latest version of an office productivity suite is a significant and needless investment unless you are in a business where the latest features are of some importance. Even then, you can download the latest version of OpenOffice or LibreOffice Suites which are available free to anyone. Both do a good job and create files that are compatible with other office suites. It does require the additional step of saving as a matching file format but that is quite simple and well worth it to save the major investment in software.

You can also keep it really simple by using the Wordpad program that comes with every Windows operating system or the Microsoft Works that comes with some computers. These are perfectly adequate for creating a draft of your book. They may lack the bells and whistles that are available with Microsoft Word or OpenOffice Writer but you really don't need them to write a book. All you need is simple software that allows you to create a basic outline and cut/copy and paste.

If you do use Microsoft Word, WordPerfect, OpenOffice Writer or any other major word processor application, set it to the Normal style. Don't attempt to format your book as you are creating it beyond separating into chapters. Just use the word processor to create a plain vanilla version of your book so it is quick and easy to edit and make changes even involving reorganization.

> *Since I provide publishing services, I have the job of layout and typesetting of books for various writers. A problem I often face is that the writer has attempted to typeset the book as he or she is writing. So, I get a draft that is loaded with all kinds of formatting and styles that are problematic when I attempt to place them into my typesetting software. On more than one occasion it was necessary to copy the entire content of the book and then paste it into Notepad so all the formatting and styles are eliminated before moving it to my software. It isn't a big problem but it is a waste of the writer's time to do all that work and then have it completely removed. I definitely suggest using the Normal style when typing a draft on any word processing software.*

Remember that word processor applications are part of an Office Productivity Suite of software programs. They are designed for office productivity not for formatting books.

Eight

The Discipline of Writing

Set aside time to write everyday if possible. Write as much as you can during each writing session. Do your best to complete each separate topic before moving on to the next. You could lose valuable ideas by stopping in the middle of a topic instead of writing out thoughts while fresh in your mind. This will help the book flow and could add value to your book.

> *I set aside some time each day for writing. If you have family responsibilities, as many people do, it is essential to set aside a time when you can have some quiet. I suggest the mornings. Get up an hour earlier and start in before things get started for the day. You may have some time in the afternoon or evening but even if you don't you will have gotten in at least one hour each day.*
>
> *Even if you only do that on weekdays it will be five hours a week. Perhaps you can do more on the weekends. I work for at least an hour each afternoon and then try to do several hours on weekends. Develop whatever schedule works for you but stick to it so you can get your book completed.*

Keep writing in that way until you have filled out every single topic on your outline. During the process you may come up with additional ideas that fit into the topic or add to it. Be sure to write them down and fully flesh them out while they are fresh. Ideas are fragile and disappear in moments if you don't capture them when they appear.

Once you have gone through the entire outline and basically have a first draft, read the entire thing while the outline listings are still in the file. During this first reading check for the chapter listings. Identify the chapter headings and the content that will appear in each chapter.

Now protect this file. Save it as it is and then click Save As and give the file the name of the book or a part of the name and add the date. For example, for this book it could be selfpublishing_4_10_12. Once that file is saved, open the new file and carefully delete all the outline listings so all that remains is the book content with the chapter headings. This is your first draft and it should be saved and backed up.

> *Because of the importance of backing up your data, chapter four is devoted to that topic. However, it bears repeating because the single most important and often forgotten thing is that backup involves two copies of data. As simple as that sounds I find that many people use flash drives or other external drives to keep their data and simply work directly from those files.*
>
> *Data in any external drive is just as vulnerable as the data in your computer's hard drive and will be lost forever if the drive becomes defective. Always maintain at least two copies of all your important data in separate storage to protect yourself against data loss. Remember, that having two copies means that, counting the original file, you actually have three copies of your book.*

Once you have completed your first draft and removed the outline listing from it you are ready to begin editing. Even at this stage you can still add to the book if you learn some new and valuable information that contributes to the topic or helps readers to get more out of the content.

Nine

Editing Your First Draft

Is it essential to hire a professional editor to edit your book? The answer depends on various factors including how you feel about your writing. If you feel that your skills allow you to do your own editing, this may work well for you. Just remember that your familiarity with the content may cause you to overlook things that could improve your book.

Hiring an editor could pose two problems. The first is financial, good editors are often well paid so professional editing could require a significant investment. Such an investment, while wise, could be problematic for some writers causing the delay or even foregoing of publishing a book.

The second issue is your voice for the book. For me writing is a personal thing and having significant changes made is uncomfortable. For an editor to find and correct typos and grammatical errors is really a help. However, doing major rewriting could make it seem like the work of someone else and could be a serious problem. Naturally, how good a writer you believe yourself to be and how important it is to maintain your voice will decide the seriousness of the issue. If you do hire an editor, make certain he or she understands what you expect before the job is started.

You can edit the book yourself but it can be tricky. It isn't unusual for writers to fall in love with their words and resist giving up any of them. If you avoid this, there is a method to edit your own work successfully.

Step one of this method is to put your draft aside for a week or two. Then, read it carefully filling in any additional information that may come to you. New ideas may popup that add value to the content. Reading your draft carefully will shed light on issues, errors, or incomplete thoughts requiring explanation. Fix these mistakes and add anything that could increase the value of your book. Don't rush through this process because you could overlook important details your readers may find valuable. After completing this step, put the draft aside for another week before beginning the next step.

Step two is to read your book aloud. This helps you hear awkward phrasing. While doing this, pick up obvious errors but don't try for perfection during the first read. Once you have finished put it down for one more week and then go through it again slowly and carefully editing and filling in any last minute ideas you may have.

If you are unsure about any section or paragraph in a chapter, try reading through it backwards. Starting from the last word in a paragraph and moving backwards works because your brain is unaccustomed to the words in this order and misspellings and other problems often jump out.

> *It's amazing how the brain works. It becomes accustomed to something and simply won't see errors. During an art class years ago an instructor taught me to make a good drawing of a photo by looking at it upside down. Your brain does not recognize what it is in that form and therefore you draw what you actually see instead of what you remember. For example, if you are drawing a chair, you already have many preconceived notions of chairs but if you turn it upside down your mind forgets those preconceived notions and you draw exactly what you see and get a much better drawing. The same is true of writing. Since you never read backwards your mind will not be able to use its preconceived notion of the content and that increases the odds of finding mistakes.*

Waiting all those weeks may cause impatience or seem like a waste of time, especially if you are in a hurry to get your book published. Instead of wasted time, it is critical for a good editing job. If you don't put it down your mind will become accustomed to seeing errors and simply overlook them. Instead of improving your draft by correcting errors, you'll assume everything is correct and ready for printing and that could lead to a book containing many errors.

Yet another thing you can do once your book is fully organized is to read the chapters out of order. Start reading from a chapter in the middle of the book and then jump around to other chapters in some random order. Change the order of the chapters each time you read through the book. This could open your mind to errors that may not be picked up reading the book in the normal order.

I think most writers, including me, tend to be too wordy. Certainly you want to add to your first draft to make it clear, concise, comprehensive, and ensure that nothing was left out, but for the most part editing should involve removing words not adding them. Your writing must be precise and easy to read and understand. It is especially important to avoid redundancies. Repeating something when you are speaking to someone to make a point is one thing but repeating it in your writing, where someone can read it as often as they choose, is not a good idea. Not only because you may be wasting your reader's time, redundancies may also insult your readers intelligence and bore them. Also avoid passive sentences as much as possible. Try to stick with action sentences that involve doing. Keep the writing active and interesting for your readers to avoid turning them off of your book and any others you may write.

A Great Editing Tool

When you have finished what you consider the final edit, go to the web site http://grammarly.com and check out this service. Grammarly is a good, solid editing program that allows you to run chapters or the entire book. Even though you could run the entire book, run the chapters one at a time. The process will go quicker. Once you have completed each chapter of the book, then you may run the entire book to give Grammarly one final chance to pick up any errors.

I use Grammarly as an app for Word. Once I open the document I can enable Grammarly and it will check for errors. You can even use Grammarly while you are typing the first draft but I prefer to clean up my content as much as possible on my own and then use Grammarly for a final review.

If you know someone you respect and trust to edit your book, ask for help. If your budget allows, hire a professional editor. Even though it can get expensive, it will be less because you have already removed most of the mistakes.

The important thing to remember at this stage is that you want the final editing to catch errors and perhaps improve the organization or structure of the book. It is often true that an editor writes in a better style but if there are too many such changes, your book will no longer have your voice. Perhaps the best way to handle it is to make certain your editor understands that you want editing services not rewriting.

Once your book is written and edited and you are comfortable with the final manuscript, you can begin the formatting and typesetting. There are two ways to proceed to final book form and the choice of tool for this depends on whether you are creating an ebook or a paperback. If a paperback or both versions, the next chapter covers how best to proceed.

Notes and Ideas

Ten

Layout, Formatting, and Typesetting

You can use a word processing program to layout and format your book but, based on many posts on self publishing blogs, it seems to create difficulties for some self publishers. A number of those posts also reflect frustration converting word processor documents into a final print ready file. Some of that frustration stems from users lacking knowledge of how to perform complex tasks with a word processing application but much of it may be caused by attempting to use an office productivity tool for publishing.

If you are determined to use a word processor such as Microsoft Word or OpenOffice Writer to create your print ready file, a search on Google will bring up many books and tutorials on the subject. In books that I publish word processors serve only to create the draft and final manuscript not for the creation of a print ready file. I always recommend using what I consider the best tool for the job to ensure a quality book with as few frustrations as possible.

There are some software applications that can render excellent results for the layout and formatting of print ready files. Many of these are created and sold by Adobe with InDesign being one of the best known. While these products are ideal tools they have a couple of shortcomings. The most significant is a high price. If you don't already own these applications, a significant investment is required. The second problem is an extensive learning curve.

In spite of the high cost and long learning curve, if you are in a position to purchase a tool set such as those in the Adobe Creative Suite and take the time to learn to use it competently, the investment is definitely worthwhile. If these are beyond your financial means it doesn't mean you can't use a publishing application to create your book.

> *For my first POD self publishing attempt, I published a children's book written by my wife. The end result was good but it took several attempts to produce a pdf file that was acceptable to the printer. After that experience I decided to use a publishing software and quickly realized the high price was an obstacle.*

I searched for one that was reasonably priced and had a shorter learning curve and found PagePlus from a British company named Serif. I started using their X3 Version, upgraded to the X4 version, and recently upgraded to the X5 Version.

As it turned out the upgrade to the X5 Version of PagePlus was unnecessary. It does have some new features that may work well for other work but for book layout, format, and typesetting it was of no added value. Because of this I continue to use PagePlus X4 and highly recommend it to anyone wanting to create books. Not only is it a quality product but, at this writing, you could download both the application and the resources software from Amazon.com for less than $20.00. It is a large download (over 1.3 Gigabytes) so unless you have a fast connection you may want to purchase the disk version also available for under $20.00 when I last checked.

About PagePlus X4

PagePlus X4 has proven to be an excellent tool for layout, formatting, and typesetting books. It has features that make the entire job of assembling the final book file for printing much easier. It also makes it easy to do final editing and even the most complex changes to your book in the final stages.

In Chapter Eleven all the steps involved in using PagePlus X4 to create the final pdf file for your book are detailed including specific instructions and valuable screen shots to guide you.

In this chapter the many features of PagePlus X4 will be described in detail. As time goes by PagePlus X4 becomes an even better bargain. As this is written, Serif, the British company that makes and sells PagePlus, has just released PagePlus X6 and there is no doubt it is an excellent product as have been all the previous versions. At only $99.00 it is a great bargain and should be considered.

In spite of the bargain price of PagePlus X6, you can get a fully functional copy of PagePlus X4 that will do everything you need to publish any book for only $19.65. The software being used for this book is this exact downloadable version. At the time it was purchased for this book, from Amazon.com, the price was over $30.00 but it went down when the X6 version was released by Serif.

A complete description of PagePlus X4 and its features is included so you can see what a complete and valuable tool it can be to your self publishing and especially if you start a publishing services business.

Here are a some of the basic features of PagePlus X4. First, it allows you to create anything from address labels to brochures, books, newsletters, business cards and posters.

> You can create any type of document using dynamic guidelines, snapping, templates, and ready-made artwork with a immense range of publishing tools.

It's compatible with images, graphics, text files and your chosen print shop.

You can open and edit documents from anywhere with excellent PDF editing.

You can print high quality pages on desktop printers, at any size including double size prints.

All-In-One Desktop Publishing Studio

Using PagePlus X4 to create this book just scratches the surface of the potential of this software. The time being spent to include a more complete description of the features of PagePlus X4 is meant to help you understand The full value of this complete tool.

PagePlus X4 eliminates the need for special editing tools for pdf files. You can simply import any pdf file into PagePlus X4 and then manipulate it any way you choose. That includes editing, merging, adding, removing, changing their order, repurposing design elements, optimizing images, and protecting content.

If your book contains photographs you can enhance them right within the book file using the built-in Photolab application. It offers dozens of adjustments, corrections, filters, effects, and artistic styles. It also has an Image Cutout Studio so you can remove backgrounds. You can professionally correct photos, remove blemishes or scratches in a specific area, and edit or undo changes.

The built-in Logo Studio includes over 400 ready-made graphics that can be edited, combined, altered and changed to create an excellent logo for your new publishing services company.

While most of you will create your drafts and final manuscript on a word processing application and then import them into PagePlus X4, you can also create all your documents within this software. With the built-in WritePlus application you can create your entire manuscript and then it will automatically import into the actual book pages.

There are excellent design templates for almost any kind of document. All the templates can be edited and altered to give you exactly what your are looking for in your document. You can make use of all these tools easily with a customizable workspace and dynamic layout assistants.

Quality Publishing

Create press ready pdfs including full-color printing using RGB, CMYK, HSL, Pantone and spot colors. Save pdf with industry-standard PDF/X-1a settings including press marks, crop marks, and bleed areas. You can also add bookmarks, hyperlinks, and security to your pdfs.

You can design pdf forms that others can fill out electronically and Serif will email you their responses free of charge. And you can create pdf slideshows with page transitions, audio, video, interactive buttons,etc

Even though Serif has an excellent Web Site creation tool called WebPlus, you can create web sites using PagePlus X4.

All in all, PagePlus X4 is an excellent publishing tool at an extraordinary bargain price and the next chapter will take you through the steps of using it for publishing but it would be worthwhile to check out the many free tutorials that will help you get even more use of this valuable tool. You can find many tutorials at the main Serif web site at: http://serif.com .

At this writing Serif has stopped updating PagePlus. They stopped at X9. Any of the versions will serve you will and you can get bargains on older versions on Amazon.com.

Eleven

Using PagePlus X4 To Create The Print Ready File

If posts in self publishing blogs are any indication, Microsoft Word and OpenOffice Writer are the most commonly used applications for creating print-ready files. Many of these self publishers produce good books so it can definitely be done with these applications.

I have always preferred using the best tool for every job. While Word and Writer will work, they are office productivity tools, not publishing tools. I believe that publishing software is a better tool for preparing files for printing books.

Most use these office productivity tools because they already own them so they can avoid an additional investment. Since many publishing applications are quite expensive, the choice to use what you have is understandable. However, it's not necessary to forego using publishing software because of cost.

PagePlus X4, an excellent publishing software, is available at a low price and this chapter will illustrate, in detail, exactly how to use it to create a quality print-ready file that will be accepted by printers the first time.

PagePlus X4 does not replace office productivity tools. They still serve many important purposes. For one thing, they are an excellent writing tool for creating your draft and final manuscripts. They allow you to create an outline and then follow it as you write your entire book. You can cut, paste, and reshape your entire book until it is exactly as you planned.

Office suites allow you to double space your drafts so they are easy to edit and improve. Plus you can create indented bullets, numbered lists, tables and many other important aspects of your book. In spite of all this potential, the wise thing to do is make use of the office suite to produce your manuscript while avoiding excessive formatting. The actual tables, for example, should be created in PagePlus X4 or other publishing software.

Not only will the time spent formatting in the office application be wasted, it will also create problems as you transfer the content to the publishing software. Instead, set the style on your office application to Normal and use the publishing software to do all the specialized formatting

To make the process of creating a print-ready file with PagePlus X4 completely clear, many screen shots are included with detailed instructions showing exactly how the print-ready file for this book was created. Each step is described in detail next to the screen shot related to that step.

The first step is to open the PagePlus X4 application and this is done in the same manner as opening any other software from the Start menu or a shortcut on your desktop.

This is the opening screen and the arrow, representing the cursor, is pointing to **Start New Publication.** The other options are **Use Design Template, Open Saved Publication,** and **Import PDF file**. The first time you open the program you use **Start New Publication**. After that first time you will use **Open Saved Publication**.

If you already have a pdf version of your book, you can use the **Import PDF** selection to import it into the program. PagePlus X4 does an excellent job of importing pdf files.

In the next pages the various steps are described in the order already used successfully with eight books. It isn't essential to go through the steps in the exact order. You can change them around as you acquaint yourself with the PagePlus X4 application. The more you learn the more you will be able to make decisions that work best for you. Each time you open the program it will ask you to register. It is not required but once you register the message will stop coming up.

Using PagePlus X4 To Create Print Ready File

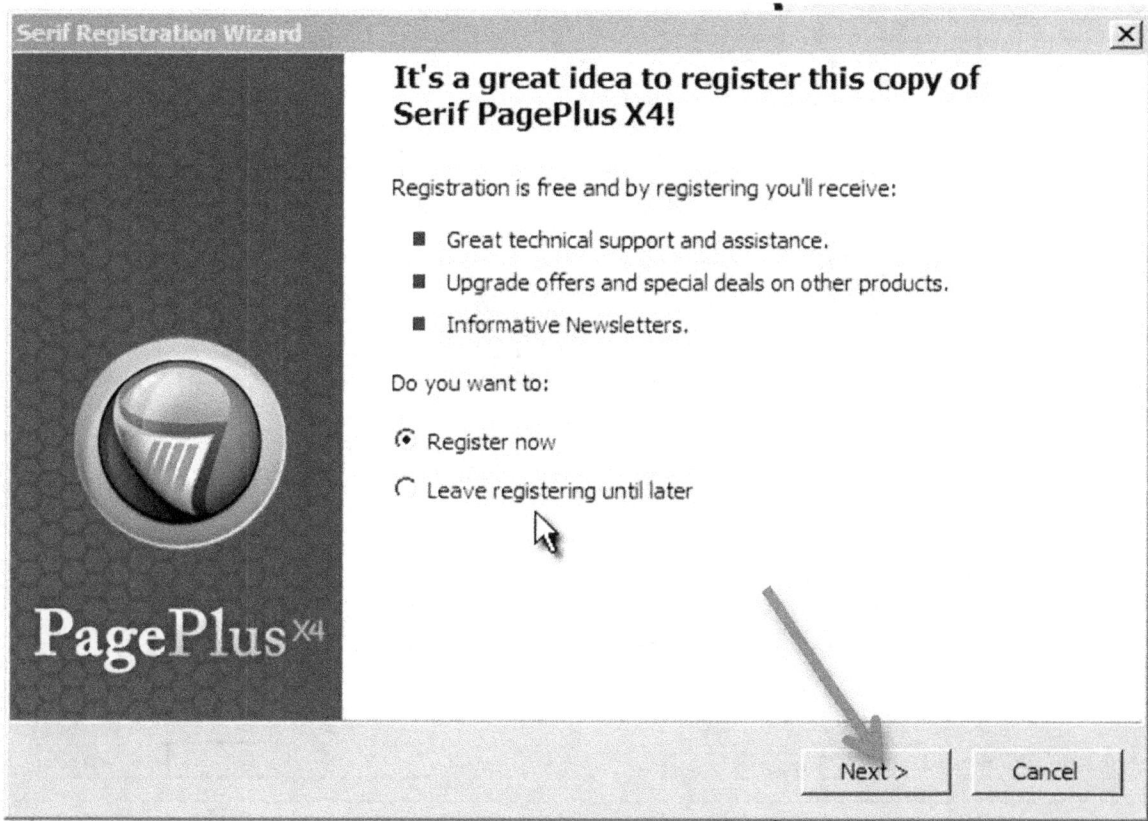

You can simply select Leave registering until later and continue to do that indefinitely.

PagePlus X4 is a flexible application and there are various ways to wind up with the same results. Until you learn the nuances of the application I suggest that you follow the steps described in the following pages

Once you click on the **Start New Publication** line you get the opportunity to make the basic selection of the size of your book. In this case, because this book is letter size, 8.5 inches by 11 inches, I selected the first default size.

Most often you will not find your book size among the standard paper sizes. This is not a problem. Just click Custom Page Setup and a new window opens, as shown by the second screen shot on the next page, that window allows you to create any size and gives you various other choices.

On the new window you have the choice of facing pages and dual master pages. If you plan to have a wider margin at the spine of your book, as I have done in this book, then you need to use facing pages. If you will be using equal margins on the spine and outside of the pages, then facing pages are unnecessary. Either way, don't select dual master pages. I find it much easier and less confusing to create independent master pages for left and right hand pages.

Notice that you also pick the starting page. It is always best to start on the right hand page. While it is definitely not a rule, I prefer to begin each chapter of my books on a right hand page.

Self Publishing: How To Publish Your Print Book or eBook Step by Step

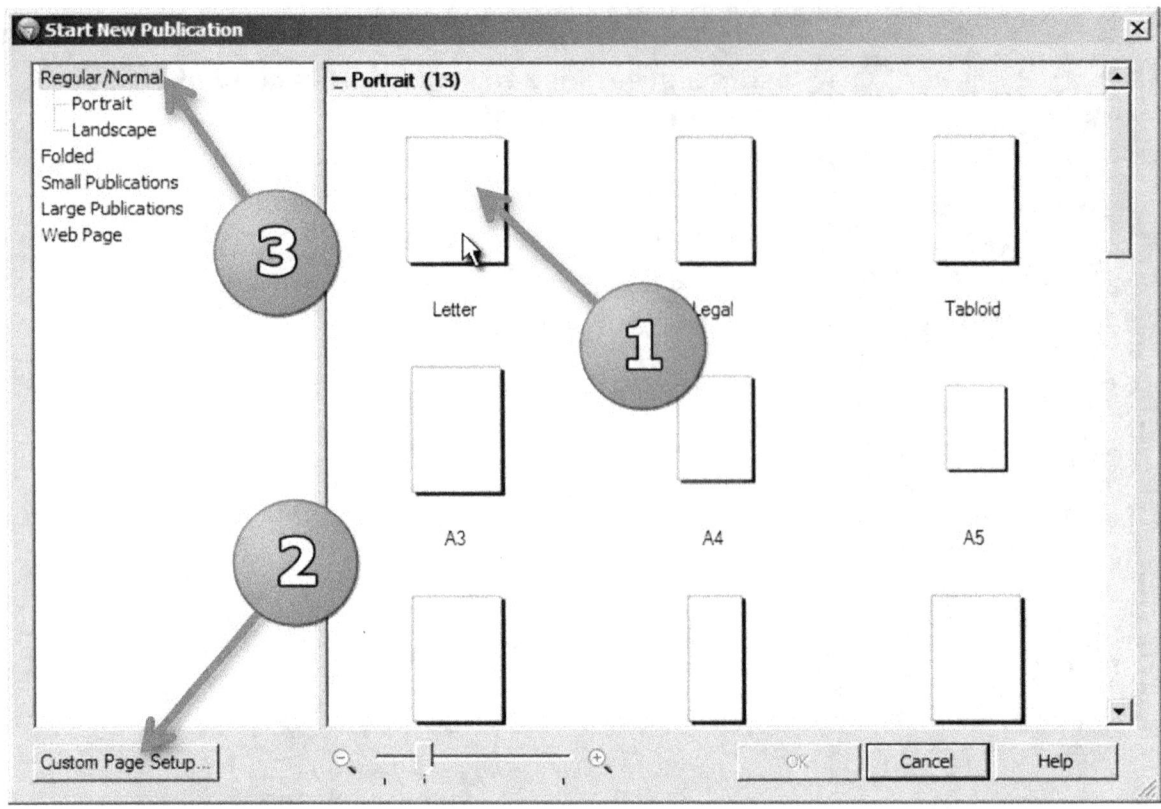

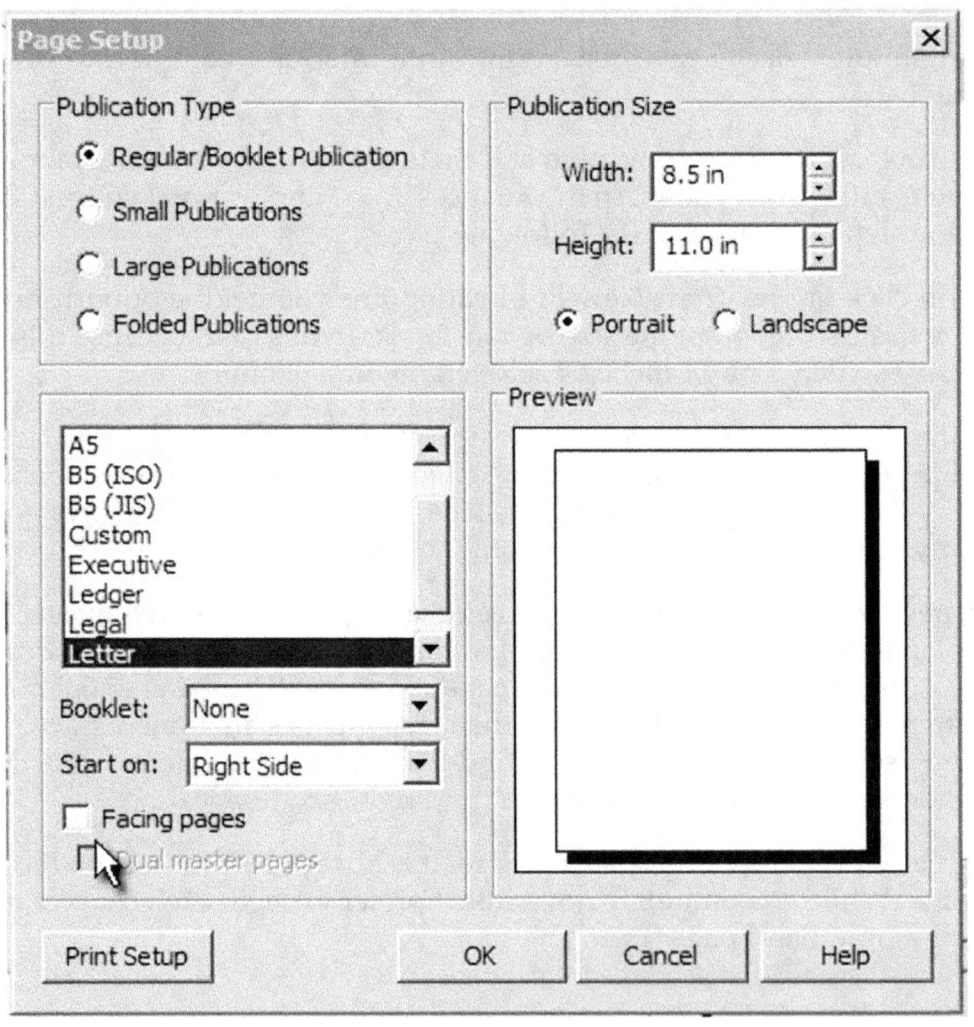

That choice requires facing pages to make the left and right pages different and sometimes a blank page is required between chapters so each chapter ends on an even page since right hand pages are always odd numbers. This is another choices you must make for your book. Regardless of the choices made, the most important thing is to maintain a consistent look throughout the book.

In the next image you will see the top portion of the first page opened. This page shows the default margins and the actual margins have yet to be chosen. Margins are best set up on master pages which are described in detail later in this chapter.

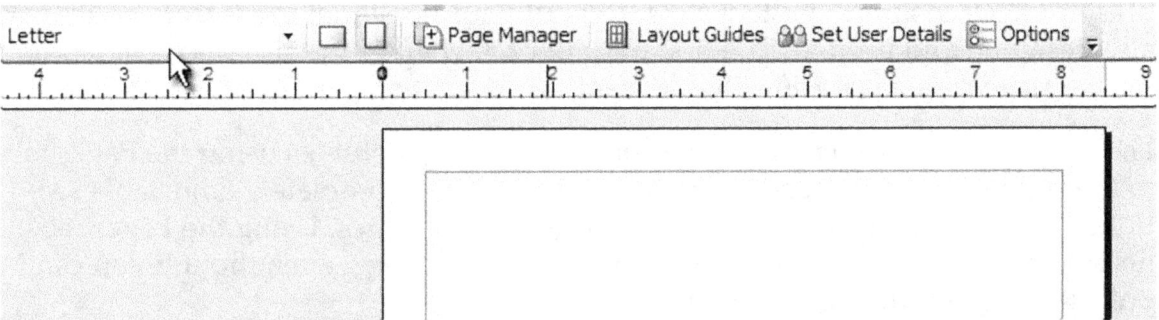

Once this page appears you are ready to start working. There are various ways to proceed. You could make your entire book in one file but the preferable method, for the best possible control of your work, is to make a separate file for each chapter. While this may sound like extra work, it actually makes the entire job much easier. Now that you are ready to start, read the caution below carefully and save yourself hours and perhaps days of layout and formatting.

Even though you are ready to start, it's critical to remember that PagePlus X4 is a desktop publishing application specifically designed to create print-ready files. Only use this application to layout and format (typeset) using the final manuscript. Avoid using it to create or edit drafts. While you can edit using PagePlus X4, especially taking advantage of the built-in text editor WritePlus, the application is intended for formatting, design, and layout and should be used for that purpose.

Create your manuscript with some text editor or word processor application and edit it until it is as good as it can possibly be. If you are employing a professional editor, give him or her the text file for editing. Wait until all the editing is complete and you believe that the file is in final form, then begin using PagePlus X4 to create the final print-ready file.

Creating a quality book requires attention to detail and great care no matter which publishing software you use and PagePlus X4 is no different. It is time consuming and sometimes frustrating to have to deal with hundreds of errors that should have been corrected before beginning the final print ready file.

Once you have a final manuscript, you are ready to start moving the content of your book into PagePlus X4, but first you must create the critical master pages.

Master Pages

Notice the top of this page and the next page. On the right hand page the title of the chapter appears. At the top of the left hand page you find the title of the book. This is consistent throughout the book. At the bottom of all the pages in every chapter, except for the first page, the page numbers are inserted and centered. All of these consistent elements are controlled by master pages. It isn't necessary to make certain these things are properly spaced or typed, they are in the master page and it is only necessary to select the correct master page for each book page and everything is correct on every page.

Master pages ensure consistency throughout your book making it look professionally designed and printed. The first page of each chapter in this book is based on a master page created specifically for them.

There are two ways to create master pages. One way involves using the Pages tab to the right of the workspace. Here you will find two completely adjustable sections. The top is Master Pages and the bottom is for Pages. Using the Pages tab helps you to keep track of exactly where you are working even though you can only see one or two pages at a time.

The illustration above shows the master pages you have created. The small icons at the top are **+ -**, they open the Page Manager and allow you to edit the master page. The **+** is for adding a master page and the **-** is for removing a master page. The last icon is for showing the name or letter of the master page.

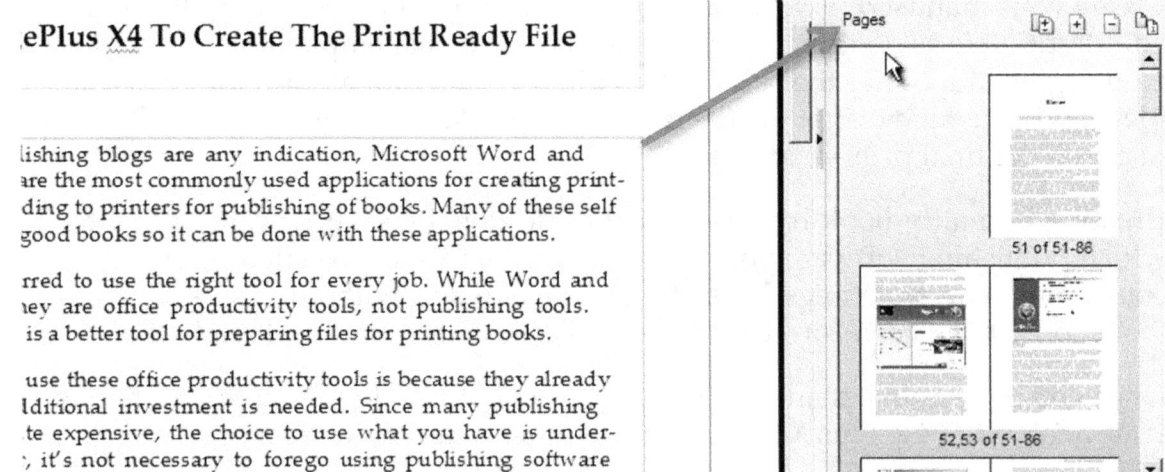

The last screen shot on the previous page shows the Pages window where all your pages are visible for selection. The small icons mean exactly the same as in Master Pages window.

Carefully create the necessary master pages for your book. Most books need at least five master pages as follows; one for the first page of each chapter, one for all the left hand pages of each chapter, one for all the right hand pages of each chapter, and one for each left and right hand page in the front sections such as the publishers page, table of contents, dedication, acknowledgements, or similar pages that either go with no page numbers or different page numbers. Some specialized books may require additional master pages and this will become evident as you learn to use PagePlus X4.

One of the most important settings on master pages are the margins. There are various schools of thought regarding right and left margins. In some books both margins are the same size. This tends to crowd the spine on a paperback and, unless the margins are wide, the book is harder to keep open. This book has a wider margin at the spine but this is not critical. The important thing is to avoid crowding the spine because if the text is too close to the spine a reader may damage the spine while forcing the book open to read.

Beginning on the next page you will find screen shots, descriptions, and detailed instructions on the creation and control of master pages. PagePlus X4 allows you to create as many master pages as you choose to control the look of your book.

Remember that these master pages should be created and edited carefully because whatever appears on them will be repeated throughout your book. So, if you make a typo or grammatical error on one master page, it could appear hundreds of times in your book. This will be much worse than a single typo within the pages of your book.

The most obvious thing to take care of with master pages is the margins of each page. The next thing is any text that will appear at the top or bottom of any of the pages. For example, on this book the title of the book appears on all the left hand pages except for the front pages and any blank pages. The title of each chapter appears on all the right hand pages except for the front pages, and any blank pages.

At the bottom of each page I have centered the page numbers. This is just one way to do page numbers. Some prefer the page numbers either to the right or left margin at the bottom. While yet others prefer the page numbers at the top opposite the book and chapter titles. All of these are acceptable methods. It is a choice that you will need to make for your book.

Master pages can also be used to add layers to certain pages. A layer can add a special feature to certain pages. For example, you may want certain pages to have a watermark or some special border. By creating this on a master page it is easy to add to any page. The important thing is to create master pages carefully because good master pages make the process of formatting and layout easier and contributes to the quality of your book.

To create a master page using the Pages tab you would simply drag the correct master page down to the correct book page. Just place your cursor on the correct master page, hold down the left mouse button, drag the master page to the correct page and release and it is applied to that page.

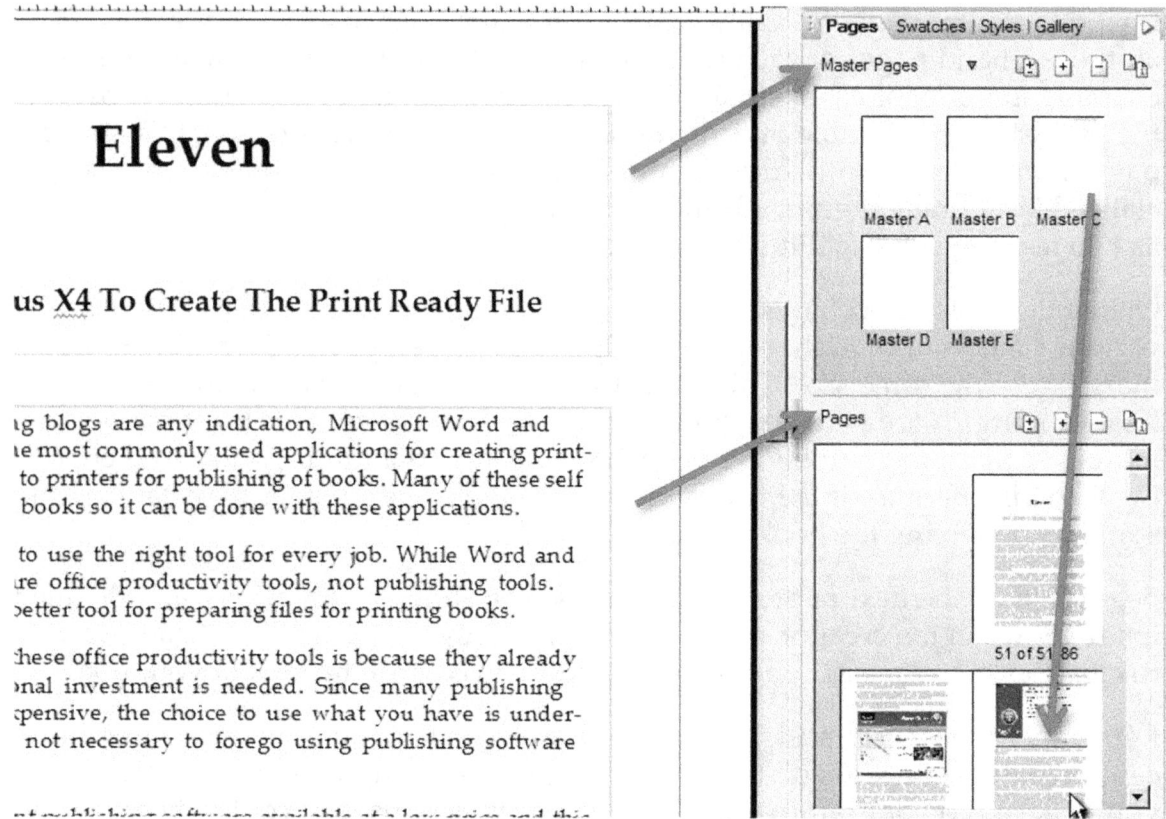

The top arrow identifies the Master Page box and the bottom arrow the Pages box. The other arrow points from the correct master page to the correct page and the master page is dragged to the book page.

This is just one way to set the master pages for each book page. There is another method that works directly from **View** in the menu line. Just click **Page Manager** above the workspace as shown below and it opens the boxes illustrated on the next page.

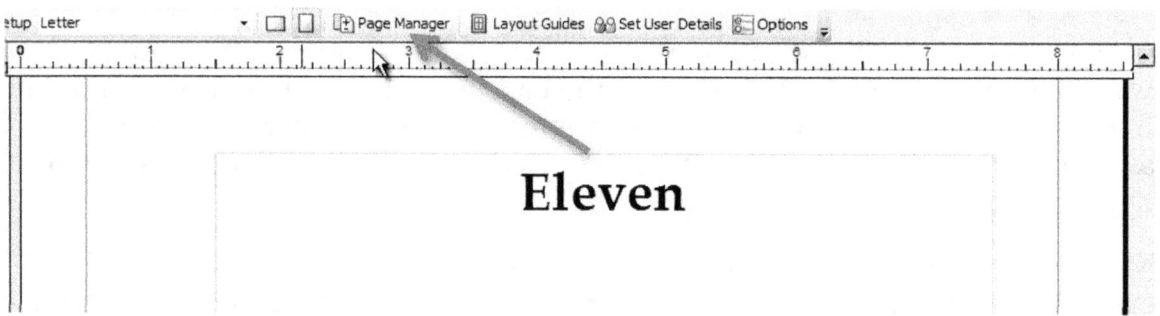

The Page Manager selection window allows you to select the correct master page for each page of your book. If you have different right and left hand pages you can simply assign a master page to all left hand pages and another master page to all right hand pages. This eliminates the need to identify a master page for every book page.

Even if you do select a master page for all left and right hand pages, you can still change the master page for a specific page if there is a specific part of your book that requires a special master page assignment.

As shown on the illustration below, you select the Set tab and then click the small arrow on the Publication Page line and the entire list of master pages available appears so you can select the correct page number. The book page outlined in blue in the pages box at the right side of the workspace is the page to which the master page will be assigned. Select the correct page number and then you get the opportunity to assign a specific master page to the selected book page.

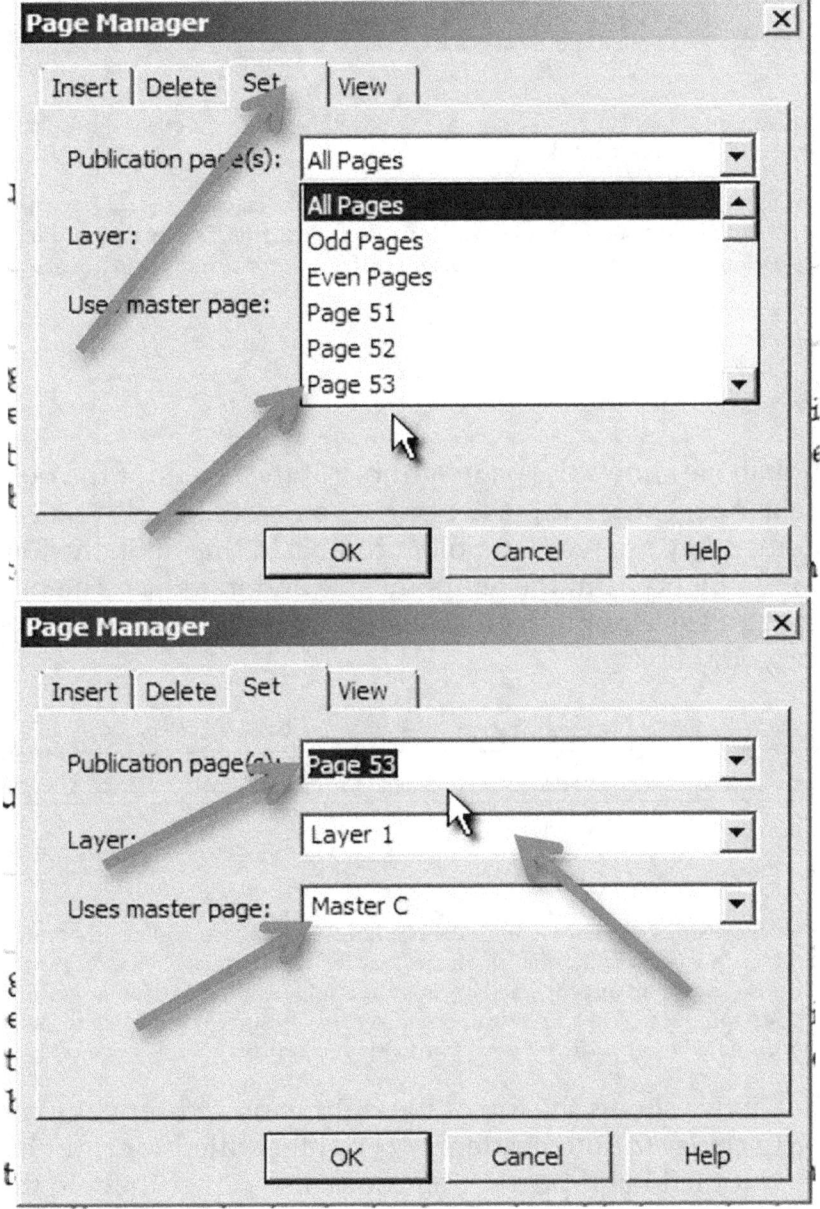

The screen shot at the bottom of the previous page shows the Publication Line indicating Page 53. The bottom arrow points to the selected master page. Here master page C is selected. It is assigned to the right hand page which is an odd numbered page. The arrow on the right hand side points to the Layer selection line. You can use layers for special publications but you seldom need them for books.

The screen shot below shows the top of a master page for the left hand page of this book. It contains the title of the book and also reflects the margins of the text.

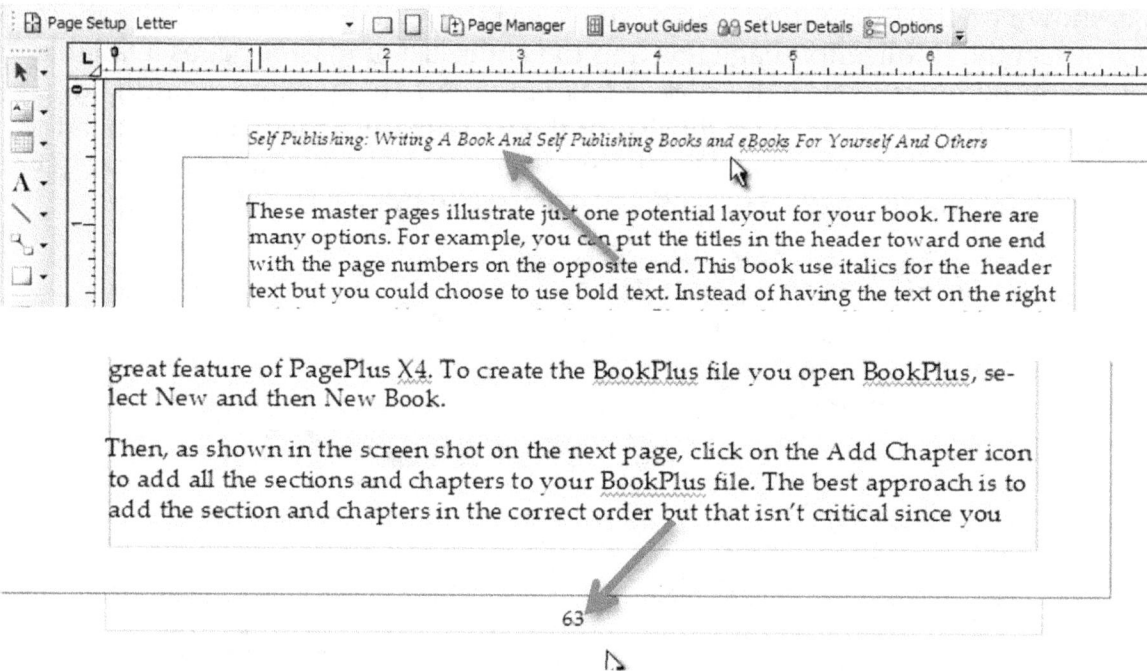

The screen shot above shows the page number at the center of the bottom of the right hand master page. On the master pages you can control the size and type of fonts and whether they are regular, bold, or italic. In this book the font for the top header is Palatino Linotype in the ten point size and in italics. The page number is in the same font and size but in regular instead of italics. These are choices you must make for your book.

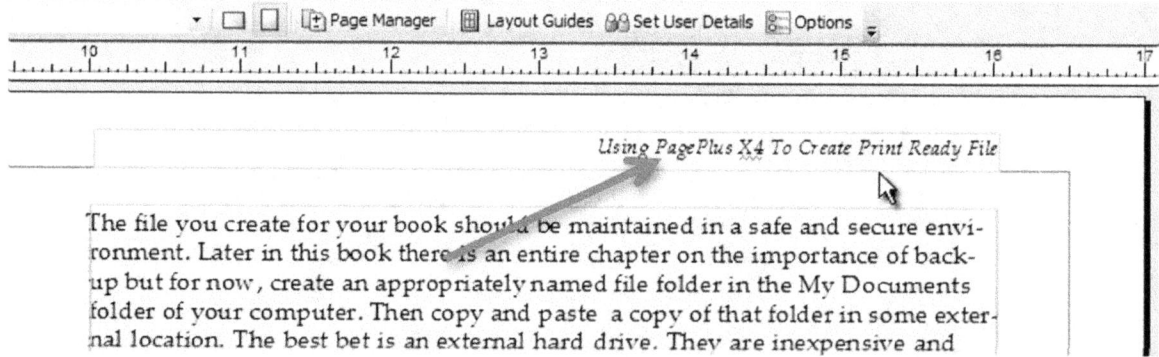

The screen shot above shows the top of the right hand master page containing the chapter title. My choice for the headers was right justified for right hand pages and left justified for left hand pages. You could also center them in the page.

In addition to the master pages with the top header and page number footer for the left and right hand pages within chapters, you need to create right and left hand master pages with the correct margins but no header or footer. These pages serve as blank pages at the end of chapters and for the pages at the front of the book.

I prefer to start each chapter on a right hand page. The pages on the right hand side are always odd numbered pages. To ensure that each chapter begins on an odd numbered page, each chapter must end on an even numbered page. Since that isn't always the case, sometimes you have to add a blank page to even up the number of pages in a chapter.

The reason to include a master page with the margins instead of just leaving the blank page without a master page is in case you add content to the chapter and that requires you to use the blank page. In that case the page would already have the proper margins and you would just have to select the correct master page.

The master page below is for the first page of the chapters in this book and it ensures that the first page of every chapter is identical. Creating a master page to guide each of the various elements of your book will ensure a consistent and professional appearance.

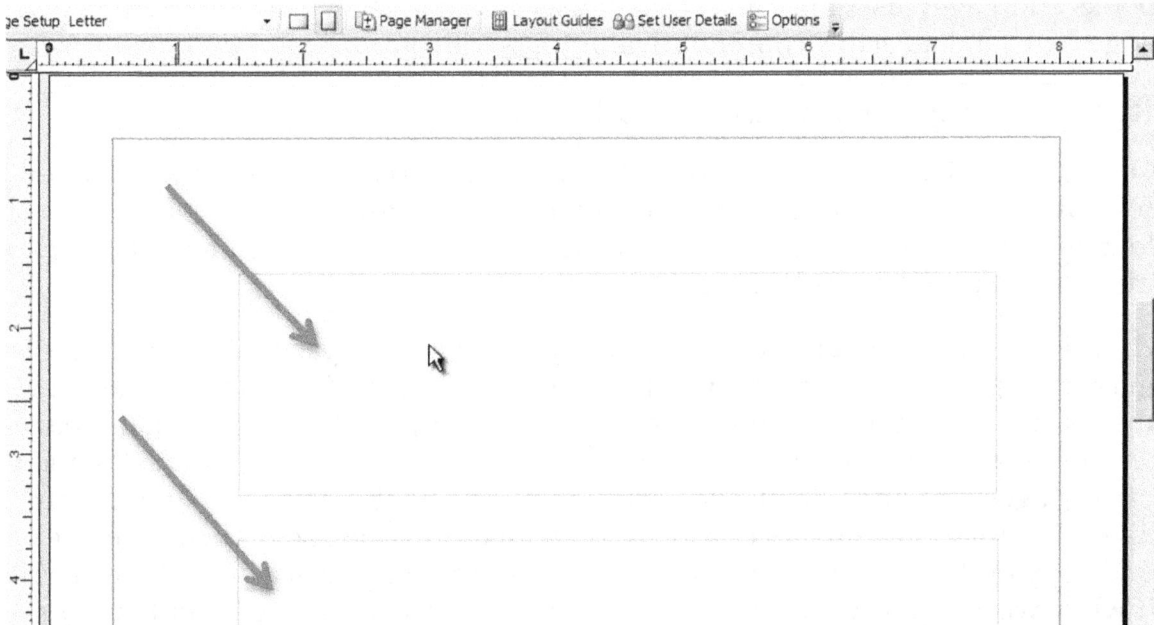

On this master page also notice the difference in the right and left margins. This is the first page of a chapter and therefore it is a right hand page. The spine will be to the left of the page and the margin on the left is larger than on the right. In this book the left margin is 1.5 inches and the right margin is 1 inch.

These margins may seem wide but I prefer to use wide margins and spaces between paragraphs on how-to books. I believe that the additional white spaces make the book easier to read.

These master pages illustrate just one potential layout for your book. There are many options. For example, you can put the titles in the header toward one end with the page numbers on the opposite end. This book use italics for the header text but you could choose to use bold text. Instead of having the text on the right or left you could center it in the header. Check the design of books you like and alter them to please yourself.

There is no one rule about designing your book. Different publishers use various designs and you can do the same. The important thing is to be consistent throughout the book.

Built-in Applications To Help With Layout and Formatting

PagePlus X4 has two important, built in applications to make the job of formatting and composing your book easier. The first is WritePlus, the Text Manager and the other is BookPlus which assembles all the chapters, regardless of the number, and creates a single pdf from them. It also rearranges chapters, renumbers pages, and has many other features.

PagePlus X4 also facilitates layers that can be assigned to one or more pages. This can be used to add a border, logo, or watermark to various pages. This book does not include details about using layers because they are not necessary for most books and PagePlus X4 has an excellent user manual, technical support, a knowledge base, and an active community at http://serif.com.

Ready To Begin Formatting and Layout

Once the master pages are finished, the next step is to create a template chapter with at least five pages. A template chapter will help keep all your chapters consistent and preclude the necessity of starting each chapter from scratch. The template chapter can be blank pages.

On the template chapter you set up the necessary master pages. The first is the master page for the first page of each chapter. The second is the master page for the left pages within the chapter. Next is the master page for the right hand pages within the chapter. Then you create the master pages for the right and left hand blank pages that might be needed throughout the book. Save this file with the name "template" in a file folder that you created for your book. Then save a second copy of the template file in some safe place in case you accidentally overwrite it while working. Now you are ready to start the formatting and layout of your book.

Before beginning those instructions, and at the risk of repetition, it's important to restate that at this point you should have a completed, fully edited, manuscript. This is critical because while word processor applications are not the best tool for formatting and laying out a book, PagePlus X4 and other publishing applications are not the best tool for editing draft manuscripts. Make things easier on yourself by using the correct tool for the job at hand.

The file you create for your book should be maintained in a safe and secure environment. Chapter Four is an entire chapter on the importance of backup but for now, create an appropriately named file folder in the My Documents folder of your computer. Then copy and paste a copy of that folder in some external location. The best bet is an external hard drive. They are inexpensive and quite reliable. You can also use a flash drive but these are easy to lose and break. To protect your book files read Chapter Four carefully.

Unless you want to import your entire file as a pdf into PagePlus X4, The copy and paste method is the simplest way, that I also consider best, to format your book using PagePlus X4. At this point you already have PagePlus X4 open and you have setup the book size, created a template file for the chapters or sections, and created the master pages for the template. Now use Save As to rename the template file and save it once for each section or chapter of your book.

The first section is the front of your book which includes the title page, the publisher's page , and other book parts such as acknowledgements, preface, foreword, dedication, and praise for your book. Of these the only ones you need are the title page and the publisher's page but you can add any or all of the others. If you have some praise for your book it should be on the first page so it is seen immediately when the book is opened.

After you create the front file, close it and reopen the template file. Then save the template file again using the Save As command and this time name it Contents. This will be used for the table of contents. Continue the procedure of closing the latest file you created and reopening the template file. Then name the file using the number of the chapter beginning with one and going through the last chapter.

If your book has an Afterword, Bibliography, Glossary, Index, etc., create a file for each one using the template file.

When you have completed this process you will have a separate file for each section or chapter in your book all together in one file folder on your computer. Now you can open each one and work on them separately but, because they were all created using the same template file, all the margins, headers, footers, and other elements of your book will be consistent. You will just have to make minor adjustments to the master pages to consider the different names of the chapters or sections.

Creating the BookPlus File

The next step is to merge all the separate files you created into a **BookPlus** file that will allow you to work on the separate sections and chapters independently but still facilitate working on them as one unit to create the final pdf file. This is a great feature of PagePlus X4. To create the **BookPlus** file you open **BookPlus**, select New and then New Book.

Then, as shown in the screen shot on the next page, click on the Add Chapter icon to add all the sections and chapters to your BookPlus file. The best approach is to add the section and chapters in the correct order but that isn't critical since you

the position of chapters and sections by simply dragging and dropping them in the correct location.

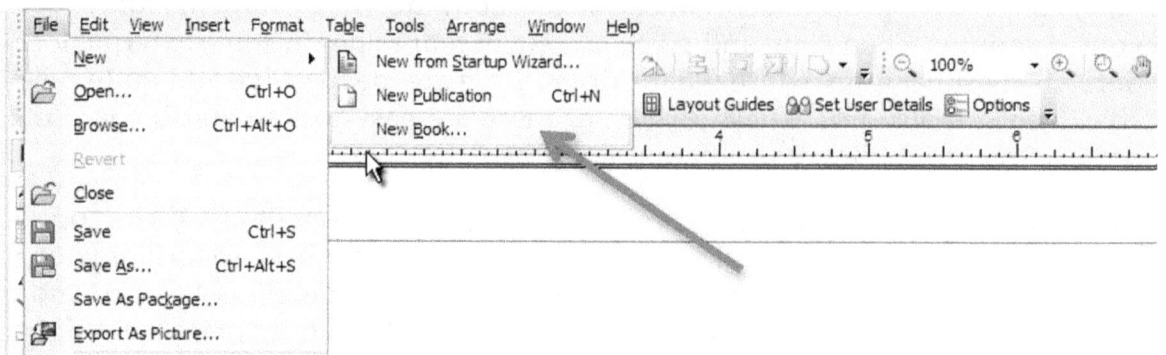

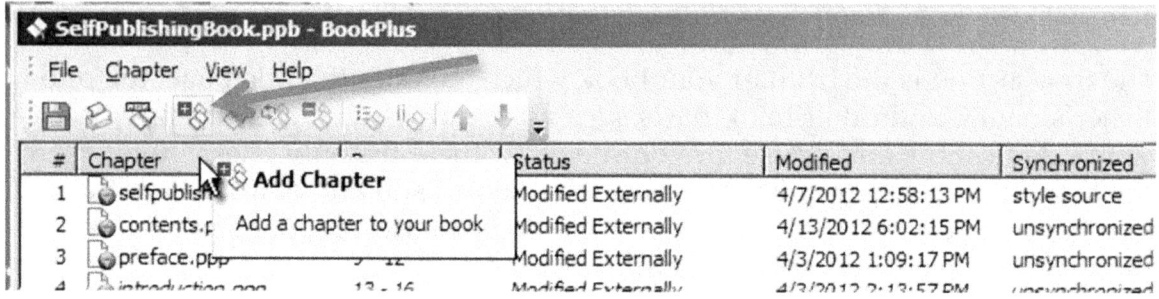

BookPlus is an excellent tool that allows you to work on your chapters independently yet promptly create a single pdf file from the entire group. The individual chapter or section files allow you to easily handle special sections and numbering without difficulty. Once you create the full pdf file you can check it and go back to individual chapters if corrections are needed and then create another pdf file.

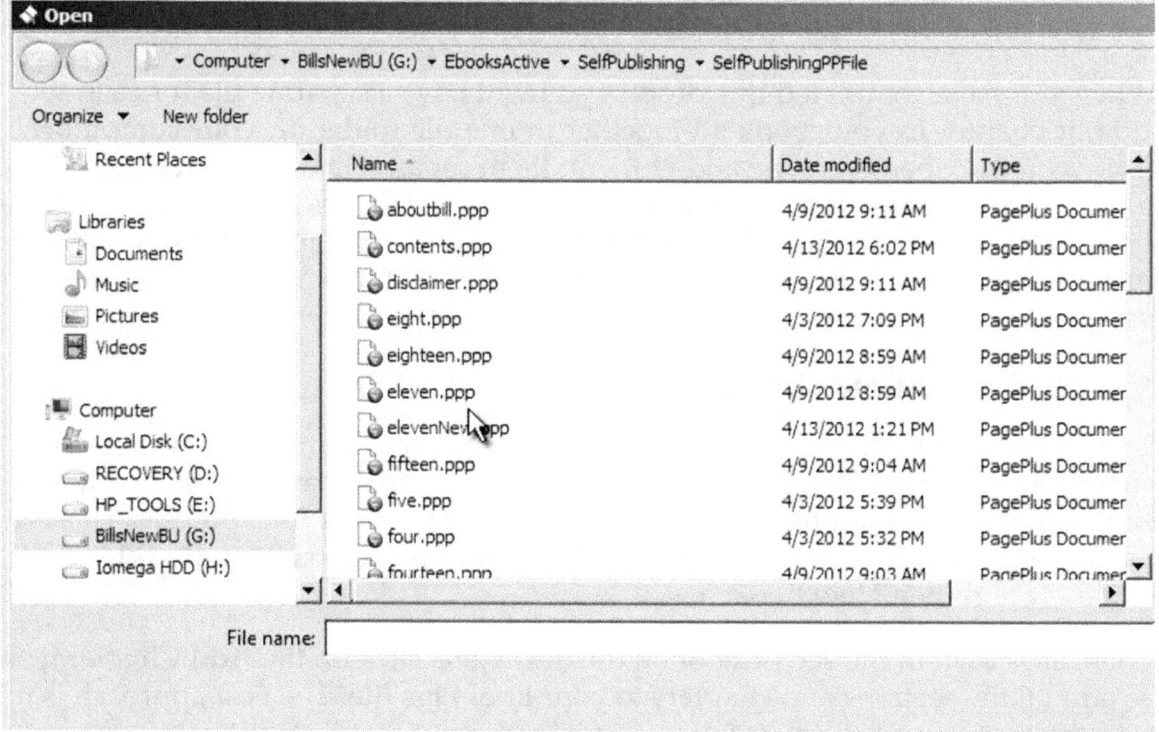

The screen shot at the bottom of the previous page is the list of chapters for this book. When you click Add Chapter in **BookPlus** you open your book folder to select the chapters to be placed into **BookPlus**. Save the **BookPlus** file with a name related to your title.

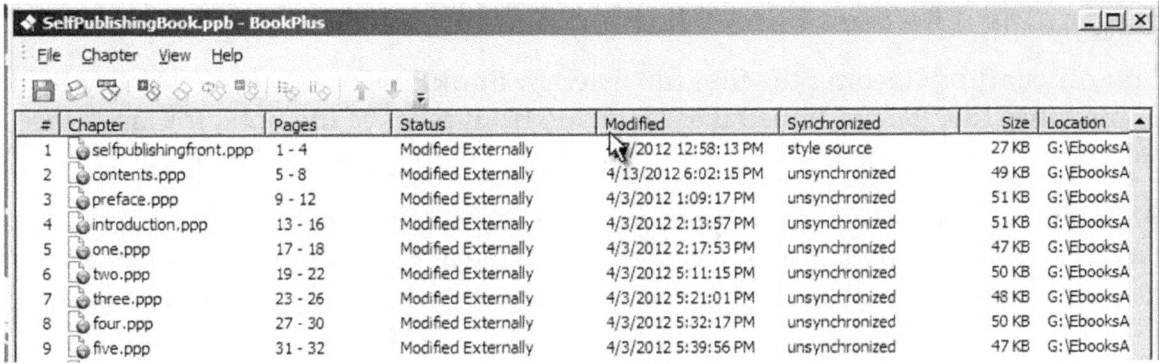

The screen shot above is a portion of the **BookPlus** file for this book. Even though the files are in correct order, they could easily be rearranged and the pages renumbered. **BookPlus** also helps you make certain that each chapter begins with an odd numbered page. The chapters are shown in their new location in **BookPlus**.

Remember that the chapter files don't actually move to **BookPlus**. These listings are only bookmarks that facilitate working with all the files as if they were one document while still allowing you to work on them independently so you can make even major formatting changes to one section without affecting any other section.

Each time you want to work on your book, you open the **BookPlus** file and use the bookmarks to open individual files to work on them. Another feature of **BookPlus** is that the page numbers are visible and you can watch them grow since they will adjust automatically and can be refreshed manually at any time. Be sure to save the **BookPlus** file each time you use it. Now you are ready to proceed with the layout and formatting.

Note: The **BookPlus** file has a .ppb file extension. The actual chapters of the book have a .ppp file extension.

> ***Design Note:*** *In this book, and all my other how-to books, my design choice has been to start each chapter on an odd numbered page and to avoid justified text. I also choose to have a line space between paragraphs with no first line indentation. I like the the additional white space this creates. The 8.5 x 11 inch book size was chosen because it allows the screen shots to be larger and easier to read. Like my choice for the headers and page numbering in the footers, these are all design choices. They are not carved in granite. Some other design may work better for your book and you must make those choices.*
>
> *I recently published a book for someone and made a proof in the 6 X 9 size. When the proof arrived it looked good but for some reason it didn't feel right. We decided to try a smaller size and redid it in the 5.25 X 8 size.*

When the proof arrived it seemed perfect. It was extra work but it was well worth the effort. Isn't your book worth that level of attention and work? Develop your design and then check it with a proof to make certain it is what you want and expect.

Beginning The First File - Chapter, Section, or Part

You can start by opening the first file listed in **BookPlus** or choose to start with some other file. It's not unusual to leave the front parts of the book for last. Once you open the first chosen file, you are ready to begin layout and formatting.

Now open your final manuscript so you can copy and paste from it to PagePlus X4. You can work on a laptop but it should have at least a 14 inch display and preferably a 17 inch display. It is also helpful to purchase a large monitor (at least 20 inches) and connect it to the laptop for a larger workspace to maintain both PagePlus X4 and your final manuscript open at the same time. Even without a larger display you can open both and keep one behind the other but it does make the work a little more time consuming.

For several years I have used laptops almost exclusively for all aspects of my writing, publishing, web site, blog creation, and graphics work. I enjoy being able to work at various locations. My largest laptop display is 15.6 inches and the laptop I use most to write has only a 13 inch display. So, I purchased a 20 inch monitor and connect it to my laptop when I am doing layout and formatting. Even though I find this a much better setup for this purpose, I sometimes do my layout and formatting work on my 15.6 inch laptop.

Begin by highlighting and copying the content from your starting point on the final manuscript. Now switch back to the open file in PagePlus X4 to begin the process of pasting in your content for layout and formatting.

You can format the various sections and chapters of the book in any order since they will be maintained in the correct order by **BookPlus**. So, if you prefer to begin formatting individual chapters and leave the front sections for last, that poses no problem. When you complete working on one section or chapter and save it, the file is saved in the book folder and has no affect on the **BookPlus** bookmark other than to alter the number of pages if the length of the section or chapter has increased.

I find it easier and less confusing to format sections and chapters in their correct order. I usually start by formatting all the front sections. I also create a basic table of contents based on the chapters by formatting the main chapter headers. Chapter sub-headers can be added later but I try to come up with a finished table of contents except for page numbers. I leave the page numbers for last as things may change when the proof is edited.

Before you can paste the content you copied from the final manuscript into PagePlus X4, you must create a text box on the first page. This is an easy step and does not have to be repeated if your content is mostly text.

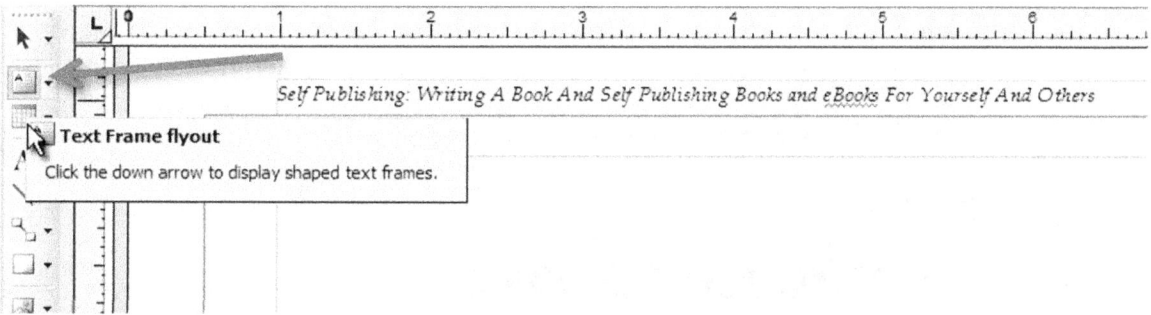

To create a text box just click on the Text Frame Flyout icon on the left side menu as shown by the arrow in the screen shot above and then use the plus sign to draw the text box on the page. Place the plus sign on the upper left hand corner and drag it down until the entire text box has been created. If you don't have sufficient room on the screen you can just stop, scroll the page down, and then use the control points on the text box to shape it to the correct size as shown below. You can also create a text box within this text box for special sections or notes.

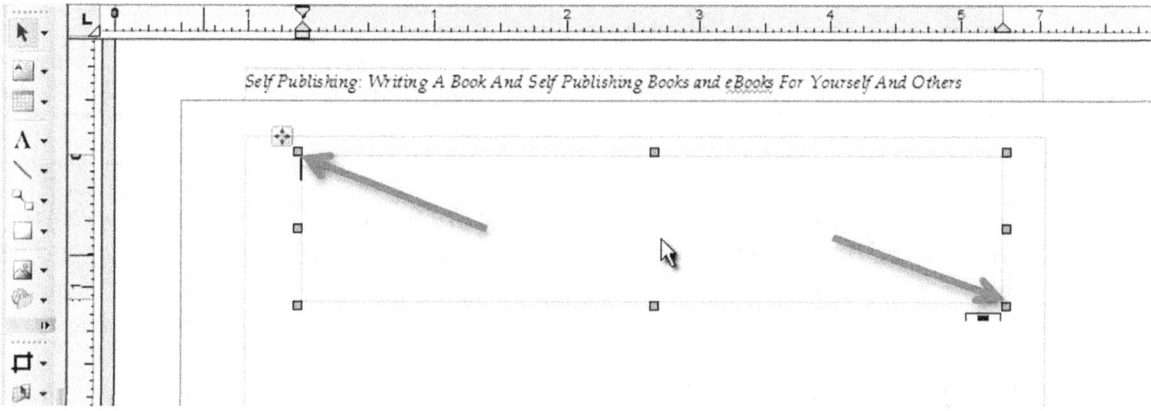

Once the text box is created to accommodate the content from the final manuscript it would seem that the next step would be to paste the content into the text box. That is workable but there is a much easier way to paste in the content for the layout and formatting.

This is where the **WritePlus** program excels. To open **WritePlus**, place your cursor at the beginning of the page or where you want the content to begin, then click the Tools menu and then select Text Manager as shown below.

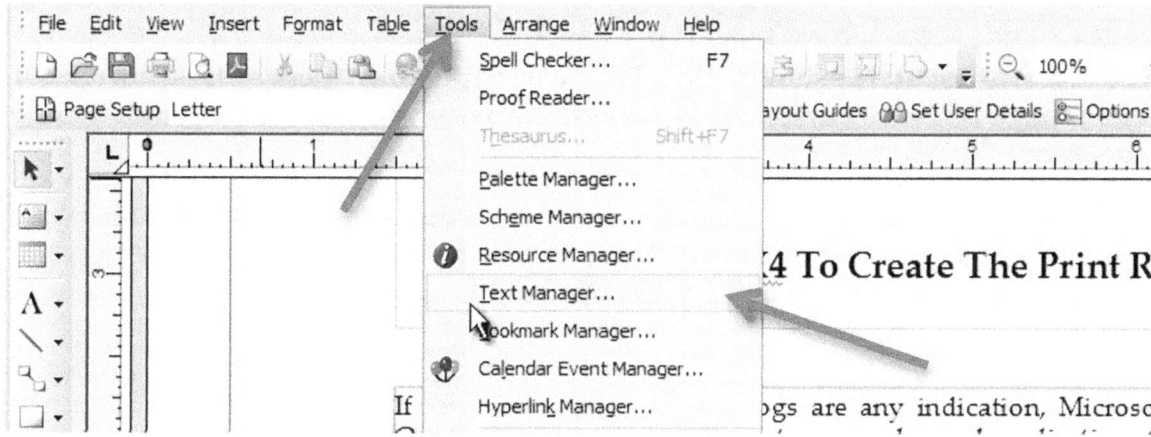

The location selection window in **WritePlus**, with the arrow pointing to the default selection, is illustrated below. You can also choose to start at any point.

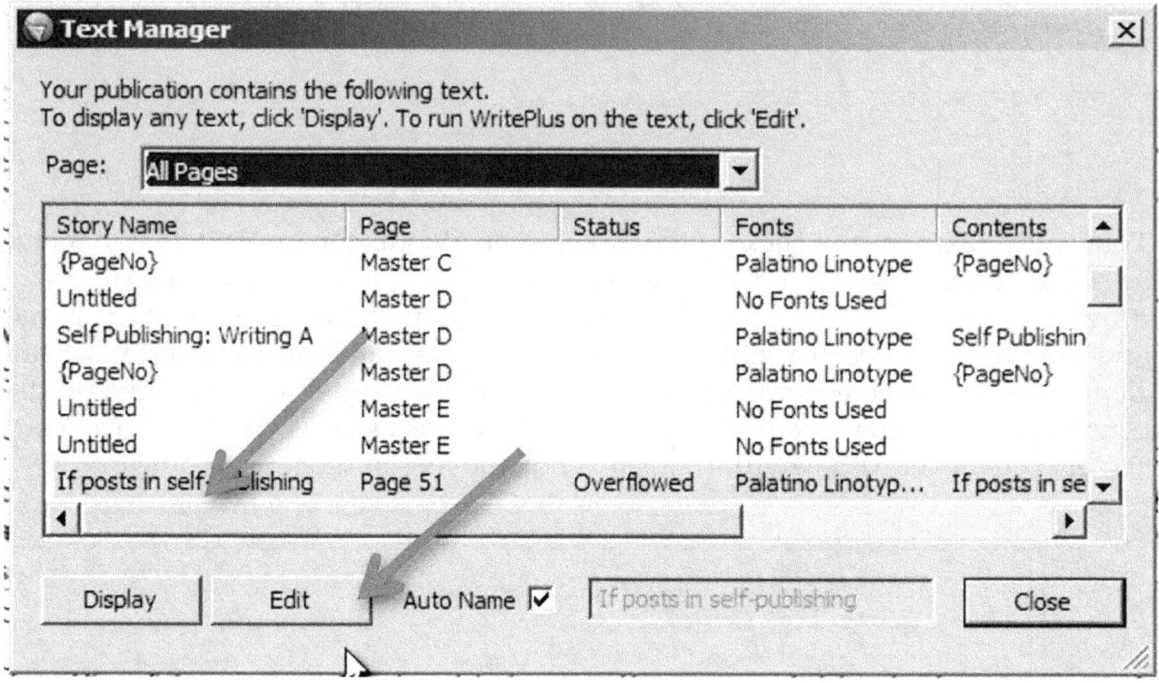

The bottom arrow points to the Edit button. This is what is clicked to place content into the **WritePlus** program for layout and formatting. If you only wanted to look at the file closely without making any changes you can click on the Display button which would show you the content in **WritePlus** but not allow changes.

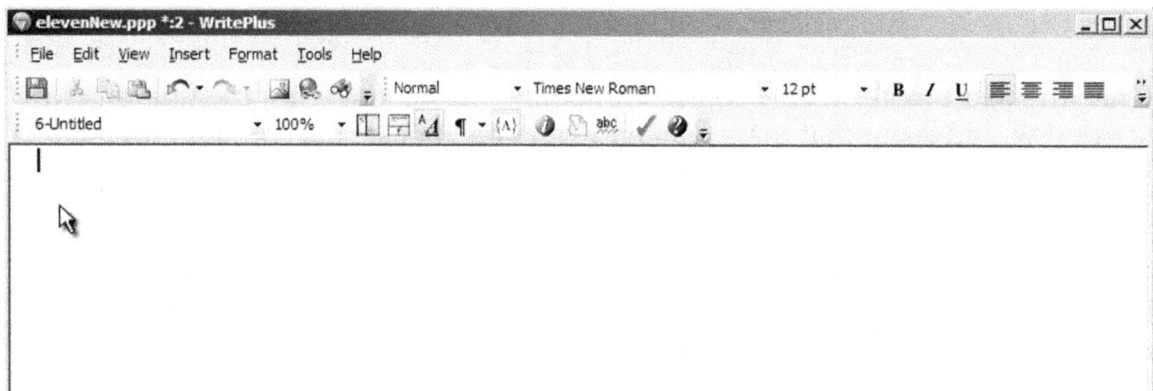

The screen shot above shows **WritePlus** when it is first opened. It is simply a blank page with the cursor ready for you to paste in as much content as you choose.

At the top of the next page is another screen shot that shows the **WritePlus** page with the content pasted in. Now your content is ready for final checking before being placed into the actual pages of your book.

Using PagePlus X4 To Create Print Ready File

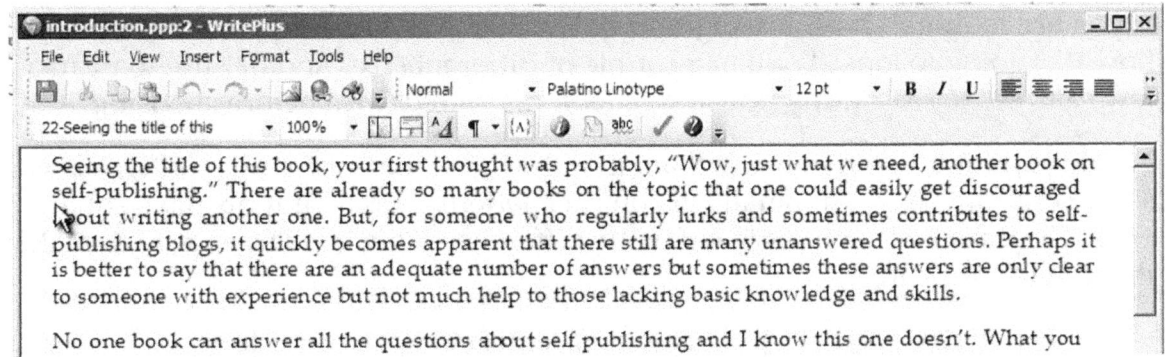

Remember that you can use **WritePlus** (Text Manager) at anytime while formatting your book. Should you decide to make a change, just open the file you wish to work on, place the cursor at the beginning of the content, click Tools and then select Text Manager and the content will open in **WritePlus**. You can edit it as you choose and once you finish just click the Save icon and the file will be saved. Close **WritePlus** and your content, with all the corrections, will appear in the various pages of the section or chapter you are working on.

In the next few pages there are screen shots and detailed explanations of the formatting that can be done using the **WritePlus** application within PagePlus X4. With this useful tool you can format your book in whatever manner you choose.

Let's begin with choosing the most appropriate font for your book. There are many options but it's easy to make a poor choice. What follows are details about various fonts and why you should or should not use them.

> *For this book I chose one of my favorite fonts called Palatino Linotype. I like it because it is well spaced and easy to read even in italics. Even though I have used it on quite a few of the books that I published, I've also used Garamond and Georgia on previous books. Obviously, Palatino Linotype isn't the only choice.*

Here is a list of fonts that work well for most books with a brief comment about each one. All of them would be acceptable for your book. All of the fonts are set to the 12 point size even though they look different.

Palatino Linotype - Can't go wrong with this neat and well spaced font

Book Antiqua- This one is tight so you may have to adjust spacing

Georgia - Second favorite. High clarity but also large and adds pages.

Goudy Old Style - This one is small and tight.

Garamond - The lower case letters are shorter and may seem smaller than it is.

Bookman Old Style - A good one for books.

Century School Book - It seems a little wider and could increase pages.

If you are in doubt, type a paragraph or two using the font you like best to see how it is going to look. Try it in a couple of different sizes and be sure to print a few samples to see exactly how it will look in printed form before choosing.

The important thing to notice is that all of the listed fonts are serifs fonts, not sans serif. Serif fonts have the small tails on each letters. Sans serif fonts have square ends. Here are two samples to show the difference. They are larger type to make the difference clear.

Palatino Linotype - The font in this book, is a Serif font.

Arial - A commonly used font is a Sans Serif font.

Georgia - Another popular Serif font.

Verdana - Commonly seen on web sites is a Sans Serif font.

Formatting Paragraphs

Now you have selected your font and have your first section of content ready for formatting your book. Start by formatting the paragraphs. This is usually fairly simple unless you plan to present your content in a complex format.

There are various ways to set up your paragraphs. The screen shot below shows how to begin by clicking on the Format menu and then selecting Paragraph. The first screen shot on the next page is from this book so it indicates no indentation for the first line in paragraphs and a 10 point space between paragraphs.

Normally, the spacing for the lines of text would be set to Single space and the default spacing would appear. However, I find the default spacing too large so the spacing was changed to Exactly and set to 14 points. I like my line spacing to be two points larger than the font size which is 12 points in this book.

All of these settings and many others are are completely adjustable to more or less depending on how you want your paragraphs to appear. This simply reflects my choices for this book.

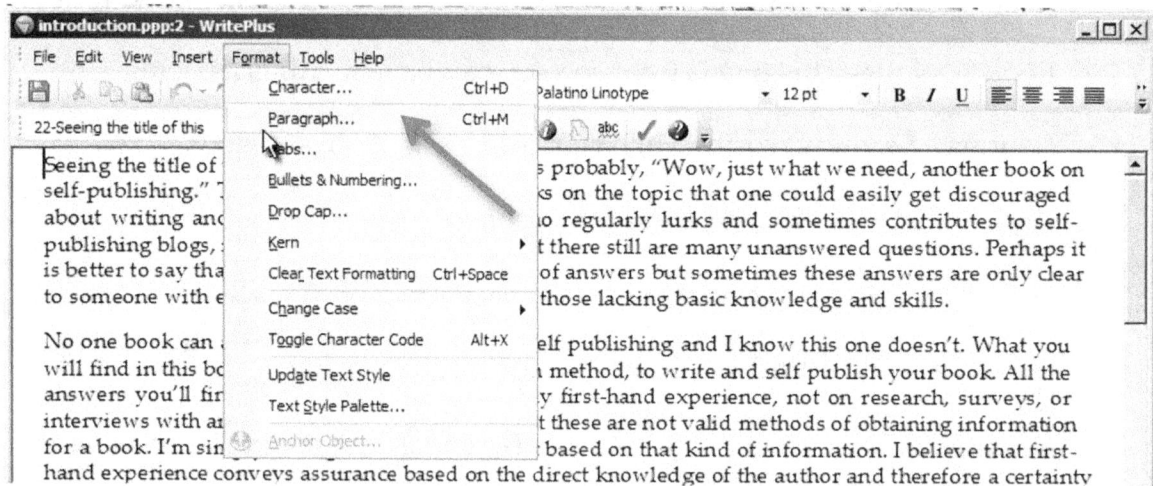

Once you click Paragraph in the Format menu the paragraph and related setting box opens and there are a large number of options.

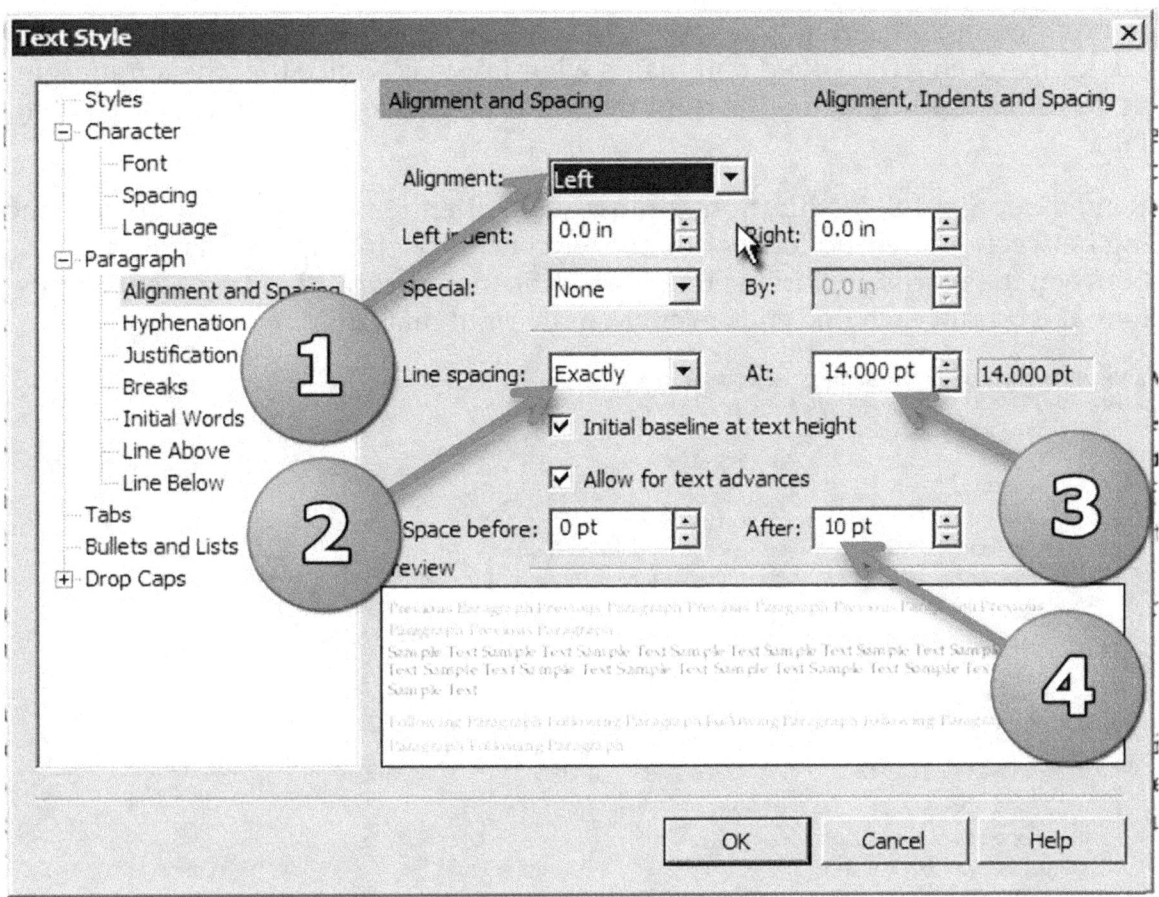

The One arrow points to the Alignment selection which includes many options including full justification where the text on both sides is square and in line with the margins. My choice for this book is Left justification leaving the right edge free but limited with proper hyphenation.

Arrows Two and Three point out the line spacing which in this book is set at exactly 14 points. You can also choose single, one and one half, double and many other multiples. You can also select any number of points when your selection is Exactly. This setting gives you a lot of flexibility.

Arrow Four points to the 10 point spacing after each paragraph. I wanted white space between each paragraph for ease of reading but I did not want a full line (14 points) of space.

All of these choices are decisions that impact the look of your book. It's important to take time to make choices that look good and professional. You can only be certain of good choices if you view them in print.

Print out several pages reflecting all your choices before ordering your first proof. It is much easy to evaluate the quality of your choices on paper than on your computer's display.

Justification is an important design consideration for the text in your book. Most books are designed with full justification which means that the right and left margins of your text are absolutely straight. This is quite normal in most fiction and in non fiction and certainly a good selection for your book. However, how-to books are often left justified and that is what I prefer. Notice that the left margin in this book is straight and the right margin is jagged so the Justification is set to Left.

Remember that full justification requires close attention to hyphenation and spacing between words and letters otherwise you could wind up with large spaces between the words on various lines as justification is carried out by adjustments to make certain each line ends evenly on the right margin.

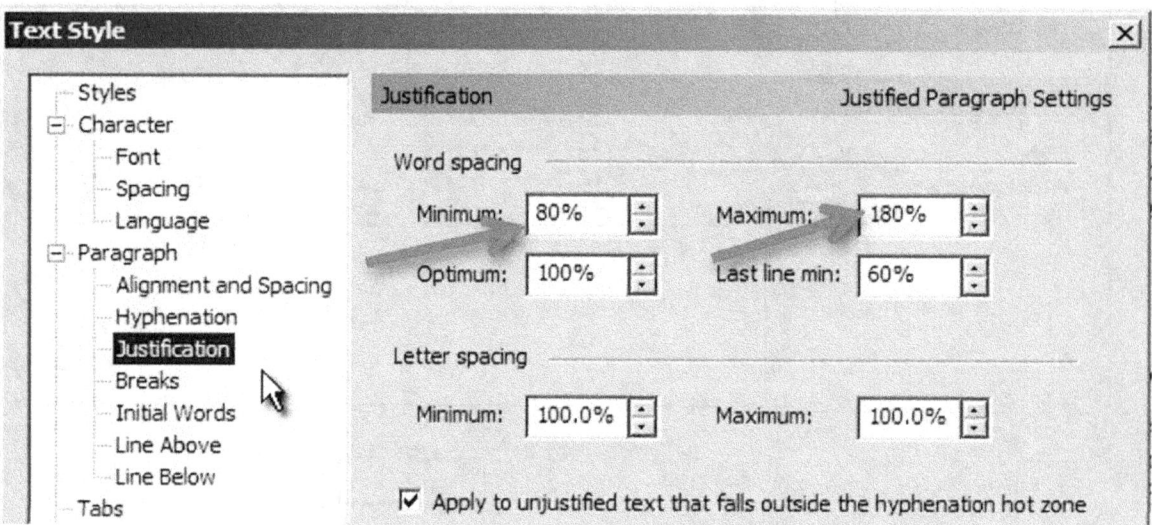

Justification settings are critical if you plan to use full justification. Notice the default selections in the screen shot above. For word spacing it would allow as little as eighty percent of the normal space and up to one hundred eighty percent of the normal spacing between words.

This is excessive variation and these setting should be changed. The minimum should be no less than ninety five percent of the the normal space and no more than one hundred and five percent with the optimum being one hundred percent of the normal spacing.

On the next page is a screen shot of the Hyphenation settings which are also found in the Paragraph settings. Here again, the default settings are inadequate whether you are using full justification or left justification as in this book. Using inappropriate settings for hyphenation will have similar effects as poor settings for justification.

Even though the settings on the next page indicate Auto Hyphenation, that simply means that you don't have to do it manually but you must still need make certain to use the best possible settings. The screen shot shows what was used for this book. The default would have listed eight letters as the shortest word to hyphenate and this is not adequate. Even with left justification you don't want the right edge to become too jagged.

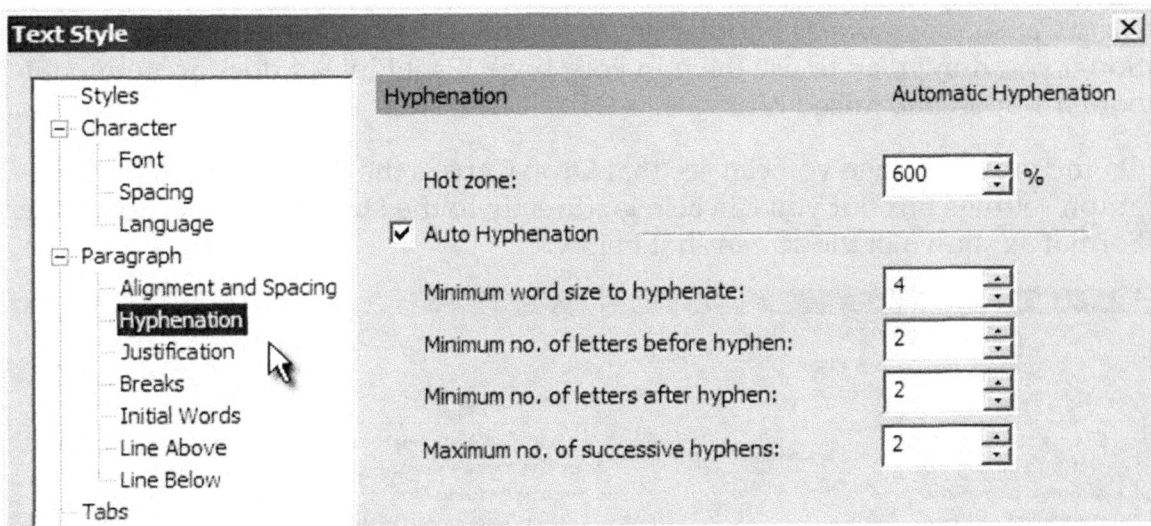

There are many other settings that appear in the Paragraph settings box including setting up page breaks, initial words, make a line above or below the text. The screen shot below is the box for line settings.

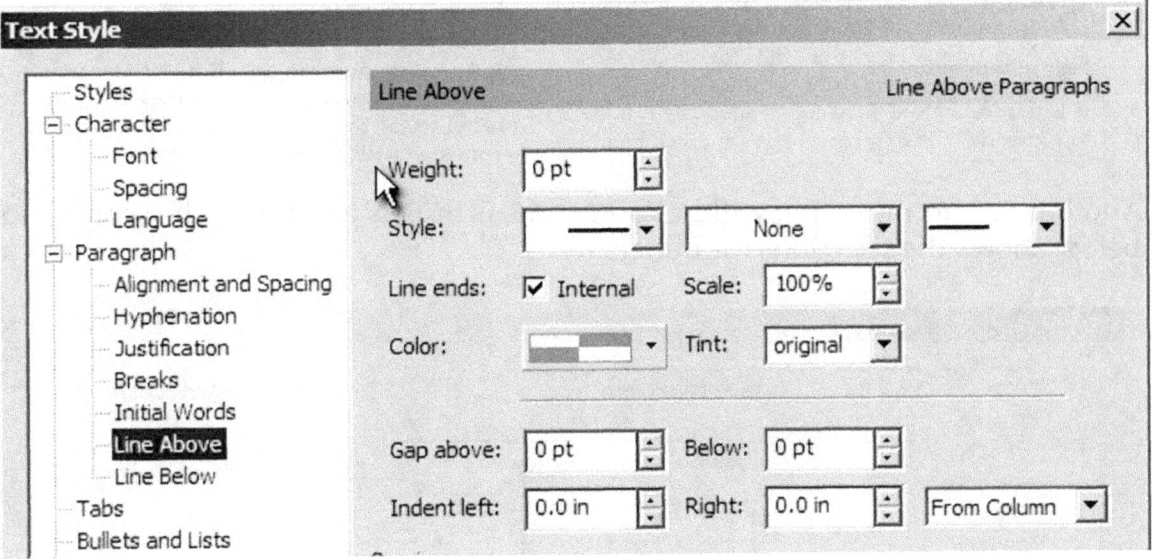

Formatting your book will require you to make many choices. If you are facing some doubts about what to choose, go to a bookstore and look at books in the same genre. You will find many different styles. Find one that you like but don't copy it exactly. Pick out the things that you like and then alter them and make them your own.

Don't want to take the time to visit a book store, check out book designs on Amazon.com. Check out the covers and then use the Look Inside feature to look at several books. You will find many books that are really attractive and it will fill your head with good ideas for your own design. There are also good books on book design and you can learn from them. Get the lessons and then put the book down and make your own decisions.

Drop Caps don't seem as popular anymore and you can probably ignore this section if you don't plan to use them in your book. PagePlus X4 does accommodate both dropped and raised caps.

On the previous page you can see that Drop Caps is the final listing in the Paragraph settings box but you can also go directly to the Drop Caps selection under Format as shown in the screen shot below.

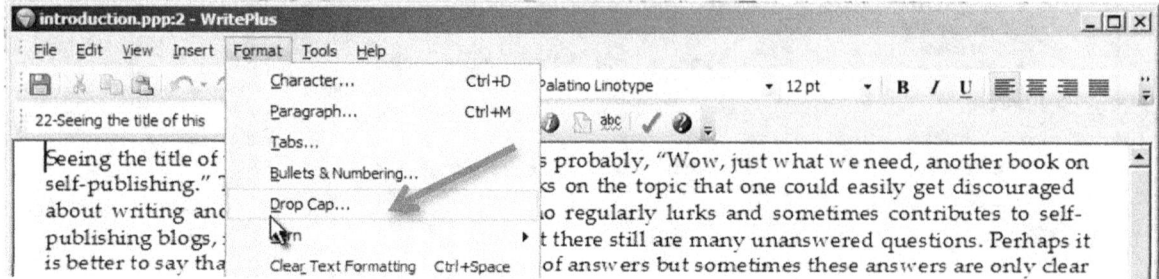

The screen shots below show a two line drop cap. These are easily created using the drop cap settings box.

Another important setting within Paragraphs is Bullets and Lists. The screen shot below shows the selections for Bullets.

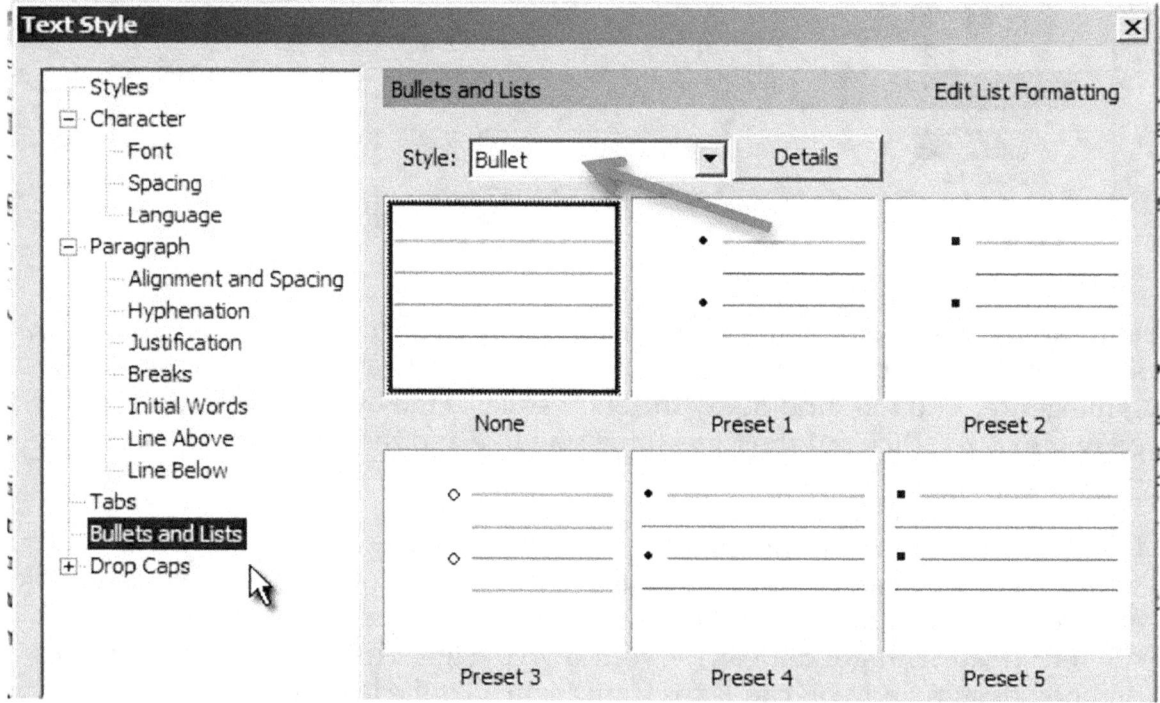

The drop down arrow in the Style line is where you would select Number. Preset number one is one of the most popular for Bullets. The illustrations on the next page show the Number and Multi-Level styles that are available.

Using PagePlus X4 To Create Print Ready File

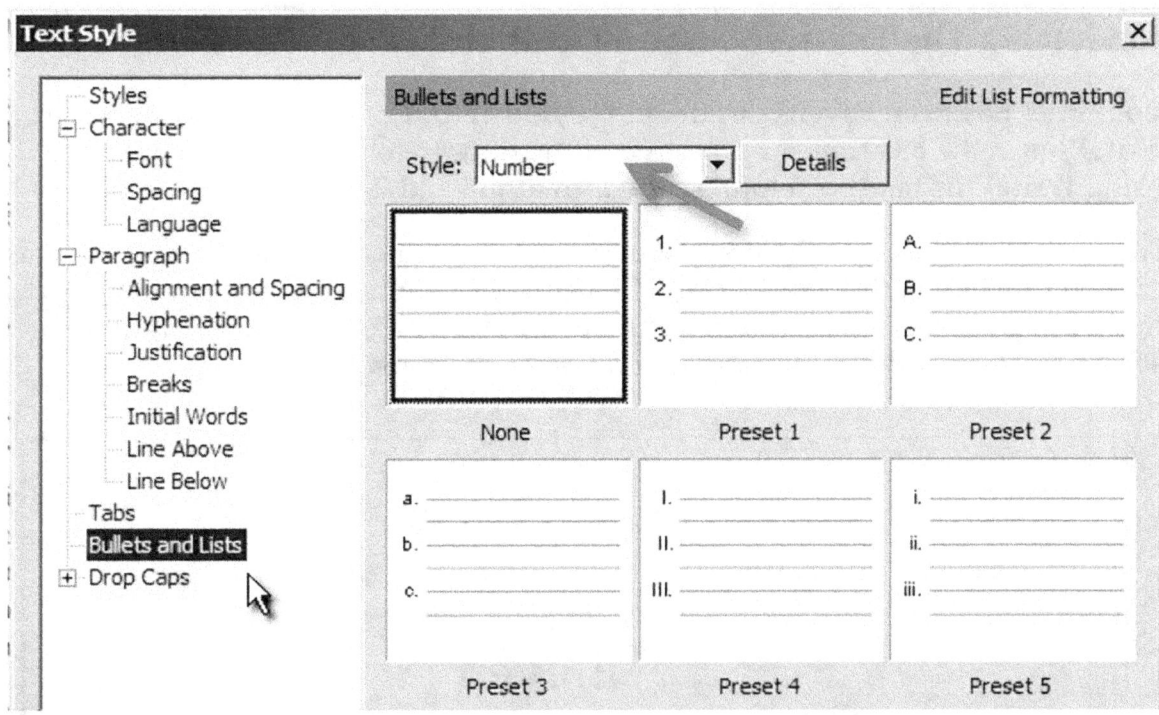

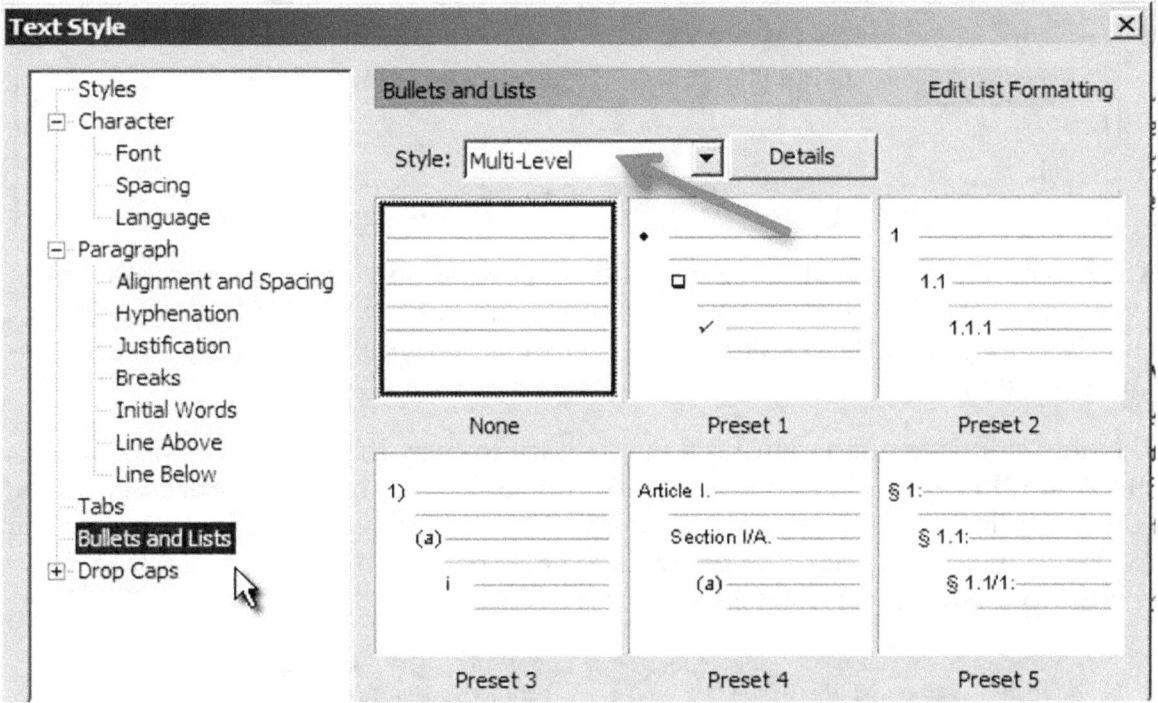

As you can see PagePlus X4 offers many options for Bullets and Lists. You can just use the plain bullets, numbers, or create multi-level lists and they will be consistent throughout your book.

Now that all of those formatting steps have been covered, the next few pages will review how to transfer content from a final manuscript to PagePlus X4 with a book that is almost exclusively text, unlike this book filled with screen shots. Graphics tend to make the formatting process more complex. However, text only can pose it own problems. Some of those have already been covered in detail but this review should help you to get your own text only book ready to publish.

Reviewing The Transfer Of Text Content To PagePlus X4

BookPlus has been covered in detail previously but a review of how to use **WritePlus** in the text transfer process and the steps to follow after you are done using **WritePlus** may be helpful so the formatting and layout flow smoothly.

The screen shot below is the first page of a chapter using the master page that was created for chapter first pages. Begin by using the chapter title box outlined by the master page to type in the chapter number and the name. This first chapter will set the location of this information for all other chapters.

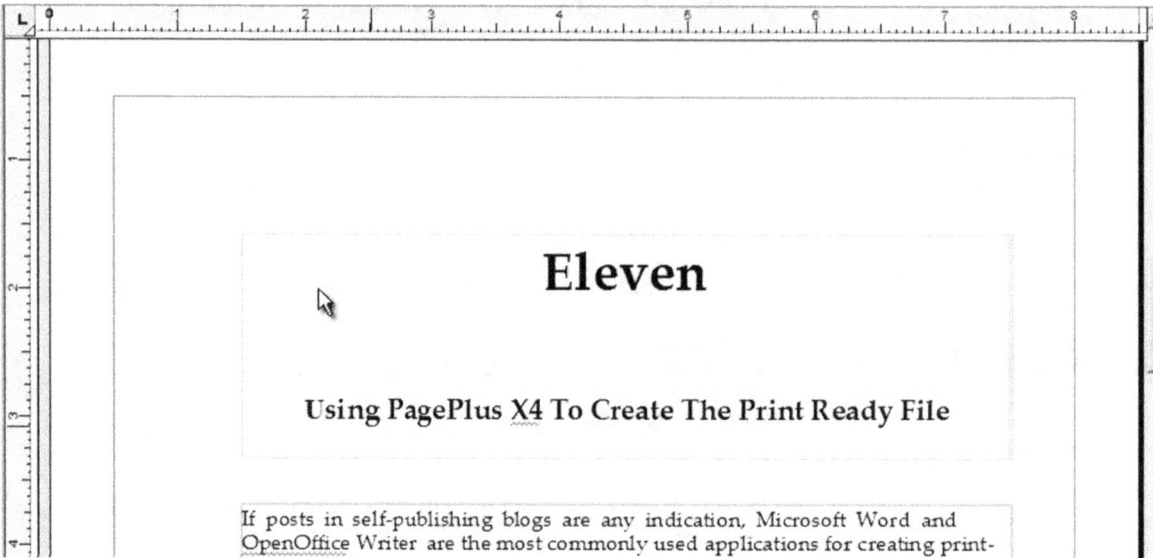

After completing the chapter or part title you can simply copy it and paste it into every other chapter title box and it will be located exactly as the first one. Then simply correct the title in place to reflect the chapter you are working on to maintain consistency.

The next step is to go to your final manuscript to copy the content for transfer to the **WritePlus** application. Your manuscript can be on any word processor or text editor application. It does not have to be formatted correctly since you can do that in **WritePlus**. The screen shot below is the first part of this book. It is not in the correct font and may not have the correct settings.

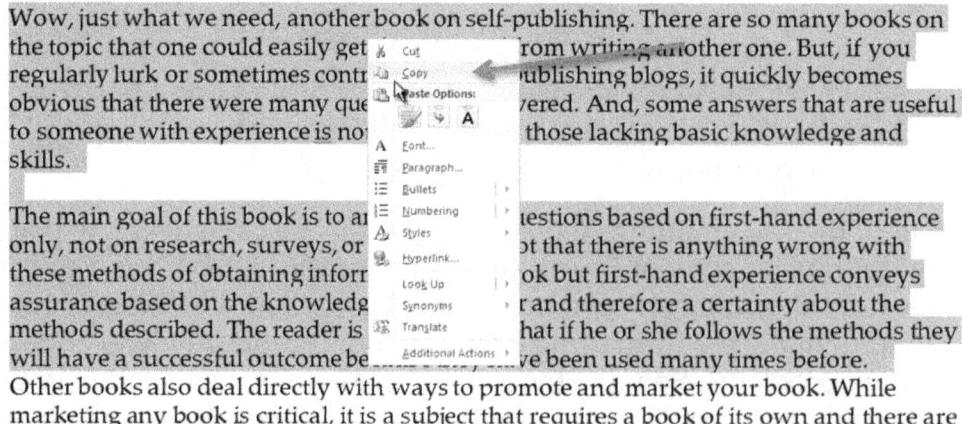

As shown in the screen shot on the bottom of the previous page, you highlight the text to be transferred, copy it, and move to PagePlus X4 to open the **WritePlus** application.

Move back to PagePlus X4 and place the cursor in the text box where the copied text will be pasted but do not paste it. Instead click on Format and select Text Manager as previously illustrated. Then paste the content into **WritePlus** as shown below.

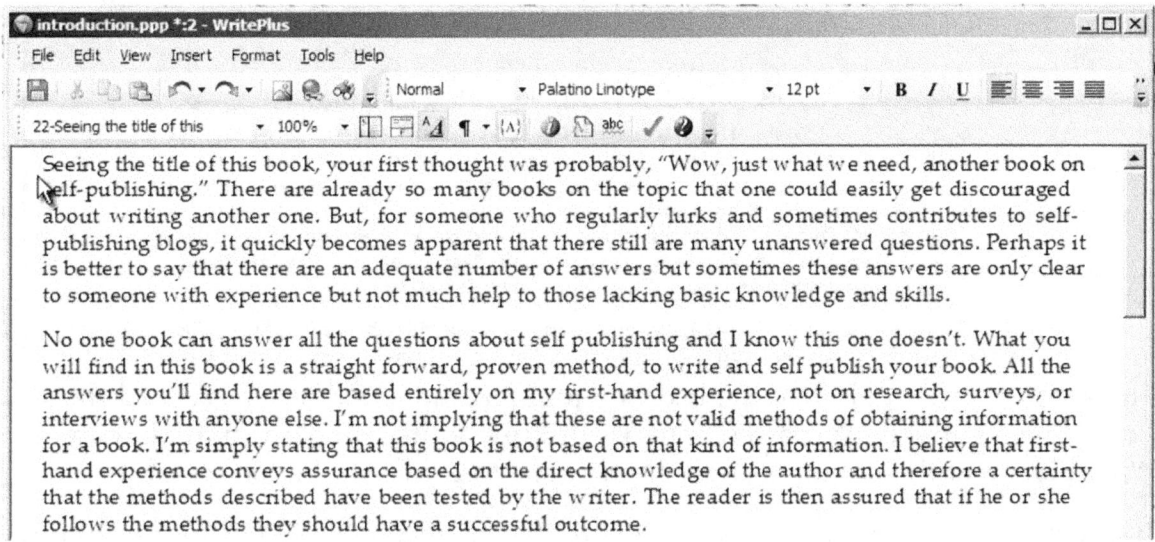

Once it is in **WritePlus**, simply highlight the content by choosing Edit and Select All. Then you can use all the previously described formatting tools to set the font type, font size, and all the related paragraph settings.

This is where extra care and time will pay off with a well designed and attractive book. There are many considerations related to paragraph settings. Most importantly is the spacing between various parts of the text.

This may involve many choices. In my book the following settings were made. The paragraph setting has no indent on the first line of each paragraph and 10 points of space between paragraphs. The Palatine Linotype font was selected and set at the 12 point size. The line spacing was set at exactly 14 points. While there is not a hard and fast rule, 2 to 2.5 points of line spacing above the font size usually works well. So, the font size for this book is 12 points and the line spacing is 14 points. To set the spacing to the size of your choice set the line spacing to the Exactly making certain every line is the same.

Once you have completed the settings in the Paragraph settings box, you save them and then save the **WritePlus** file. Once you save the **WritePlus** file the changes are made in your book file so you can close **WritePlus**.

Once **WritePlus** is closed you will see the text appear complete in your book file. On the first screen shot on the next page, the top arrow points to the part of the first page of chapter one that was created directly in PagePlus X4.

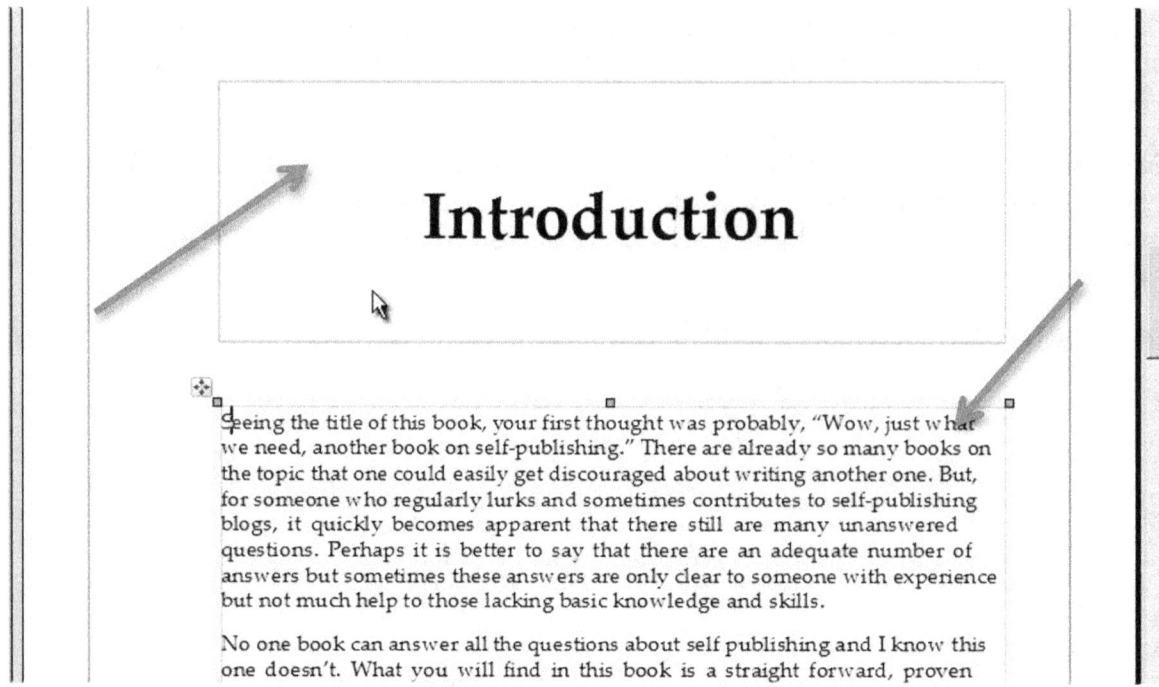

The second arrow points to the text box that has the text that was copied from your final manuscript, pasted into **WritePlus**, edited and formatted with **WritePlus**, and then automatically transferred to the file in PagePlus X4.

It's best not to assume that because you edited correctly in **WritePlus** everything will fit perfectly into the final file. Remember that **WritePlus** is one single document page upon which everything fits. The book file for each chapter will consist of many pages so you must make certain that the pages flow correctly and that each page looks good.

When you are going through the pages there are several things to watch for but the most common problem is a single line from a paragraph at the top or the bottom of the pages. You should always make certain that there are at least two lines of a paragraph at the beginning and end of each page. The only time one line alone is acceptable is in the case of a one line paragraph.

Another important thing to watch for is spacing between words and letters. This is seldom a problem with books like this one where the text is left justified. Full justification, where the right and left margins are fully justified requires compromising of space since each line has a different number of words and letters. Most publishing programs, including PagePlus X4, do a fairly good job with this but you do have to be vigilant in case the program creates lines with poor spacing.

This may sound like a minor issue but lines with wide spaces between words or letters look unprofessional. This should be important when publishing your own books but especially so when you are publishing a book for someone else since they are depending on you to create a professional product.

When you are transferring entire chapters of text from **WritePlus** to the individual PagePlus X4 chapter files you will find that the text ends on a page and doesn't include all the content that appeared in **WritePlus**. This happens because

WritePlus is a continuous single page of content and your book is comprised of many pages. When the text seems to end and fails to continue to the next page, this doesn't mean that the text did not transfer. If you extend the text box you would see that the text continues.

This is an easy fix and merely requires clicking on the content of the last page so that the frame of the page appears. Then you will see a small rectangle at the bottom right of the page with a small green plus sign.

The green plus sign indicates there is more content that doesn't fit in this page. To resolve this problem, just select the next page in the Pages box at the right to identify it as the location where the text should be continued. Then reselect the page with content and click the green plus sign and it will give options and show where the content will go, normally the next page. If it indicates an incorrect page that you chose by placing the blue border around it, click to cancel or the text will continue into the wrong location.

Normally this means either the next page lacks a text box or there is something wrong with the text box. Should that occur, just select the problem text box, delete it and then create a new text box and retry clicking the green button. This usually resolves the issue. Then you click OK and the content will continue to move forward even if it has to create more pages.

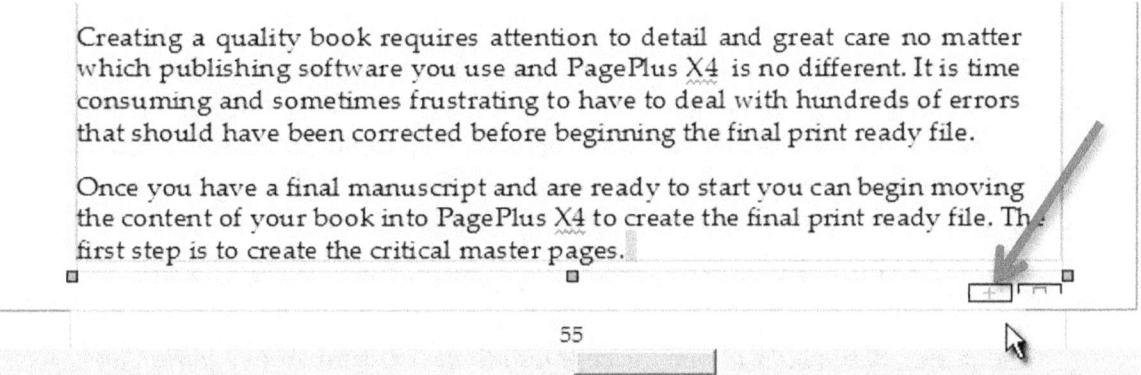

When the green button is clicked the message below will appear giving you the opportunity to make certain that the next page of text will be placed correctly. Don't just blindly click because it will simply mean more work to get rid of the text from the wrong location. Check first and then click Yes when ready.

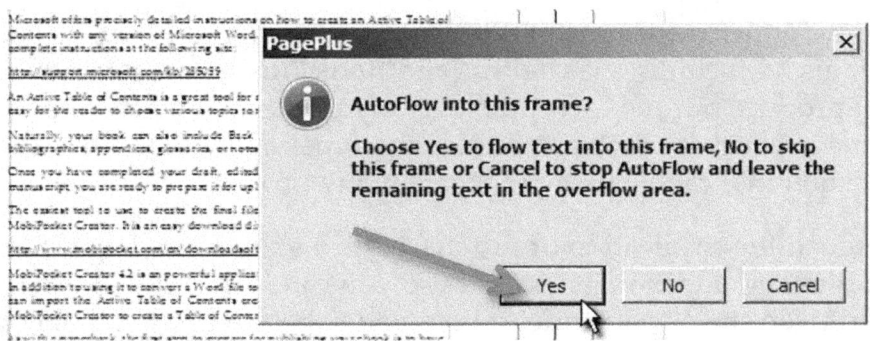

When you click the Yes button the text will flow into the correct page and continue to flow onto other pages until there is no more text to transfer. If you don't have sufficient pages a message will pop up asking if you would like it to create additional pages and frames to match the one you are on. If you click Yes it will continue to flow the text after creating as many pages as necessary to accommodate the pasted text.

Successful formatting and layout require attention to detail. Check the details of each page as you go along to make certain of the correct results. This is especially important with the master pages. Selecting the wrong master page will create issues that are quite obvious to the reader.

When Not To Use WritePlus

WritePlus is an excellent and powerful tool and should be used in most cases to transfer content to PagePlus X4. However, there are times when it's necessary to transfer content directly into the book pages. Sometimes it may even be best to type your book directly into the PagePlus X4 files.

This chapter is a prime example of a situation when **WritePlus** shouldn't be used to transfer content. Because of the extensive number of illustrations, the text flow is consistently interrupted. Unlike an all text book, it requires other methods and is a prime example of how you must be prepared to make the best possible use of the tools you have.

> *Because of the large number of screen shots in this book I developed a method to make the best possible use of PagePlus X4. I did type text drafts for many of the longer sections. Then I would copy and paste those directly into PagePlus X4 without using WritePlus. Because of the brief length of each transfer I was able to work well in the individual files.*
>
> *I also found that it was much simpler to just type the short descriptions between the screen shots directly into PagePlus X4 as I added the screen shots. But that would not be the case for an all text book or one with few screen shots or other illustrations.*

Using the method of working directly within PagePlus X4 did not interfere with editing the content. Even when major changes were made it was easy to either move the screen shots or simply copy and paste them from one page to another. PagePlus X4 accommodates various methods of working.

Using the instructions and screen shots in this chapter you should be able to successfully use PagePlus X4 including **WritePlus** and **BookPlus** to format and layout your book and produce pdf files acceptable to any printer. Nevertheless, you should take the time to learn as much as you can about using PagePlus X4. It is an excellent application that can be using to create many projects.

Whether you download the application or purchase the disk version, PagePlus X4 has excellent help files and additional resources so you can learn how to use it effectively. The Serif web site also includes a knowledge base with searchable information and a really helpful community of users who are always willing to help you resolve any issues you encounter with the application. There are also some excellent tutorials. Check out the web site at:

http://serif.com

Using PagePlus X4 To Format Books For Others

By now you realize that during the creation of your drafts and final manuscript is not the time for detailed formatting. Unfortunately, writers who have excellent skills with word processor applications often feel the need to format their original manuscripts as they create them.

Regardless of the format used by the writer you can use PagePlus X4 to create a print ready file for any printer. You can even accept files in the pdf format.

> *After I contract with someone to either create a print ready file or publish a book, the first step is to obtain the final manuscript. This can pose two problems, the first is that the file I get is not actually a final manuscript. This is a serious problem because it will require significant editing after the book has been formatted. While this can be done, it takes time and causes a great deal of duplicate work. So, if you are doing this work, make certain that the writer understands you must have a final manuscript.*
>
> *The second problem is that some writers will attempt to format their book as they are typing the manuscript. I have received manuscript with so many formatting and style alterations as to create significant problems when transferring the content to PagePlus X4. With one manuscript I had to copy the entire manuscript and paste it into Wordpad to eliminate the excessive formatting before I could copy and paste it into PagePlus X4. I always caution writers to use only the Normal style and only Basic formatting on their manuscripts.*

You can import a pdf file into PagePlus X4 and then either work on it as one file or use **WritePlus** to divide it into the various chapters and then use **BookPlus** to work on the entire book. This allows for many options. You can create the entire book as one section and then add a separate section for the front which could include the Preface, Foreword, Praise for the book, and Table of Contents. Then you could add a separate section at the end of the book section to include a glossary or an index. All of the sections could then be put into **BookPlus** and a single, print ready pdf could be created easily.

Creating A Table Of Contents

It's not possible to know all the parts that will be included in your book but for most books a Table of Contents is essential so the creation of it is explained below.

> *Like office productivity software, PagePlus X4 has a tool and instructions for creating a Table of Contents. These tools work well but I prefer more control over the appearance of my Table of Contents. I still use PagePlus X4 but I do it manually. It takes a little extra effort but I can make it look*

exactly the way I choose for each book. So, the instructions here are for the manual creation of a Table of Contents. If you prefer the automatic method, the instructions are clearly outlined in the PagePlus X4 help files.

To manually create a Table of Contents you use the PagePlus X4 Table tool. To give you an idea of how this works there is a screen shot of a partial table of contents below from a book published by Positive Imaging, LLC. I have chosen to show all the Table margins so you can see exactly how it is done. The Table image is followed by detailed instructions for producing a Table of Contents.

		Introduction	11
	1	**Is The Handyman Business For You?**	17
		Self Employment	
		No large investment needed	
		Set your own hours	
	2	**Inventory of Your Skills**	21
		Learning and Training	
		Making a list of your skills	
		Using your strongest skills	
		Working on doors	
		A few other ideas	
	3	**Inventory of Your Tools**	25
		Power tools	
		Hand tools	
		Carbide tipped blades and bits	

Notice that when all the table margins are visible it gives a clear idea of how the table is created. On the next page is another image of a table like the one above but empty and with instructions about the various cells to help you create your own Table of Contents.

Start by clicking Table from the Menu line and then selecting Insert and then Table. This will bring up a window that allows you to select what kind of table you wish to use.

Select the default because it gives you complete control of the design. And, select the number of rows and the number of columns you need. You may have to do this more than once if your Table of Contents is lengthy and spans more than one page.

This first time pick the number of rows and columns you need for the first page of your Table of Contents. Don't worry if the number is not exact as you can add and remove rows as necessary to make a perfect fit.

You can also adjust the rows and columns to suit you needs. The table on the next page has only eleven rows but it can have as many rows as you need for the Table of Contents for your book. This is how it looks before any adjustments.

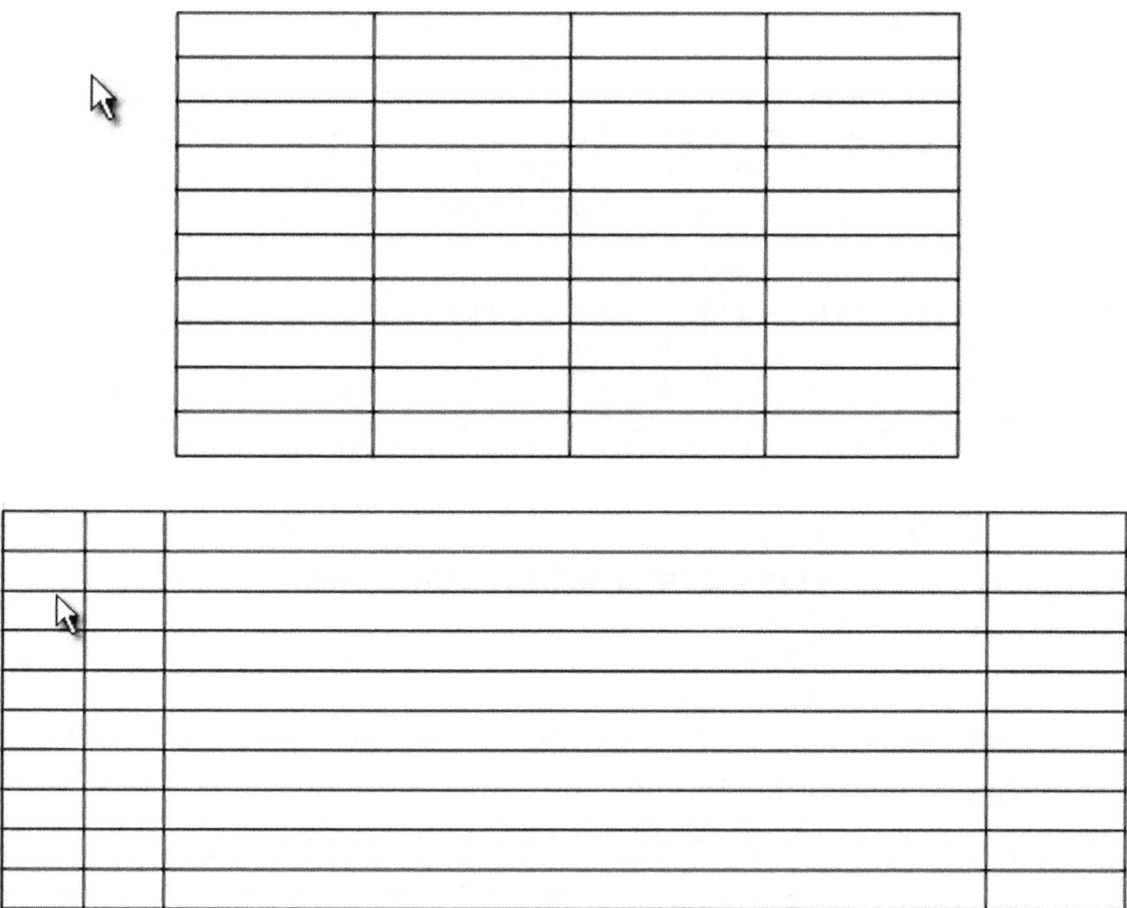

The table above has been adjusted to the correct proportions for this Table of Contents by moving the column lines around. Once that is done you need to change the shape of the individual cells to accommodate the various text.

Cells can be changed in several ways. A cell can be merged with another cell highlighting both and then selecting Table from the Menu and selecting Merge Cells. You can also split cells if necessary.

You can see how this was done on the screen shot below and then Introduction was typed in the cell.

Just follow those steps for each item in your Table of Contents and you can control every aspect. Also notice that the height of each row adjusts automatically to the size of the text. However, if the row looks incorrect, you can adjust the height of each row manually giving you full control of how your Table of Contents looks. PagePlus X4 has detailed instructions on making these adjustments. The last step is to remove the visible margins as explained below.

By clicking on Table in the Menu line and then selecting Cell Properties you can choose to remove all visible margins. Since the default table begins with invisible margins, it will not be necessary to do that. In this case I have made the margins visible so you can see how to create the Table of Contents. Once the margins are not visible the Table of Contents appears as shown below.

		Introduction	11
	1	**Is The Handyman Business For You?**	17
		Self Employment	
		No large investment needed	
		Set your own hours	
	2	**Inventory of Your Skills**	21
		Learning and Training	
		Making a list of your skills	
		Using your strongest skills	
		Working on doors	
		A few other ideas	
	3	**Inventory of Your Tools**	25
		Power tools	
		Hand tools	
		Carbide tipped blades and bits	

Another thing to notice is that this Table of Contents is just one design and the choice here was to put page numbers only on the Chapters and not on the sub headings within the Chapter. This is a choice that I made on that book but on this book I chose to number the Chapters and the subtopics. You can choose either method for your book. This is another of the many decisions involved in the self publishing process.

Using the details in this chapter you should be able to create an excellent print-ready file but it is advisable to take some additional time to learn all the potential of PagePlus X4. The more you learn about it the more flexibility you will have in the preparation of the print ready file for your book.

Twelve

The Free Options

Because this book is based entirely on the method I use to write and publish books, the emphasis throughout is the use of what I believe is the best tool for each part of the publishing process. Using these tools, after going through the learning curve, makes the job easier, more accurate, and less frustrating.

The main products recommended, PagePlus X4 and PhotoPlus X3 or X4, are not free but are inexpensive compared to many products used for publishing and photo editing. I find these products, with their ease of use and excellent support, help me do a better and faster job.

In spite of the low cost of these products there are some who prefer to avoid even this limited expenditure. While this book will not explain how to use some of the free products, it will mention them with some helpful details that can also be found on their web sites together with personal observations.

As I mentioned previously, creating a draft manuscript does not require an expensive word processor capable of handling complex office productivity. While Microsoft Office with the MS Word processor is an excellent tool, if you don't already own it, there is no need to make the investment to publish books.

Open Office

Open Office is a perfectly adequate office suite that is comparable to MS Office and capable of doing anything necessary to produce an outline and a draft manuscript. It is an easy download from the following web site:

http://download.openoffice.org/

OpenOffice is open source software making it completely free and the web site contains a great deal of valuable how-to information and a community of users that participate actively.

In addition to being adequate for preparing manuscripts it is an excellent office productivity suite that serves small businesses well.

The learning curve for Open Office is similar to that of Microsoft Office but for basic creation of a manuscript it is quite easy to use.

Scribus

The introduction to the Scribus application on their web site states the following: "Scribus is an Open Source program that brings professional page layout to Linux/UNIX, Mac OS X, OS/2 Warp 4/eComStation and Windows desktops with a combination of press-ready output and new approaches to page design."

"Underneath a modern and user-friendly interface, Scribus supports professional publishing features, such as color separations, CMYK and Spot Color support, ICC color management, and versatile PDF creation."

> *Scribus has fascinated me for sometime and I plan to learn how to use it and begin with publishing a small booklet for practice. I have played around with it and it seems to be great application with infinite potential and, most importantly, it is open source and therefore completely free. The application can be used for both formatting and layout but is also an excellent tool for creating book covers. As a good, all-in-one tool it merits the time to undergo its significant learning curve. I definitely view that as a worthwhile effort and in time it may replace the Serif applications in my publishing business.*

Scribus can be downloaded free at: http://www.scribus.net/canvas/Scribus

Gimp

Gimp is an excellent application that is available free to anyone. It seems to be the equal of Photoshop, an excellent but expensive application from Adobe. On the Gimp web site you will find the following details, "GIMP is the GNU Image Manipulation Program. It is a freely distributed piece of software for such tasks as photo retouching, image composition, and image authoring. It works on many operating systems, in many languages."

"It has many capabilities. It can be used as a simple paint program, an expert quality photo retouching program, an online batch processing system, a mass production image renderer, an image format converter, etc."

"GIMP is expandable and extensible. It is designed to be augmented with plug-ins and extensions to do just about anything. The advanced scripting interface allows everything from the simplest task to the most complex image manipulation procedures to be easily scripted."

"GIMP is written and developed under X11 on UNIX platforms. But basically the same code also runs on MS Windows and Mac OS X."

> *Gimp seems to have all the advantages of Photoshop without the high price tag. I have used Gimp many times but am still in a learning phase. Since I own Photoshop and PhotoPlus X4, there isn't much motivation to learn a new graphics program. However, for those willing to meet the challenge of*

a lengthy learning curve, Gimp is the best deal around. It is another one of those applications I will get around to learning when time permits and I definitely recommend it to anyone.

Gimp can be downloaded free at: http://www.gimp.org/downloads/.

Photoscape

This is another good photo editing application. CNET editors gave it four stars and wrote the following about Photoscape: "Add another name to the roster of feature-rich freeware image editors: PhotoScape. Although it eats and leaks about as much memory as Firefox, this editor is perfect for those making the jump between JPEG and am-pro dSLR work."

"It supports RAW, as well as all other major image formats from JPEG and PNG to animated GIFs. It comes with prebuilt templates for users to create photo collages, fumetti, and Web comics, and has a standard set of red-eye removal, light/shadow, and contrast-editing features. One warning about the RAW processing: although it looks like you can drag and drop, the converter doesn't change RAW to JPEG unless you load the RAW file from within the native file navigator. It's a minor bug, but one that can lead you to believe that there's no RAW support at all. You can also batch edit images, combine them, and print them out one at a time or several at once."

In all honesty, I have only used Photoscape to process my vacation photos. I returned from Spain with over 1,300 digital photos and thought that I would face a nightmare editing, culling out, and preparing a slide show. Instead Photoscape easily facilitated batch editing and made the job quite pleasant. So, if you need to edit a large number of photos, this is an excellent tool. It is also capable of much more in the hands of someone willing to learn how to use all of its features.

Photoscape can be downloaded free at:
http://download.cnet.com/PhotoScape/3000-2192_4-10703122.html

Inkscape

This is an excellent and free scalable vector graphics editor. The Inkscape web site states: "An Open Source vector graphics editor, with capabilities similar to Illustrator, CorelDraw, or Xara X, using the W3C standard Scalable Vector Graphics (SVG) file format."

"Inkscape supports many advanced SVG features (markers, clones, alpha blending, etc.) and great care is taken in designing a streamlined interface. It is very easy to edit nodes, perform complex path operations, trace bitmaps and much more. We also aim to maintain a thriving user and developer community by using open, community-oriented development."

This is an application I recently found and have only used it to create a few lines with arrows on the end. Clearly it has immense potential for anyone willing to learn how to use it to advantage.

Inkscape can be downloaded free at:
http://inkscape.org/download/?lang=en

NVU

This is an excellent WYSIWYG web site creation software. The publisher accurately describes it as: "Nvu (pronounced N-view, for a "new view") makes managing a web site a snap. Now anyone can create web pages and manage a web site with no technical expertise or knowledge of HTML. Finally! A complete Web Authoring System for Linux Desktop users as well as Microsoft Windows and Macintosh users."

> *I used NVU for years and still manage some of my web sites with this easy to use application. Admittedly, I now use Serif's WebPlus for many of my web sites because, like PagePlus and PhotoPlus, I find it easy to use and enjoy good support for the product. However, I highly recommend NVU as an excellent, free web creation application.*

NVU can be downloaded free at:
http://download.cnet.com/Nvu/3000-10247_4-10412423.html

About Free Software Applications

If you spend any time on the web, you have received information about free software. It is definitely readily available and much of it is quite good. Unfortunately, many such applications come with hidden dangers including Trojans that can damage your computer.

Since so much of this software is quite good it is a good idea to make use of it to publish your book or to perform other computer based tasks. There is a simple and safe way to make certain that the free software you download is safe and effective. You simply have to make certain that you only download software from safe locations on the web.

There are quite a few safe places to get free software but listed below are two that have been around for years and never include anything dangerous with the free software you download. These two are CNET and SourceForge and their main web sites are listed below.

http://www.cnet.com/ - this is the main site so just click the Download tab.

http://sourceforge.net/ - this is the main site where you just select your category and find free software.

While on the subject of free software is a good time to deal with the issue of viruses. It's critical for those who work with computers, as do most writers and publishers, to protect their computers from viruses. This makes perfect sense but it's amazing how many people ignore the need for antivirus software or install the software and fail to update it on a regular basis. And, with the continued virus attacks across the Internet, updates are required almost everyday.

Virus protection has become a growth industry and there are many excellent tools on sale from reputable companies. One such reputable company that has proven itself over many years is Avast. In addition to their popular professional and reasonably priced antivirus and Internet security software, they have an excellent free product available for a simple registration.

Avast is available at the CNET web site listed previously and at Avast.com. The CNET site states: "Avast made great strides in its previous update. Version 5 set the stage for the modern, massively popular, and free security suite with a new interface that ditched a quirky, late-'90s jukebox style for a more polished look. Easier to navigate, it also became easier to add new features."

"Make no mistake; Avast 6 adds features both big and small. Some that had previously only been available to paid upgrade users are now free for all versions, and newer features have been seamlessly added to the interface experience. If you're familiar with Avast 5, upgrading to Avast 6 won't be that big of a leap."

> *I have used Avast for almost five years now on both my computer and my wife's and have always been well protected. What I like most is that it continuously updates itself and regularly prompts you to download the latest version only requiring free registration every fourteen months. Definitely an excellent cost saving product.*

Especially in a tough economy, it makes excellent sense to take full advantage of free quality software such as OpenOffice, Scribus, and Gimp. However, it is critical to search for safe products from safe locations to avoid having your computer contaminated by viruses.

Notes and Ideas

Thirteen

Getting Your Own ISBN

An ISBN number uniquely identifies books, audio books, and ebooks. The ISBN is a 10 digit number in four parts. The first part is a group identifier that usually identifies the country. The second part is the publisher identifier or prefix which as a self publisher, will identify you. The third part is a title identifier which is a number assigned to the title of the book. The fourth part is a check digit usually between 2 and X where the X stands for 10.

The main purpose of the ISBN number is to specifically identify one title or one edition of a title from a certain publisher. If you are self publishing a book, you are that publisher and the ISBN should be in your name. Without an ISBN most booksellers will not consider selling your book.

For anyone planning to sell their book at Amazon.com, bookstores, or almost any bookseller, an ISBN is an absolute necessity. However, you do not need an ISBN to publish a book. If you are intent on selling your book entirely on your own without placing them in bookstores, wholesalers, or Amazon, an ISBN is not required. The ISBN number is not the copyright registration.

Getting an ISBN is wise even if you don't plan to use these sources to sell your book as things may change if demand increases for the book. In that case, you would be prepared to reach all of these sources if your book already has an ISBN number.

Bowker, The Official ISBN Source in the USA

ISBN numbers can only be purchased from ISBN agencies. In the USA, Bowker is the only official source of ISBNs. Even though Bowker can only issue an ISBN for books being published in the USA, you can sell your book anywhere in the world with the USA purchased ISBN.

You will find that many companies who help self publishers offer to give you an ISBN at no cost. This seems like a great deal to the inexperienced but it's problematic. ISBN numbers cannot be transferred so if you get an ISBN from anyone other than Bowker, you are not the owner of that ISBN and this could create problems should you decide to print your book elsewhere. Owning the ISBN gives you the flexibility to have your book printed anywhere you choose instead of being stuck with the first printer you chose.

> *To publish my first POD book, my wife's children's novel, I chose a company other than Createspace. Fortunately, I had already read enough to know that I should own the ISBN. It wasn't long before I realized that the prices of my first choice were considerably higher than I needed to pay. I quickly found another company (Booksurge, now merged with Createspace) to print my book and it was not difficult to change the ISBN to the new printer because it was mine. I could have been stuck with paying too much for the books indefinitely had I not realized the importance of using my own ISBN. In publishing, as in most things, you find out quickly that there is no free lunch.*

Save With Ten or More

If you only plan to self publish one book, just buy one ISBN number. It will cost you $125.00. However, if you plan to write or publish more than one book, purchase 10 ISBN numbers for only $250.00. Even if you only plan to publish two books, you may as well purchase the 10 ISBNs since it cost the same as two purchased separately.

If you have plans for many books, the ISBNs become a real bargain. One hundred ISBNs cost just $575.00 (only $5.75 each). Larger enterprises can purchase 1000 ISBNs for just $1,000.00 (only $1.00 each). For really large publishers who can purchase either 10,000 or 100,000 ISBNs, there are even bigger bargains. Clearly, when these large companies offer you a free ISBN they aren't giving you much in return for controlling where you print your book.

To purchase an ISBN directly from Bowker, go to http://myidentifiers.com and begin by creating an account. Before creating the account, decide the name under which you plan to publish. If you are just going to use you own name, then proceed. However, if you plan to create a small publishing services company, you should set up the name of the company before creating your account and then create the account in that name.

If you are publishing an ebook version of your book, it must have a different ISBN and that must be a standard ISBN. There is no such thing as an eISBN especially for ebooks. As with paperback books, you don't need an ISBN to publish an ebook but lacking it will keep you from selling through most major ebook outlets and curtail your sales.

Remember that only publishers can obtain and assign ISBNs. Distributors, manufacturers, and vendors are not authorized to assign an ISBN. When companies like Createspace assign an ISBN to your book they are doing it as publishers and it is their company name that will be listed as the publisher even though you are self publishing your book.

Once you assign an ISBN to your book it is critical to log into your Bowker account and fill in the necessary information about your book. Until you do this the book will not be listed in the bibliographic databases at Bowker and appear in "Books In Print" so it will be available to bookstores, libraries, and other companies looking for books.

Regardless of your initial plans for your book or ebook or whatever you hear from the POD printer or ebook publisher, obtain an ISBN in your name or the name of your company for every book you publish. This is the only sure way to keep your options open allowing you to respond to the market for your book in the most profitable way.

Notes and Ideas

Fourteen

Publishing With Createspace

Once you decide to self publish a book there are many companies offering you the best way to proceed with your project. For me the only sensible route is to use a POD (print on demand) printer. They may call themselves publishers but that is an incorrect title for them. If you are self publishing then you are the publisher so they can't be the publisher. They are POD printers and you need a printer for your book.

You don't want just a company that will print your book. They have to do much more than that. Printing the book is only step one. They have to fulfill book orders completely so when someone purchases your book they will receive it promptly. They have to make your book available through many channels other than just online. This includes retail bookstores and other outlets. They have to list your book in Amazon.com because they sell more books than any other company in the world. And, they have to do all that at a reasonable price allowing you to make a fair profit on your book. Finally, they have to provide good customer service when problems arise. These are essential to successful publishing.

That is a lot to ask and it's not easy to find. After several attempts and much firsthand experience, I have found a company that meets those requirements in Createspace, an Amazon company.

This entire chapter is based on how to get started with Createspace and completely details every step of the process to get your book printed by them and have them fulfill all the orders. In addition to the instructions, there are many screen shots that will help you avoid confusion so your first experience will be successful and satisfying.

Start by going directly to the Createspace web site at:

http://createspace.com

At the top of the next page is a screen shot of the Createspace home page where you can begin the process.

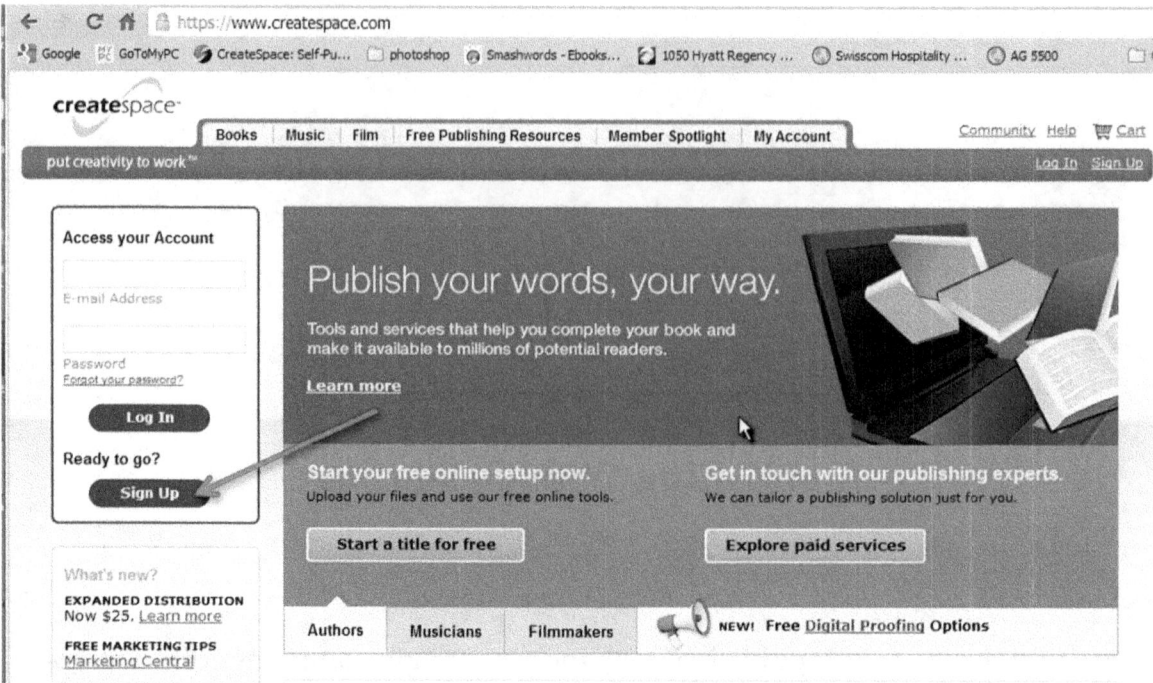

Start by signing up with Createspace. There is no fee involved. If you take a few moments to read the home page you will notice that it allows you to begin the process for your book at no cost. If you only intend to sell your book over Amazon.com, the only cost to you is the printing of each book and the commission when a book sells. You can publish your book without any front end cost. However, I describe many options that do involve some investment but are wise choices if you intend to make many sales.

The screen shot below is the sign up page. Here you will create the account on Createspace that you will use for all your books. As part of your membership you get many useful tools to help you get published including digital proofing of your cover or book interior, 24/7 member support, reasonable royalty rates, and good customer service if you ever experience a problem with a book.

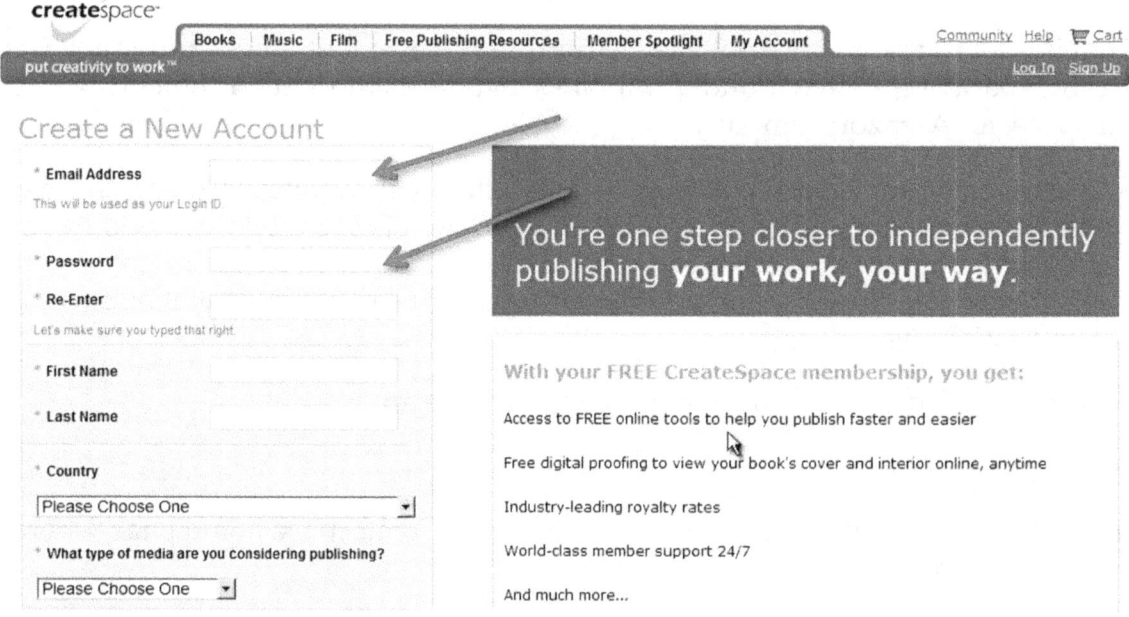

Publishing With Createspace

Once you have an account setup, you can log in at anytime to either work on your book project or use some of their training materials. You simply use the same email you setup initially and the password that your created to enter the web site.

As a member of Createspace you have a dashboard where you can keep track of your book or books. This includes reports on sales and a way to purchase your books at wholesale prices so you can use them for book signings or to place them at local outlets if you choose. The screen shot below shows my dashboard with all the figures removed since there are many books written by others.

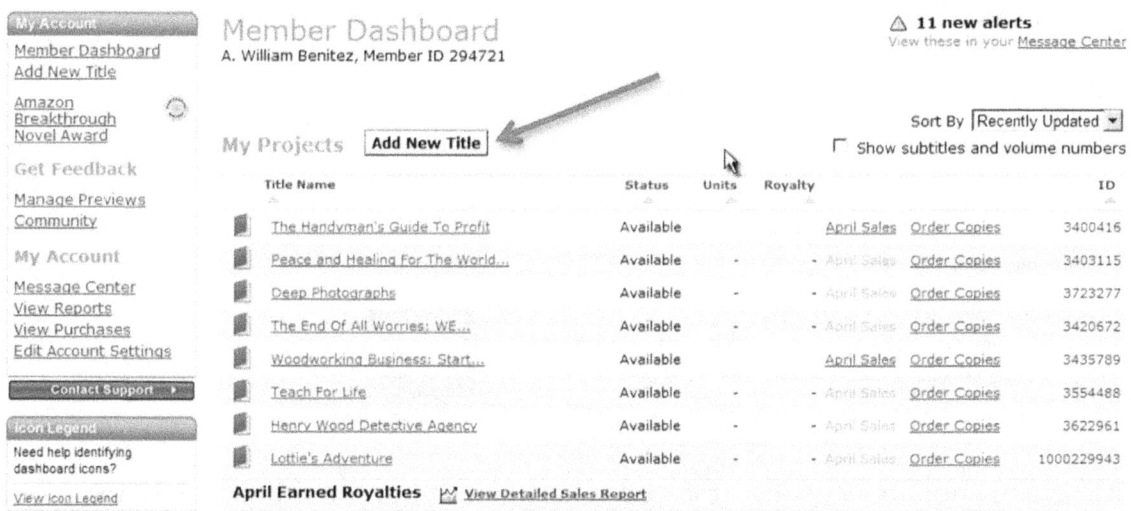

In addition to beginning a new title, you can check the status of any title by clicking it. And, you can see the number of books sold and your royalties at any time. On the left side is a Contact Support button and this will take you to the page shown on the screen shot below. You can ask your question by email or have them call you promptly.

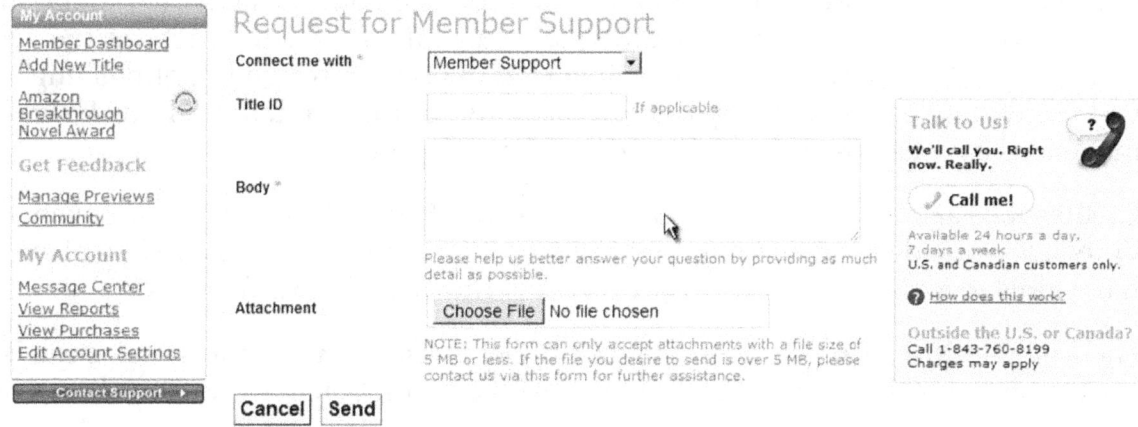

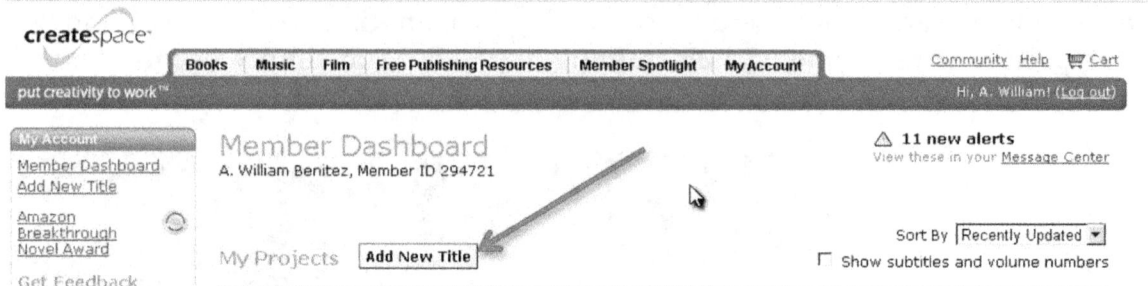

Once you click the Add New Title button you are ready to start publishing your book. The screen shots that follow will take you step by step through the process.

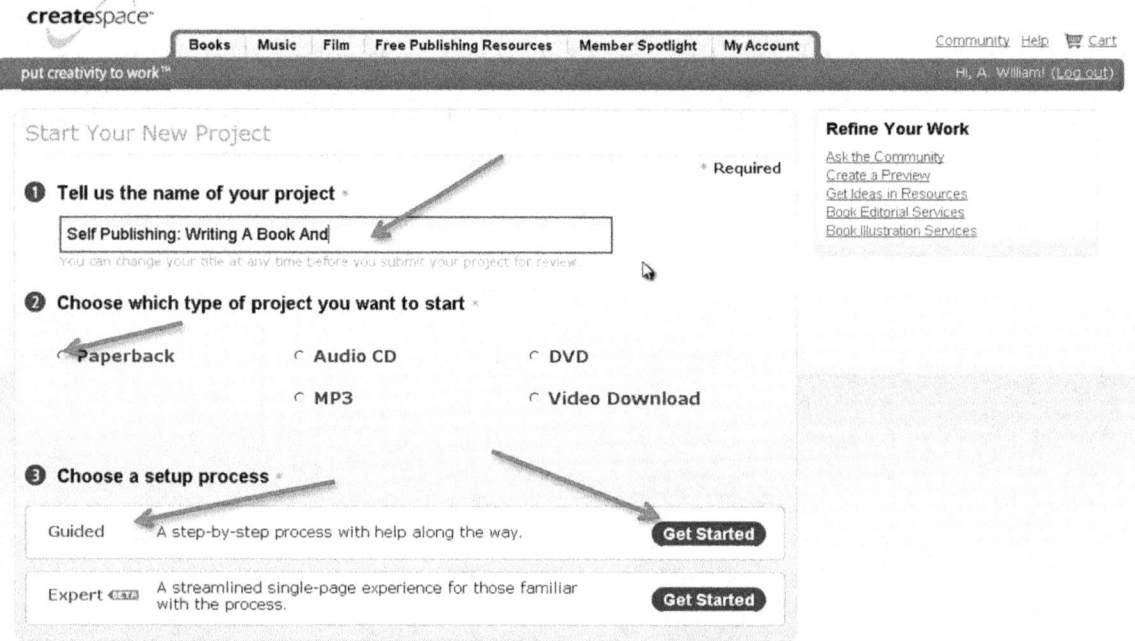

The screen shot above is the first step where you fill in the title of the book. Notice that I started to include the entire title and found out that title length is limited to a reasonable number of characters. I then removed everything but the title and found it best to put the subtitle on another page.

Createspace works for all kinds of publications but I selected paperback. Also at the bottom are two choices of how to proceed. One is Guided and the other is Expert. I normally choose Expert and you can also once you learn how to handle the entire process. This time I chose Guided so you could see the instructions they include to help you. Until you are well versed in going through the publishing process with Creatspace, I suggest you make use of the Guided method. They make it as easy as possible to take each step in the process.

Createspace also facilitates the creation of Audio Cds, MP3s, DVDs, and even Video Downloads for those who create other than paperback books. They also have tools to assist you in making your book into any of those formats.

The first window to appear after you select Get Started in the Guided selection is shown on the screen shot on the next page. I have numbered the various items on the screen shot to help with clarity. Notice there are two ones. I included this to show that the mistake I made on the previous page by trying to include the subtitle on the same line as the title shows up in the project identification box at the upper left hand side of the window. The one on the left shows the incorrect title I typed on the first screen. The second one is the correct title without any part of the subtitle included.

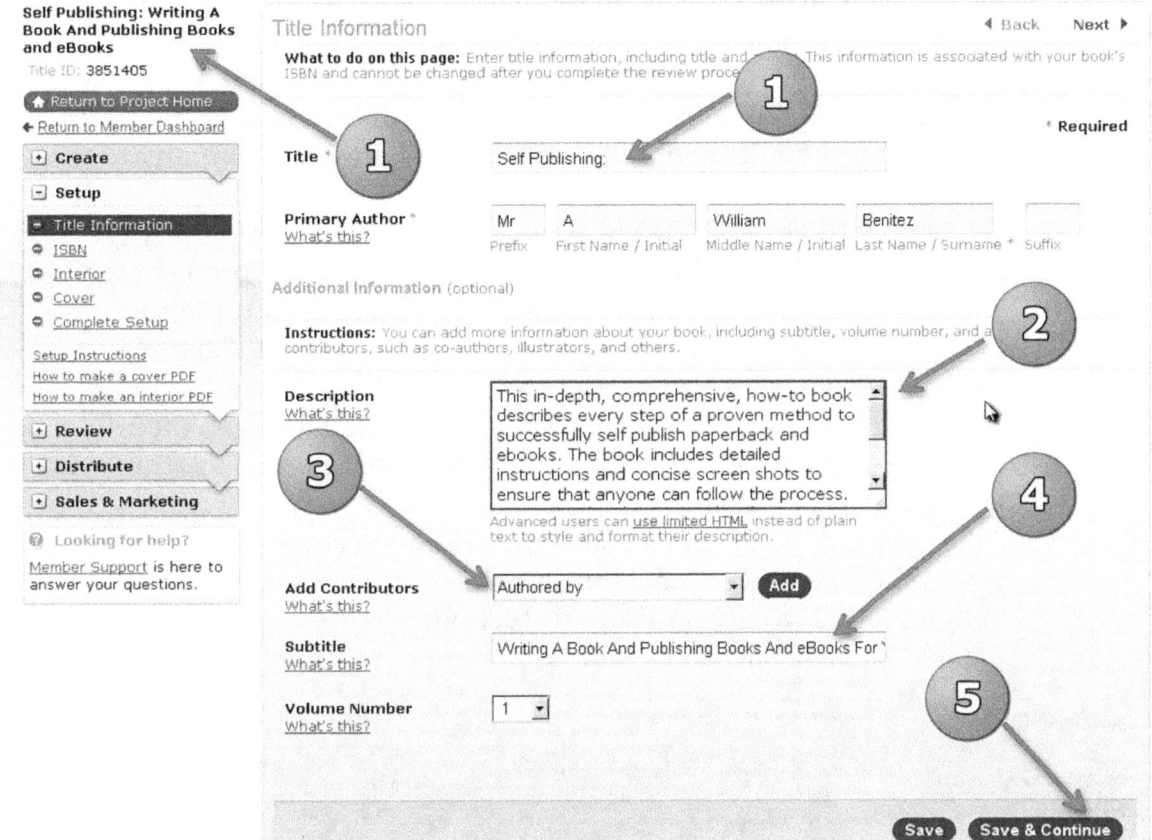

Number two on this screen shot is the description of your book. This is an important statement because it appears in Amazon.com every time someone looks up your book. This description should be written to peak the interest of prospective readers. It should clearly identify the benefits of the book to a potential reader. Make it as interesting and concise as possible. Don't just type it at the spur of the moment. Draft it carefully before you enter it here. Use a separate page and edit it well before inserting. If you are not ready to fill this in carefully, bypass it and go on. You can come back and fill it in later.

The author's name, your name if you wrote the book, should appear as the Primary Author. Be sure to include your name exactly as you want it to appear.

Number three is for Contributors. This could be coauthors who worked with you to write the book, photographers who took any pictures for the book, artists if you have drawings or other artwork. Don't include a name unless you want it to appear on Amazon.com. The information in this section will appear as you have written it with the book during every search.

Number Four is where you write the subtitle of your book and number five is button to Save and Continue to the next part.

The next section is critical to your ownership of the book being published. Making the wrong choice here will remove you as the publisher of record. Chapter Thirteen contains complete information about obtaining an ISBN but based on the numbers on the screen shot below, here is a brief explanation of the options.

1. Free ISBN - This ISBN is not free because if you accept this offer from Createspace, or any POD Printer, you will not be the publisher and you will be stuck with them as the printer of your book.
2. Custom ISBN - This one is only $10 and you are listed as the publisher but you cannot take your book to another company to print.
3. Custom Universal ISBN - This one does make you the publisher and you can take the ISBN elsewhere. If you are only publishing one book, this is a good price at $99. However, if you plan to publish several books, you can do better by reading Chapter Thirteen.
4. Provide Your Own ISBN - This is the best option to give you full control as a publisher. If you are only publishing one book this will cost you $125.
5. This is part of the Provide Your Own ISBN selection. Here you list your ISBN and if you have an Imprint name such as Positive Imaging, LLC, you enter it in this section.

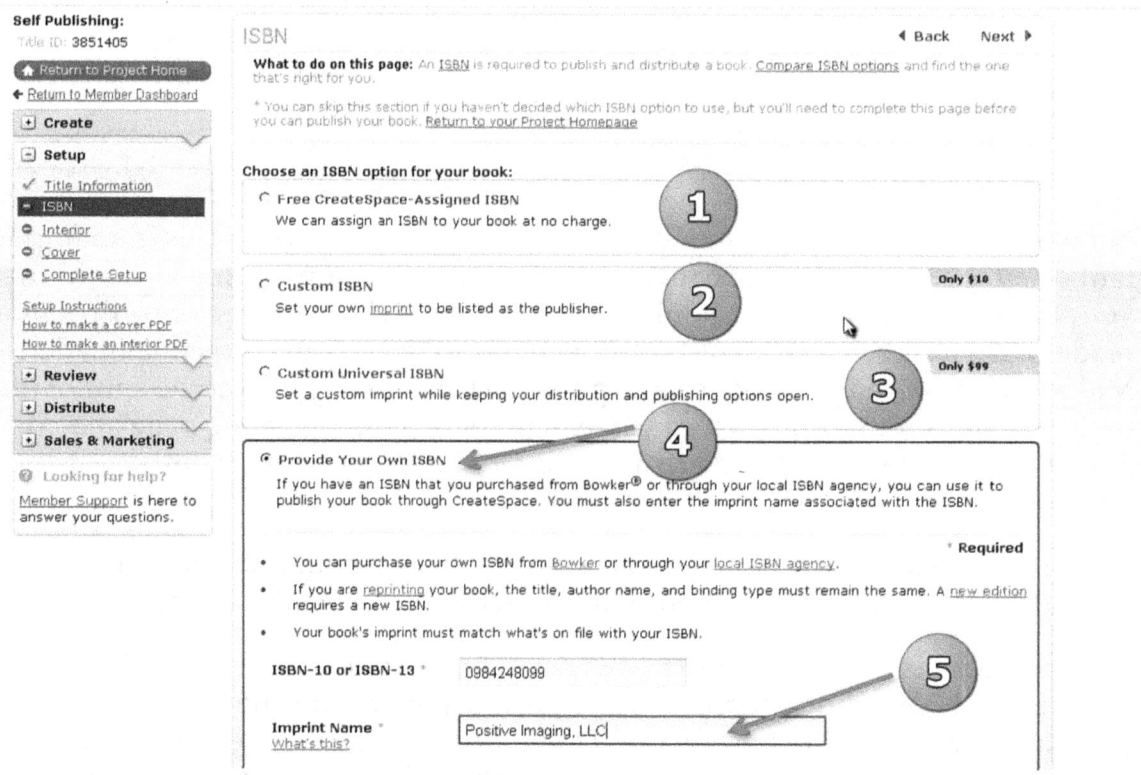

Notice that now the title of the book in the upper left hand corner of this window is correct. Also, as you work on your book you can move to other sections by clicking on the section you choose in the left column. From that column you can also access member support which is information posted by other self publishers.

Once your have concluded work on the ISBN section you click the Assign This ISBN button and your book now has an ISBN as shown on the second screen shot below.

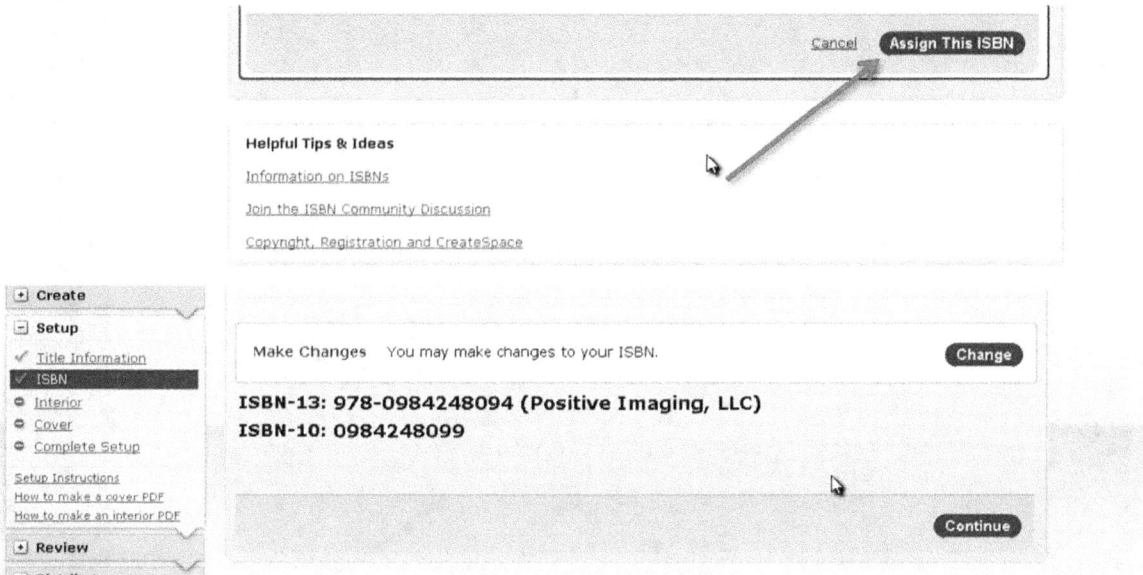

As shown in the screen shot below, the next section is where you make more choices about your book. Here you choose the size of the book, the paper color, and whether your book interior will be black and white or full color. The default book size is usually 6 inches by 9 inches, a common trade size. In this case I clicked Choose a Different Size because my book is 8.5 inches by 11 inches. You may have to select a different size also. If you don't know the size you have in mind, check out a bookstore to see the various sizes. I have published books ranging from 5.25 inches by 8 inches to a full 8.5 inches by 11 inches. The choice is entirely yours.

Choosing the color of the paper is not critical. I always prefer white but for some books cream may give a better impression. Once again this is a personal choice.

Whether your book interior is black and white or full color is a critical choice as there is a significant cost difference and you will have to price your book much higher to realize a profit perhaps pricing yourself out of the market. The thing to remember is that the number of color photos is not important to Createspace. If you need one or more color photos or drawings on the interior pages, it is considered a full color book and priced accordingly.

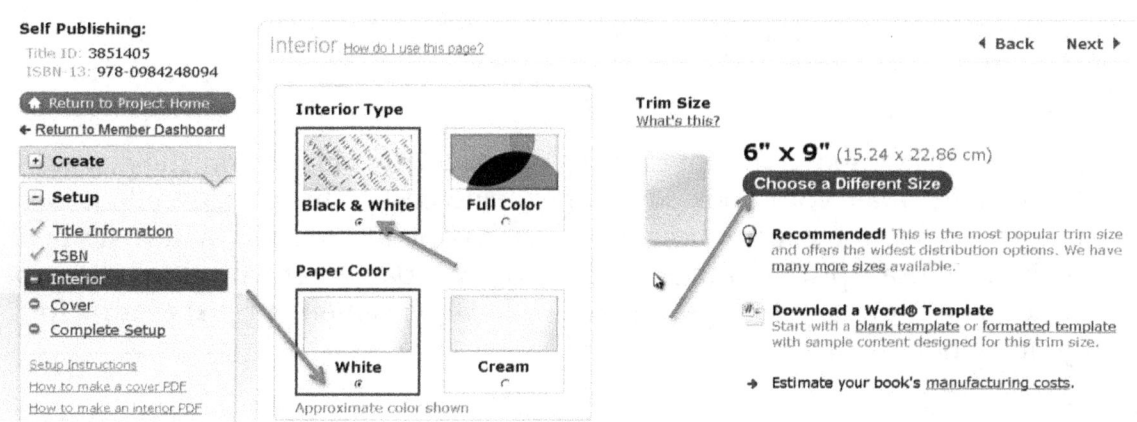

When you click choose another size, a window with the various options appears. I selected the size of my book. Some sizes are not visible on this screen shot.

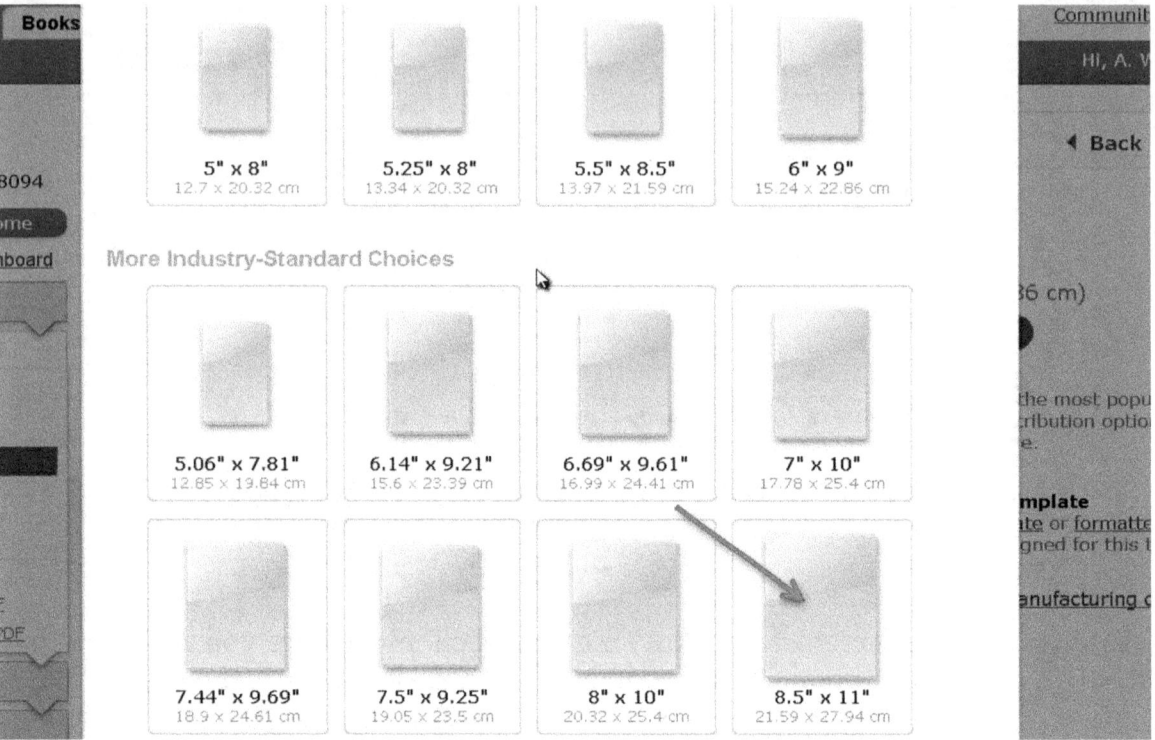

While there may be some common sizes for the kind of book you are writing, chances are there are several options open to you. Naturally, as the size of the book gets smaller, the number of pages increase and this will affect the final wholesale cost of the book. Other factors influence the size of the book as in my case the importance of clear screen shots required a larger book size.

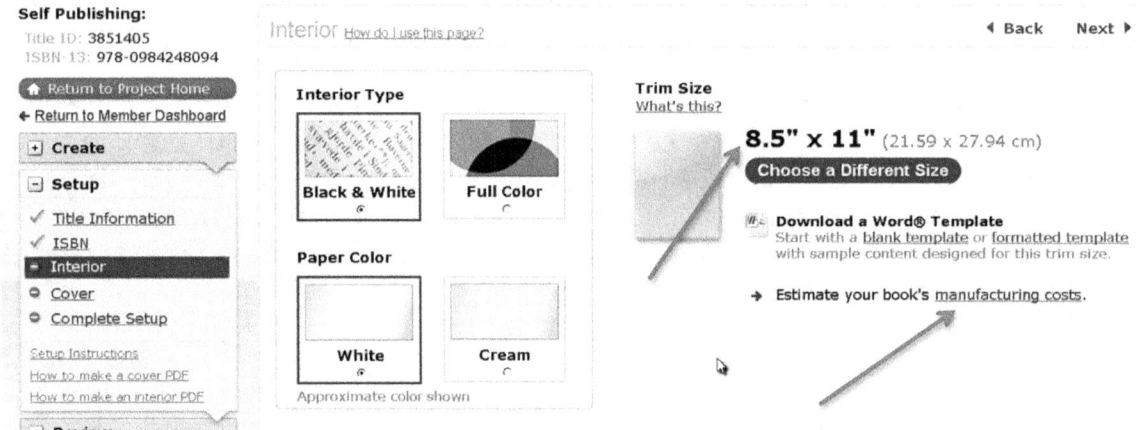

On the screen shot above the first arrow points to my choice and the second points to the Estimate your book's manufacturing costs. This is an excellent tool because it will tell you exactly how much each copy of the book will cost you. This is the wholesale price of the book that you will pay when you purchase copies for yourself for book signings, reviewers, local placement, or just as gifts for family or friends.

Publishing With Createspace

The screen shot below displays the wholesale price of my book based on 166 pages. The final book turned out to have more pages and the final wholesale price is higher. Remember that the wholesale price is only for you when you purchase directly from Createspace for your own use. When anyone purchases a copy of your book from the eStore or from Amazon.com, there is also a commission to pay and that increases your cost considerably.

You can also calculate the shipping cost that buyers will pay when they order a copy of your book. They can choose to wait up to five days or have it delivered in just one day by paying much more for the shipping.

Createspace has made some changes since I first started working with them in 2008. For a long time they would only accept .pdf files for book printing and I still believe that is the best way to submit a print-ready file. However, as indicated in the screen shot below, they now accept .doc, docx., and .rtf files. From the standpoint of controlling the final result, .pdf is still the best since it doesn't require conversion before beginning the actual printing of your book. As is probably obvious in this book, I like to maintain control of all aspects of the publishing of my books and .pdf allows me to see the final product.

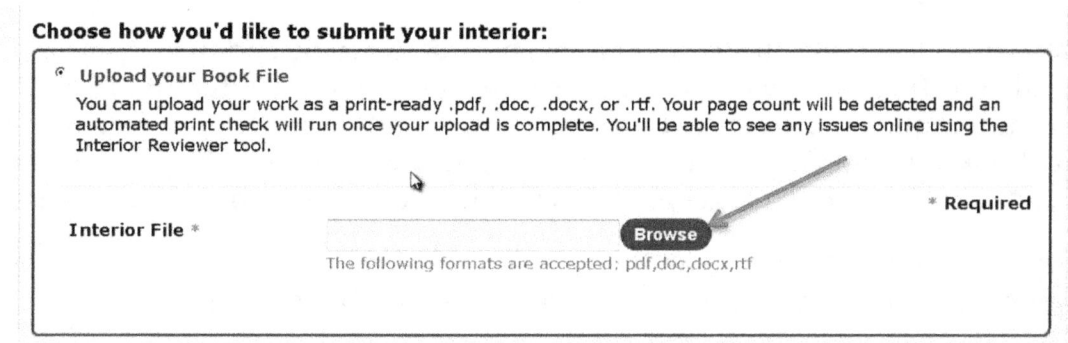

As shown on the last screen shot on the previous page, you browse for your final print-ready file and then you are ready to upload it for your book.

Once you have found the print-ready file it appears in the Browse line ready for upload. Then you have to choose how to handle the edge of the paper. I always prefer to end the page contents just inside of the edge of the paper. For certain kinds of book it might be acceptable to allow the content to bleed beyond the edge of the paper.

The third arrow points to Run automated print checks and view formatting issues online. This is an excellent choice for inexperienced publishers. It will give you valuable information. Naturally, you can choose not to do that.

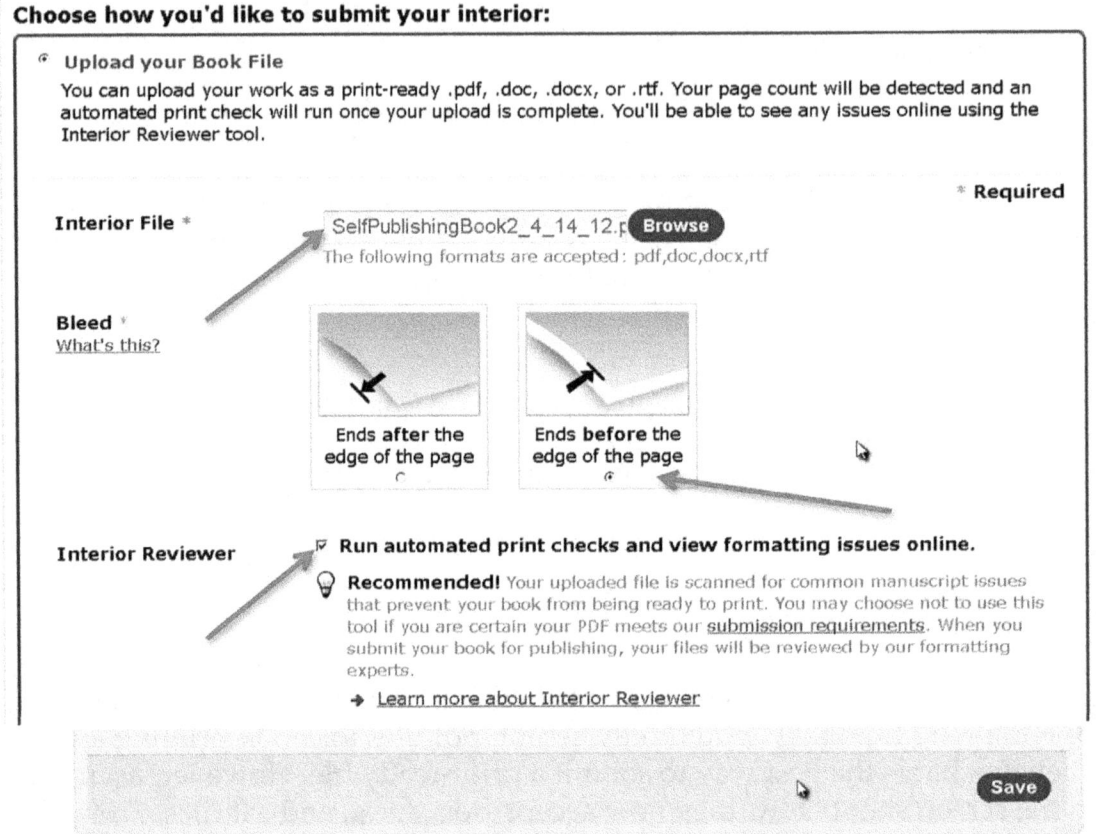

Clicking the Save button is the final step to upload the interior of your book. This prepares things for the next step. The screen shot at the top of the next page shows the name of the uploaded file. Here you have options that you will continue to use until you have completed preparing your book for publishing.

For now, just click Continue to go on to the next part. At the end of the process, when all your files are submitted, Createspace will review your files to determine if they meet required standards. This step is important to protect you from poor quality books. If your files are not satisfactory, they will explain the problem so you can fix it. If the files are accepted you will then order a proof of your book.

The proof is a complete book with the word Proof on the final page. Proofs give you an opportunity to review the book exactly as your buyers will.

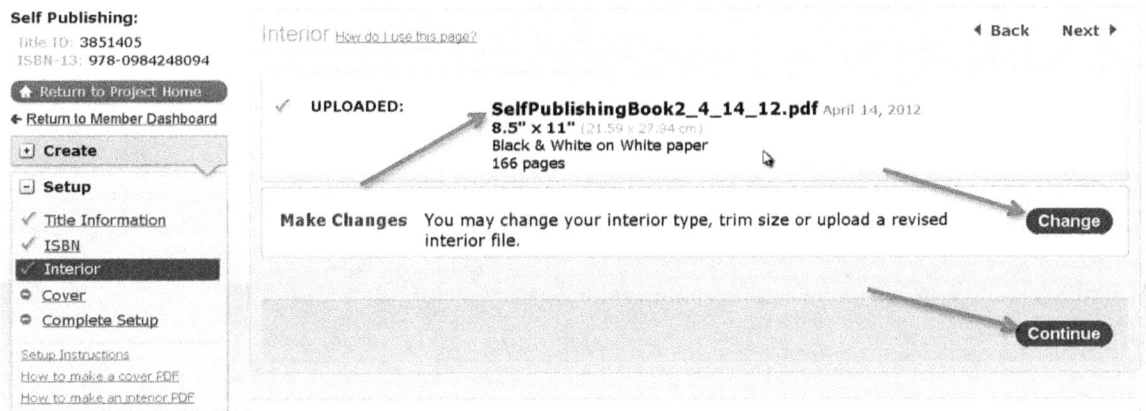

The review process is critically important and the proof should be checked carefully for any mistakes. Have someone else look at it also. I try to have several people look at it because fresh eyes often find errors that I didn't catch.

The screen shot above is where you will go to upload a new file if you have to correct some mistakes after checking the proof. You click the Change button and then upload a new file. Createspace will review the file and then you will order another proof and check it as you did the first. I normally do three proofs to make certain I catch every mistake but this is a choice you must make.

After you develop your standing with Createspace, they will allow you to publish without purchasing proofs. Even though I have reached that stage, I still view proofs as a critical step in the publishing process as they allow me an excellent opportunity to make certain my book looks great before I publish.

Creating The Cover For Your Book

The cover is the final file that you need to publish your book. Two methods for creating a quality cover are described in Chapter Eighteen. The first method involves using graphic software such as Photoshop, PhotoPlus X4, or Gimp to create a cover from scratch. The second and much simpler method is to use the Createspace Cover Creator. This is an excellent tool that allows you to create an attractive cover online using templates and either their photographs or your own. The screen shot below shows how to launch the Cover Creator. For complete details on how to use the Cover Creator go to Chapter Eighteen and follow the instructions and the screen shots for a great looking cover.

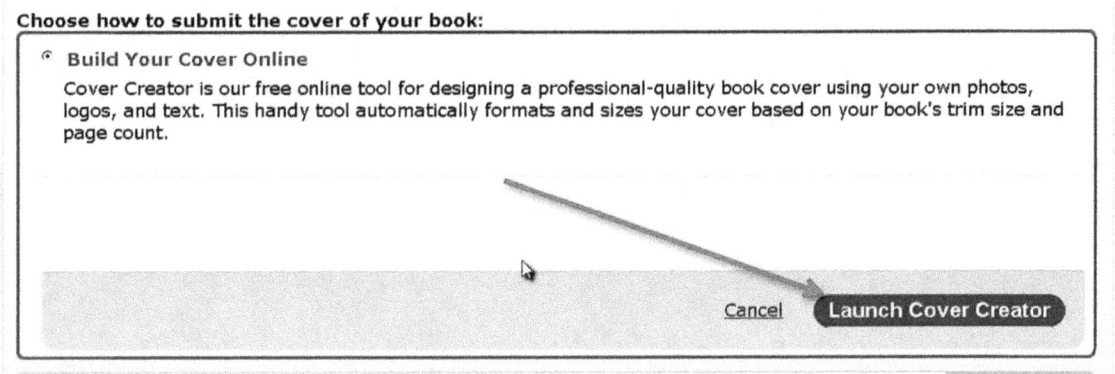

Notes and Ideas

Fifteen

Creating and Publishing eBooks For The Kindle

Amazon Kindle is a great market for almost all books. It can be a secondary ebook market for your paperback books or it can be the sole market for your ebooks. Either way it works great because your books are listed on Amazon. If you begin with a paperback that is listed on Amazon and then create an ebook version, both of them will be available on the same sales page so your prospects have the opportunity to purchase either one.

There are some books that are not ideal for the Kindle. This book falls into that category, not only because of it large 8.5 inch by 11 inch size but also because it contains a large number of screen shots. The book was published in this large size to make the screen shots as clear and easy to view as possible. I believe that publishing it as a Kindle ebook would render those screen shots too small to be of real value.

Books of this size and type can still be sold as ebooks using other formats such as pdf and epub. Chapter Sixteen covers other ebook options for books such as this one which don't fit well within the Kindle format.

The Kindle publishing program is called KDP (Kindle Direct Publishing) and they provide complete instructions and all the tools you need to convert your book file to a Kindle eBook file and begin earning up to 70% commission on every sale of your eBook.

Once you publish on Kindle your eBook will automatically be available for the iPhone, iPad, PC, MACs, Blackberry, and Android. No matter how your customers want to read your book it's available and this increases sales.

In addition to the normal sales channels, Kindle has created a new lending library that, while controversial, has the potential to increase a self publisher's profit on eBooks. As part of this Lending Library Kindle has created a fund that begins with a half million dollars and increases to over six million to pay for the use of the books in the Lending Library. It may not mean much for some books but for popular books it can mean a windfall in addition to sales.

Joining the Lending Library program called KDP Select in no way affects your commission on books sold through KDP. Instead it helps you to make money from readers who seldom purchase books. KDP Select can expose you to more customers and can increase your profits. You can get complete details about the KDP Select program at: http://kdp.amazon.com/self publishing/KDPSelect

Creating a Kindle eBook

There are several easy to follow methods to create a Kindle eBook. One involves creating the manuscript using Microsoft Word and creating a .doc file. This is important to remember because the newer versions of Microsoft Word create .docx files by default and these seldom work well because of additional built-in code that may create issues when converted. To create a .doc file you have to choose **Save As** instead of just **Save**. This gives you the opportunity to save your manuscript as a .doc file. This doc file is the one to use for all of your editing.

There are several important things to remember in creating this .doc file. Start at the KDP web site at http://kdp.amazon.com by becoming a member. It's free and gives you full access to some great tools and lots of free advice.

Kindle converts many formats to the final format for eBooks. These include Word, ePub, plain Text, MobiPocket, and HTML. There several ways to arrive at the final Kindle format and many companies willing to handle the entire process for you for a fee ranging from quite reasonable to fairly unreasonable.

Since the KDP site is so informative, this book will only cover the one method used at Positive Imaging, LLC to create the final file for conversion. This method works consistently and should work well for you and preclude the need to hire someone to do the conversion.

This method uses two applications to prepare the file for conversion. The first is Microsoft Word 2010 but any version of Word will work well. Here are a few things to remember in creating the manuscript in Word.

One – Use the normal template and avoid creating any unusual styles. These will present problems for the conversion. This is the same issue that comes up with manuscripts for Createspace paperbacks. Writers sometimes attempt to format their book by creating complex styles while typing the draft. Keep it as simple as possible.

Two – Make certain that you are saving the file in the .doc format not the .docx format. This can add complications to the conversion process.

Three – You can use indentations, bold text, italics, and headings but avoid bullet points, special fonts, headers, and footers because they will not be transferred and the final result will not look good.

Four – Use a page break after each chapter. This keeps the text from running together in the Kindle reader. Remember, there are no specific pages in a Kindle reader since the user can alter the size of the font and can also read in both the vertical and horizontal position which alters the length of the lines. A page break will push the beginning of a chapter to a new page in the Kindle.

> **Note:** The importance of the page break in creation of a professional looking Kindle book can't be overemphasize. To create a page break in Word simply click the Insert Menu at the top and the select Page Break.

Five – The Kindle automatically indents the first line of each paragraph and it displays the text fully justified so you don't have to handle that aspect of the formatting. However, if you want a specific indentation at the beginning of a paragraph, do not use tab spacing. This does not convert into the Kindle format. To control the indentation use the Paragraph Formatting to set the first line indent. Since this is automatically done it is best to leave it alone.

Six – Images may be used but it's important to center them on the page and to control their location using page breaks. For example, if you want the picture to have a page of its own, place a page break after the text and then after the image. This will devote a full page to the image. If you would like an image set at the beginning of a chapter, put a page break at the end of the previous chapter, place the image and then use the Enter key to add one or two line spaces after the image and follow that with the rest of the chapter text.

Seven – Use .jpg images exclusively and insert them into the manuscript. Do not copy and paste them into the manuscript. This is an important distinction to remember. Even though many Kindle devices only see images in 16 shades of gray, you can leave the pictures in color because they can be viewed in color using the free Kindle apps for PCs, MACs, iPad, iPhone, Android, and the Kindle Fire.

Eight – Like a paperback, Kindle books can have a Title Page, Copyright Page, Dedication, Preface, Prologue, etc. You should have at least a title page and each of these pages should be separated by page breaks to make them individual pages in the Kindle book.

There are several things that should be added to your Kindle book to make it a much better product. These are not required to upload your book and should not be used for short and simple books. However, longer and more complex books will definitely benefit from having both a Table of Contents and Guide Items. These guide items work with the Kindle Go To feature to make it easy to navigate the ebook.

The easiest tool for creating an Active Table of Contents is Microsoft Word. If you are already using Word to create your manuscript then it's easy to begin the process. Before starting to work on the Active Table of Contents, use the Save As command to save the completed manuscript under a different name. You can simply add the numeral 1 at the end of the file name and save it. Then any changes you make to the file will not affect your completed manuscript just in case you encounter difficulties while creating the Active Table of Contents or any other aspect of the file.

Microsoft offers precisely detailed instructions on how to create an Active Table of Contents with any version of Microsoft Word. You can read or print out these complete instructions at the following site:

http://support.microsoft.com/kb/285059

An Active Table of Contents is a great tool for a How-To book because it makes it easy for the reader to choose various topics to read at any time.

Naturally, your book can also include Back Matter which are things like a bibliographies, appendices, glossaries, or notes.

Once you have completed your draft, edited it fully, and deem it a final manuscript, you are ready to prepare it for upload to Kindle.

MobiPocket Creator is the easiest tool to use for creating the final file to upload to the Kindle site and it is an easy download directly from:

http://www.mobipocket.com/en/downloadsoft/productdetailscreator.asp

MobiPocket Creator 4.2 is an powerful application that is available free of charge. In addition to using it to convert a Word file to the correct format for Kindle, you can import the Active Table of Contents created in Word or you can use MobiPocket Creator to create a Table of Contents within the imported documents.

As with a paperback, the first step to prepare for publishing your ebook is to have a completed final manuscript. You can follow the instructions listed above or, if you prefer, you can build the Table of Contents after you have imported your file to MobiPocket Creator.

Your file should initially be saved as a .doc file as previously indicated. The final step before importing is to save the Word file as a Web Page, Filtered (htm or html) file. Once you have done that it is ready to import.

From there you go to the page with all the direct links to the tools needed to convert you manuscripts to the final Kindle format. For more details checkout: https://kdp.amazon.com/self-publishing/help?topicId=A17W8UM0MMSQX6

Easy Kindle Formatting Kit

To help me with formatting files for Kindle publishing I created a complete kit that makes the job quicker and easier and that kit is available at a low price from **http://easykindleformattingkit.com/.** If you find formatting difficult this kit will help you to get your files accepted quickly. You can do the job without it but sometimes a simple kit helps.

For OpenOffice Users

OpenOffice creates a .odt file as the default but is also capable of creating a .doc file if you use Save As instead of just Save. There is an excellent application called Jutoh that allows you to convert .odt files to Kindle ready files but Jutoh is not a free program. It costs $39.00 and is well worth the price. However, since you can convert files for the Kindle with free applications provided by KDP, there is no need to pay for an application.

Sixteen

Creating and Publishing eBooks For Smashwords

Smashwords; the name definitely doesn't strike an inspirational note at first glance, unless you remember that Smash also has a positive meaning. Take a few moments to checkout the details on the Smashwords site and it may sound too good to be true but everything on the site is quite accurate.

http://www.smashwords.com/

Self publishers often start out publishing ebooks because creating them is simpler and involves little if any cost. It once meant setting up your own fulfillment and credit card processing arrangements which were sometimes difficult to obtain and costly. But now, with Paypal to serve as your credit card processor and sites like Clickbank who can handle the entire process for an ebook, it is much easier.

Many ebook self publishers progress to paperbacks using Createspace because it is relatively easy and doesn't require a significant investment to get a paperback book published. Because of this ease, some self publishers lose interest in the ebook but that is a financial mistake. Ebook growth has been astronomical and Amazon is now selling more Kindle books than paperback books. Now self publishers can publish not only ebooks for the Kindle but also make certain that their ebook is available to any interested reader in any format they choose by using Smashwords, a company who has improved ebook creation and marketing significantly.

The success of the Kindle rekindled (no pun intended) interest in ebooks. A recent report indicating they were selling 1.8 Kindle books to every paperback book, proves that it would be unwise to ignore ebooks.

> *I had already begun reformatting my wife Barbara's children's chapter book for the Kindle when I heard about Smashwords. I immediately changed over and now have it published as an ebook with Smashwords. It simply made sense because Smashwords is the world's leading indepen-*

> *dent ebook publisher and distributor with well over 400,000 titles already published.*

There is no question that Smashwords is a quick and simple path to getting an ebook published and noticed. Please remember to read the format requirements before submitting your books for acceptance. Some have experienced difficulty successfully formatting their book even though it's really not difficult. Fortunately, Smashword's helpful owner, Mark Coker, is clearly someone who knows how to create comprehensive how-to information. You can download an invaluable Style Guide and follow it carefully so your ebooks will get accepted the first time.

If you've created ebooks, even for the Kindle, you'll find Smashwords unique. You submit only one properly formatted manuscript and Smashwords, using a computer affectionately called the meatgrinder, turns it into a multi-format ebook that can be purchased and read on many platforms. This multi-format availability is based on a two-step process.

Step one takes place immediately when your manuscript is accepted as properly formatted and becomes available to the public in the following formats: Html and Javascript for online reading, Kindle (mobi), ePub for stanza readers and others, Pdf and Rtf for computers, lrf for Sony Readers, Pdb for Palm reading devices, and plain text. Think about that for a moment, once your manuscript is accepted, it is available in all those formats and immediately downloadable. Remember, even though your Smashwords ebook can be read on Kindle, it is not listed in Amazon and that will affect sales.

There is nothing else you have to do other than get the word out about your ebook. Smashwords handles all the sales for you, creates a sampler version of your ebook, and you choose to provide from 20% to 50% of your ebook to potential customers before they buy. You can also create coupons for special deals, like a certain number of free copies or special discount for a certain time, to encourage sales. Smashwords also does a great deal of marketing for you by showing your other books, should you have more than one. Plus, they show your book when someone is searching for related topics similar to Amazon.

If you are a writer with several books, then your standard profile is fine. If you publish books for other writers, you have to join as a publisher. Either way, there are no fees to join and no cost to publish. Being a publisher is slightly more complex but it allows you control of all your books. Depending on the arrangement, you will get between 70% and 85% of the income from the sale of your ebook. Smashwords makes their money from the balance.

Premium Level is the ultimate step in Smashwords and it is a good idea to strive for this level. There are significant advantages and it's a little more difficult to get your manuscripts accepted at this level but there is still no cost involved. The most important advantage of the Premium Level is that your ebooks become available on more markets including Apple (iPad and iPhone), Barnes and Noble within their Nook ebook format, and Droid. You don't have to attain Premium Level to be a Smashwords author but it could make a significant difference in sales.

For those considering self publishing, Smashwords is an excellent way to start. It's easy to create an acceptable manuscript using Word and you can make revisions and upload a revised copy at any time. This facilitates making sales of your book and learning a lot before you get to the paperback stage. It also helps you determine if your book is salable before making a larger investment. With the present trend towards ebooks, Smashwords is definitely a good place for self publishers.

Notes and Ideas

Seventeen

Creating and Publishing eBooks Using Other Options

Kindle and Smashwords are not the only games in town for eBooks. Clickbank is also a good place for .pdf based eBooks. You can use exactly the same methods that you would use for creating a print-ready file for Createspace except that you would add live html links to your book and also a front and back cover file. Then the book is uploaded to Clickbank and if it is approved, they will sell it for you.

Clickbank provides a unique service in that they not only set up a place to store and sell your eBook, they also have thousands of affiliates who may decide to sell your eBook through their own web site in order to get a commission from the sale. You decide the amount of the commission you wish to pay and then place your eBook in the database. Any affiliate interested in selling your eBook obtains a link to use on their sites and that link identifies them so when anyone buys the eBook using their link, you make a profit and they collect a commission on the sale. If your eBook is on a popular topic and leaves a reasonable commission it may be sold by hundreds of affiliates thereby multiplying your sales significantly without any effort on your part.

You can learn all about Clickbank at their main site:

http://www.clickbank.com/index.html

In addition to their informative home page you will find a large collection of valuable articles that will help you use Clickbank successfully to sell your own eBook and you could even sell other eBooks related to your topic by becoming a Clickbank affiliate.

Your Own eStore

For any of you who already have web sites set up and a list of potential buyers, you may consider handling everything yourself. You start by creating your own eBook in the .pdf format. You can simply use the letter size, 8.5 X 11, that is so common but I suggest separating yourself from the pack. Create your eBooks in a size that is best viewed on a computer. The 6 X 8 or 600 pixels high and 800 pixels wide will fit on one screen of any monitor. Using a format in this size allows the reader to see one page at a time without scrolling.

Another positive thing for your eBooks in the .pdf format is to create a bookmarks table of contents. That allows your reader to open the bookmarks on the left hand side of the .pdf document and select the topic they wish to read. This helps those readers who may know a great deal about the topic but just need some specific information.

You can make your eBooks even easier to use by adding links on each page. For example, each page can have a small button at the bottom for the next page, the previous page, and going back to a table of contents. Or a Go To specific page which allows you to select a page in which you are interested. None of these things are essential and they do require software capable of working within .pdf documents. While many believe that only Adobe makes such software and at a quite high price, actually there are many companies that make this software for more reasonable prices including PDF Converter Professional 7 available at the link below where you can also download a free trial version to test for yourself.

http://www.nuance.com/products/pdf-converter-professional7/index.htm

In addition to Adobe Writer and PDF Converter Pro, you can simply make use of PagePlus X4 to create the entire document for your ebook and once converted to PDF all the links you created will work. Since you may have already invested in PagePlus X4, this will eliminate the need for any additional software.

There are many free tools you can use to create .pdf files and office suites such as OpenOffice and Microsoft Office have built in tools to create .pdf files from the documents created with them. However, for editing and improving .pdf files a program such as PagePlus X4 is invaluable.

The main advantage of selling your own eBooks directly is that all of the profits are yours. This is a significant advantage but requires you to have considerable skills and a payment process to collect for your sales.

Most ebooks should be created to be viewed on a monitor. There are two reasons for this. First, monitors are only capable of 72 to 96 dpi (dots-per-inch). PDF documents prepared for printing are at least 300 dpi and are therefore much larger files. This works well when uploading to a printer but is problematic as a downloadable ebook. Your ebook customers will be downloading their purchase and some may have slow connections. Large downloads quickly become frustrating and some will simply quit the download and demand a refund.

You must have the skills to create your own web site with a great sales page for your book and an easy to use purchase and download page. Everything should be single click. One click should take the buyer to the purchase page to fill out the credit card information and one more click should start the download. Make it as simple as possible. Paypal is a great way to begin taking credit card payments. It is easy to sign up with them and easy to prepare the buy links for a web site.

The payment process is not as complex as it sounds. For a minor fee you can get set up with Paypal to collect for the sale of your book or eBook. With Paypal you can even set up a shopping cart if you have several books or eBooks to sell. Get complete details about Paypal at their main web site:

http://www.paypal.com

Remember that you are selling a download and that should be explained clearly on your sales web site. It's not rare for someone to purchase your ebook thinking that it is a paperback and then send you an email indicating that he or she never received the book. I have experienced this and once told that it is a downloadable ebook they want a refund because they never purchase ebooks. Save yourself this potential problem by making certain your sales site and the credit card page state that they are buying an ebook and must download it to their computer.

You can find a simple way to create your own web site in chapter nineteen. You also need the skills to market your book by creating traffic to your web site and conducting many other marketing activities beyond the scope of this book.

One disadvantage when publishing your eBooks is that they are not secure. That is, someone can purchase one copy and share it with friends and anyone else they choose. Worse than that, if your book is a good seller someone can simply buy one copy and then duplicate it and sell it on the Internet. If you have a copyright there are some legal remedies but they are costly and time consuming and by the time they are over your book may be available at sites across the Internet.

Another disadvantage of handling all your own sales directly is that it requires you to get much more serious about running a business. You have to make arrangements to collect and pay the sales tax on your sales. You also have to set up your own credit card payment process as previously indicated because sales will not be handled by a company like Clickbank, Amazon, Createspace, or Smashwords, who would take care of everything and report your income to you. This makes accounting fairly simple as you need only keep track of your expenses.

This is an important consideration. Running a business takes time and effort. It also means that you have to be available to your customers when they have a problem. You need to be able to answer emails promptly even while on vacations or if you become ill. For those reasons I much prefer to handle all my books using Createspace and my ebooks using Kindle, Smashwords, or Clickbank. They are open 24/7 and prepared to deal with your customers at anytime while you simply collect your royalties and pay your taxes.

Notes and Ideas

Eighteen

Creating A Cover For Your Book

The level of difficulty involved in creating your own book cover is directly related to your skills with graphic software. For those who own Photoshop and know how to use it, creating a nice cover will be relatively easy. Only you can decide if you have or can attain the skills to create your own cover.

There are many options for creating a nice cover for your book. In this chapter I cover two of those options. One involves using a good graphics program to design and create your own cover. The second is to use the Cover Creator software that is built into the Createspace publishing web site.

For the screen shots in this chapter I used PhotoPlus X4 even though I own Photoshop. PhotoPlus X4 is an excellent and, most importantly, inexpensive graphic software application developed and sold by Serif, the same British company that created PagePlus X4.

At this writing, PhotoPlus X4 is available from Amazon.com for under $25.00 in either download or disk format but that could vary over time. This is a great tool for creating book covers but it is capable of much more including:

- Editing any photo in a myriad of ways
- Add a large number of creative effects to any photograph.
- Portrait retouching to create better images of friends and family
- You can work on RAW photos
- Even works on videos

So, for a small price you get a tool that will easily handle all your cover work and many other photo related tasks.

Of course, a third option, hiring an artist to create a cover for you, is always available. Check out the rest of this chapter for ways to do it yourself and then decide how you want to handle your own book cover.

The image above shows the entire workspace for PhotoPlus X4. All the screen shots that follow were created and then copied from this workspace. PhotoPlus X4 is a reasonably priced, high quality, graphics editing and creation tool that will serve you during the creation of any book project. This screen shot was placed in the vertical position to make it large enough to see the details.

The Book Size

Before beginning a cover you must know the size of your book. In addition to the width and height of the book, you should know the number of pages. Once these dimensions are established, go to the Createspace web site and download a book cover template. This makes the job of creating the cover much simpler.

In this book the instructions do not involve a template because the book size is 8.5 inches by 11 inches and the largest template available from Createspace at the time of this writing was 8 inches by 10 inches. However, the steps for creating your cover with PhotoPlus X4 (or Photoshop if you have it) are the same except that you would begin by opening the template instead of creating a new image as outlined in these instructions.

One final note before we begin creating the cover with PhotoPlus X4. There is an excellent graphics application available free and capable of doing everything that PhotoPlus X4 or Photoshop can do related to covers. That application is called GIMP. Gimp can be downloaded free at: http://www.gimp.org/downloads/.

If you are not using a template then you must make some calculations before creating the initial image for the cover. There are several things that are included in these calculations. They are as follows:

1. The width and height of the front and back cover. You will need the total size of both of these side by side. With an 8.5 inch by 11 inch book the size is 17 inches wide by 11 inches high.

2. The size of the spine of the book which is based on the number of pages. On the Createspace web site you will find a calculation wizard that makes this easy. Or, Createspace also provides the exact thickness of a white or cream page and you can use this figure and multiply by the number of pages to determine the spine size.

3. You must then add the bleed size which is normally .25 to the width and .25 to the height. This adds .125 to each side of the cover and .125 to the top and bottom of the cover.

4. Use these dimensions to determine the exact size of the image you will create for the background of your cover. For this book the total width of the cover is 17.75 inches and the total height is 11.25 inches. The size of your cover will probably be different. Even if your book is 8.5 inches by 11 inches in size, it is unlikely it has the same number of pages so the size of the spine will alter the size of the background image.

On the next page you will see the background image created for this book. As I write this, the final design of the cover has not been determined and it may vary from this somewhat but the method of creation remains the same.

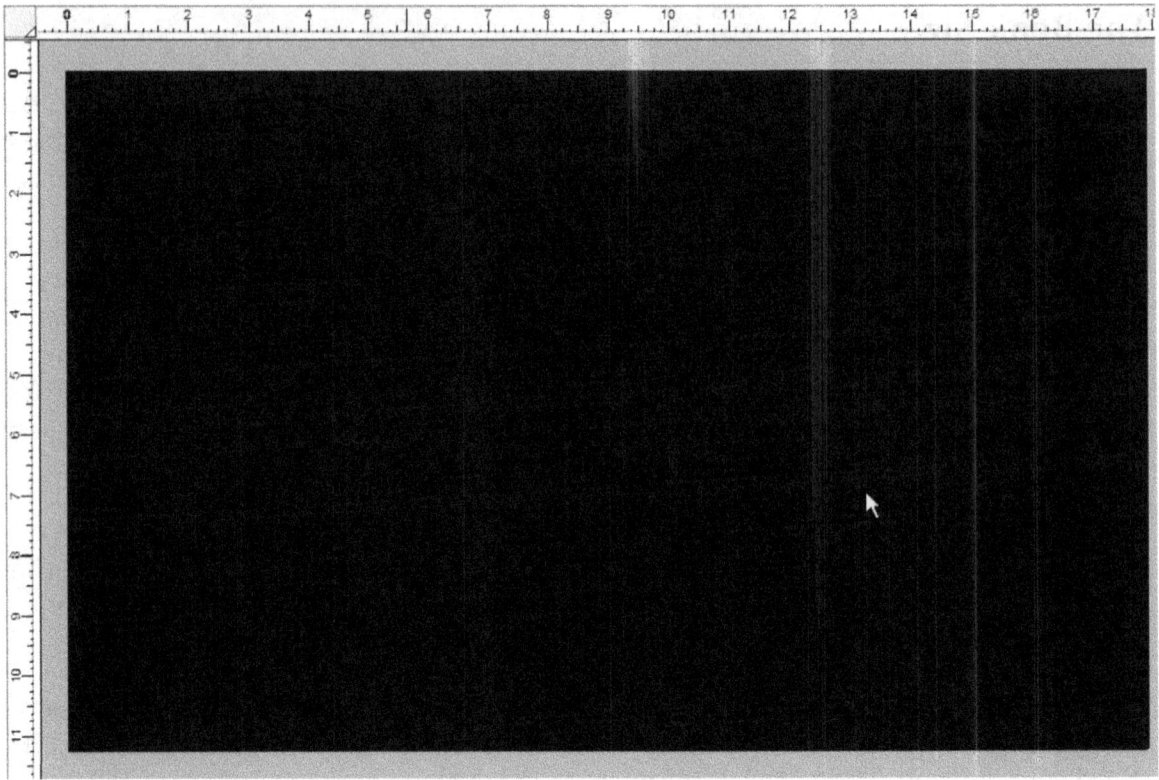

Let's go over the background size again for clarity. The size of this book is 8.5 X 11 inches. After making the calculations described on the previous page, the size of the background must be 17.75 X 11.25 inches. This is how that breaks down. The front and back covers will be 8.5 X 11 so for the background to cover both it must be 17 inches wide. The spine, based on the number of pages calculates to .50 inch. That makes the background 17.5 inches. Finally, you must add .125 inch to each side for the bleed which adds .25 inch total making the width of the background 17.75. Adding .25 inch to the 11 inch height gives you a cover height of 11.25 and adds .125 inch bleeds to the top and bottom of the cover.

Once you have the size worked out you must be sure that you set the correct color for the background since this will be the base color of your cover.

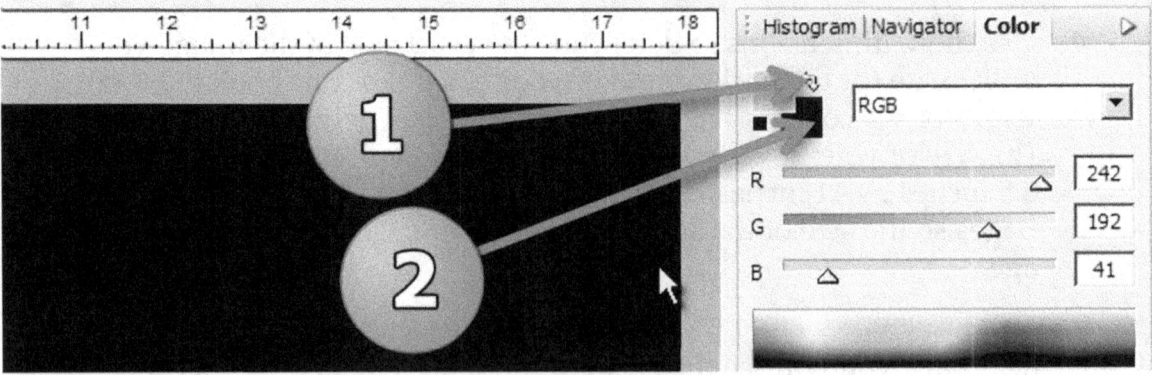

Number 2 above points to the background color. To change it to the correct, dark blue color, you click on the curved arrow and the colors are reversed. You can do this for each layer to maintain the colors you choose.

Once you have completed the background, you are ready to start adding the various objects and text to your cover. For ease of working with the various objects and text it is critical to create a new layer for each. Usually, you will have to create a new layer for each object manually but each time you begin a new text location, a layer will be created automatically. In the screen shot below you can see the rectangular selection tool icon with the basic instructions in the pop up menu.

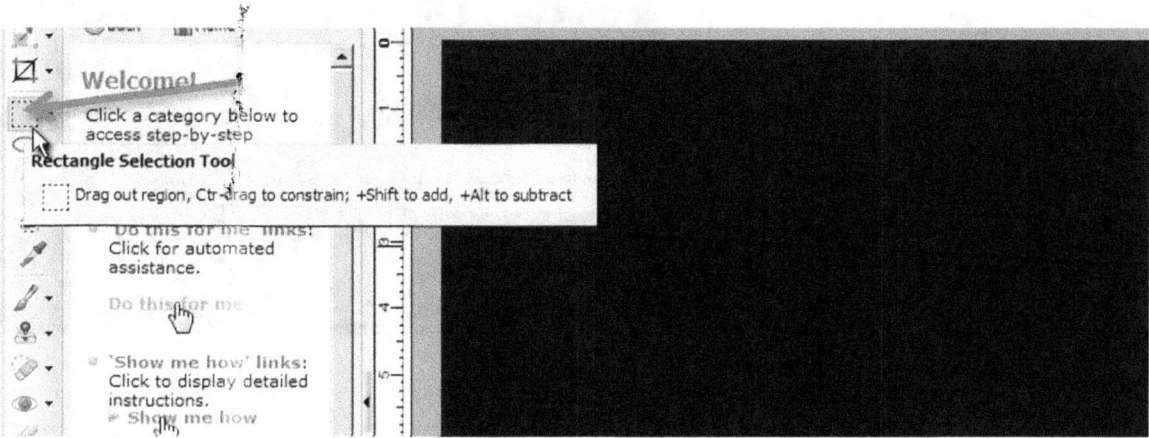

The screen shot below shows the first shape that I created. The size of the shape is actually 6 inches wide by 6.5 inches high. Shapes are created by placing the small plus sign anywhere on the background, holding the left mouse button and dragging it to the final point. If you have created a layer first, it is not essential to place the shape in its correct location. The important thing is to use the rulers to make certain the shape is the correct size. Once the shape has been completed it has to be filled with the correct color and dragged to its correct location. You can do those things in any order. I usually fill with the correct color and then move the shape.

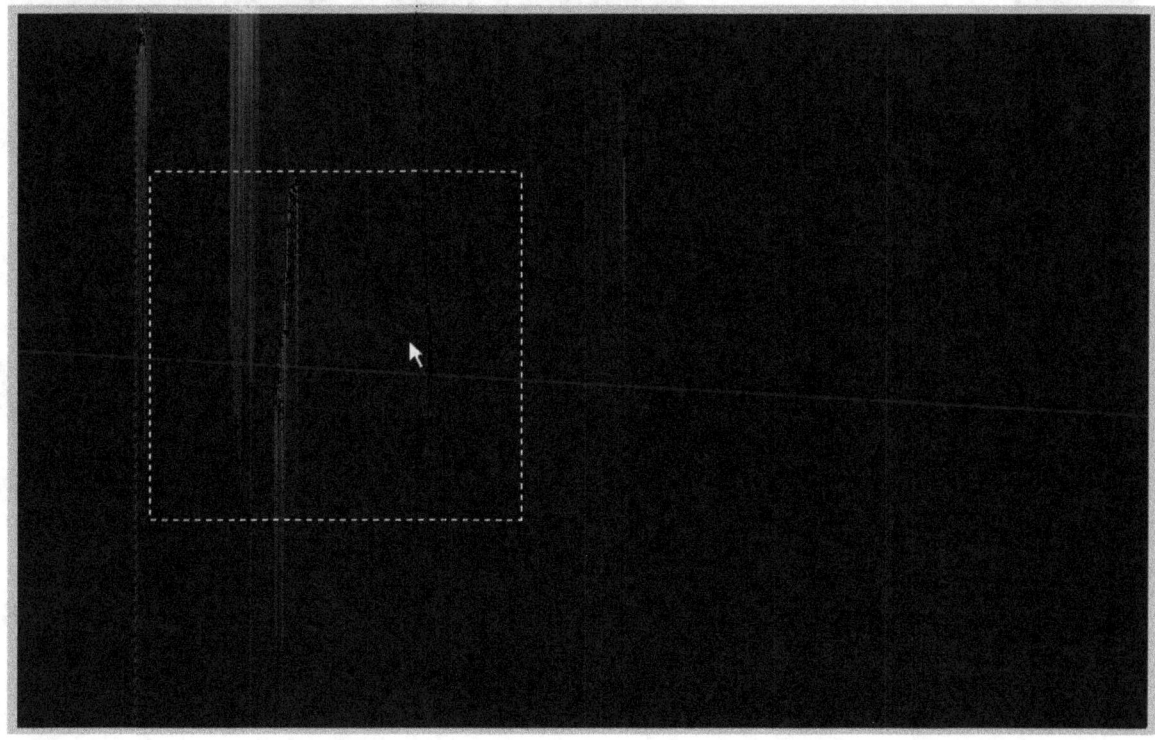

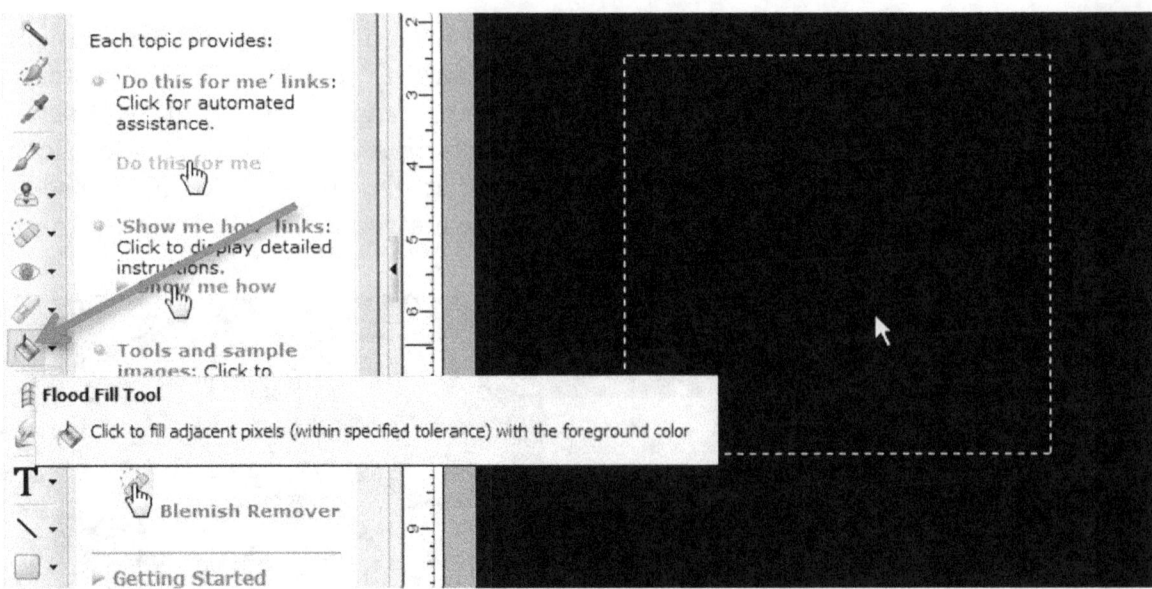

The next step is to fill in the shape with the color you have chosen. On my cover I only use two colors, the foreground and the background. For the same effect you need only select either one of these colors as covered on a previous screen shot. Once you have clicked the Flood Fill Tool as shown above, you just move the cursor within the shape and click. The color will appear as shown below.

Notice that the shape is still not in the correct location. However, the shape was created on an independent layer. This allows me to move it to any location on the background without considering any other shape or object. In addition to moving a shape around to whatever location you choose, you can also move it above or below other objects or shapes as long as they are all on separate layers. This gives you great design flexibility.

The next step is to move the shape to the correct location on the background. Two things to remember when doing this. The first is to use the top and side rulers to control the location. The second is to remember that this first placement need not be perfect. Since the shape is on an independent layer, it can be moved at any time by selecting the layer and then using the move tool as shown below.

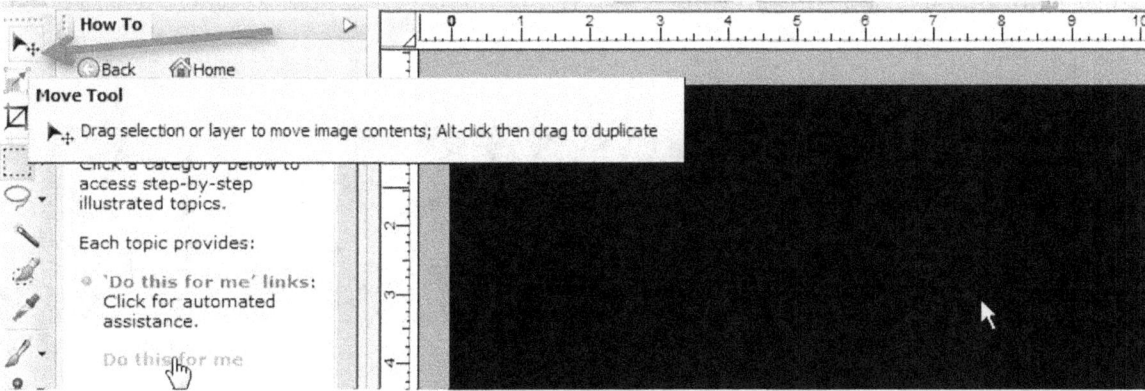

Notice in the screen shot below that I have use red arrows to identify the places on the ruler where the shape should be located. The ruler on top guides you to the horizontal location and the ruler at the left guides you to the vertical location.

The location of the plus sign of the move tool is always shown in the top and bottom rulers so you can easily maintain control of the exact location of the shape on your cover. You can move the shape slowly to its correct location and then continue your design. Remember that this location is not necessarily permanent. If you change the design or merely wish to move the shape, simply select the layer and the move tool and then you are free to change the location of the shape.

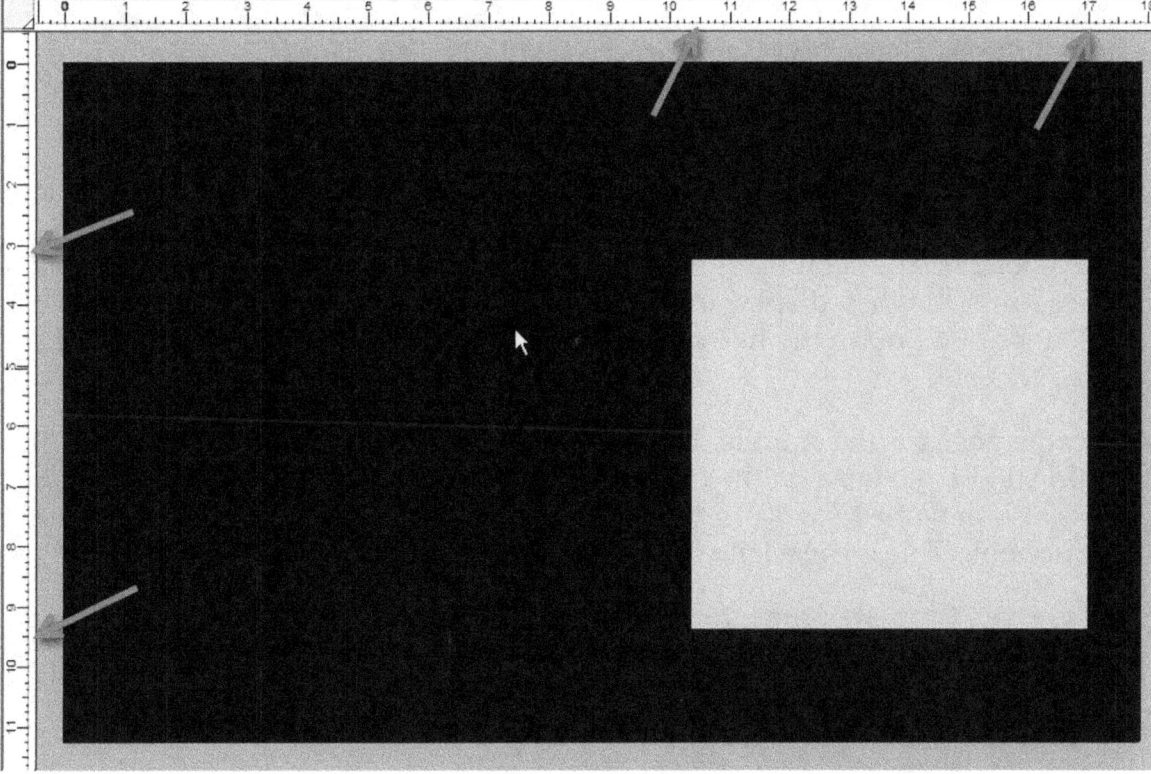

As you have probably noticed by now, creating a cover involves making many choices. I prefer to add all the shapes to the background before beginning the text. In the screen shot below you will see the second shape added. It was added to the background in exactly the same manner as the first shape except that it is a different size and is located in a different place. However, it is also on an independent layer that allows me to move it as needed.

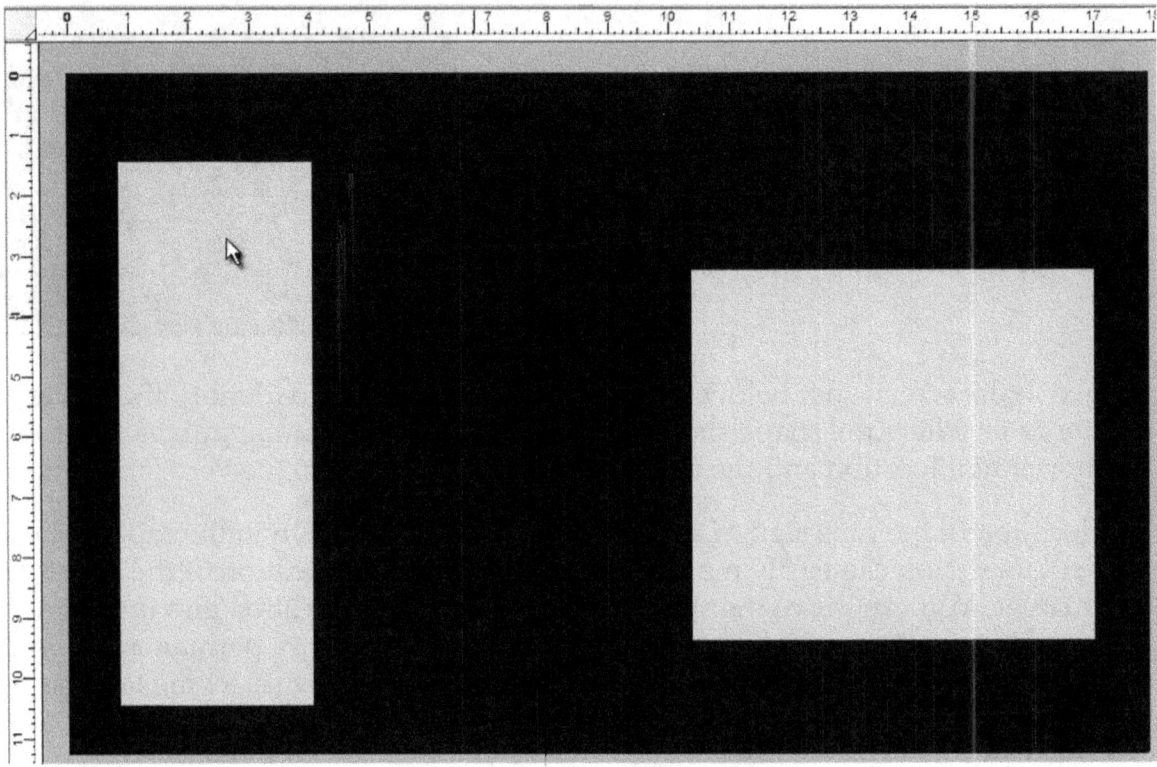

After all the shapes are in place, I proceed with the text. This is a critically important part of the cover and advance planning is essential. You should know exactly what you want your cover to convey to potential buyers.

The most important thing is the title of the book and that is handled in more detail in Chapter Five. The major consideration at this point is the font size for the title of the book and the subtitle. Remember that your book cover will be dramatically reduced in size when displayed on a web site and on Amazon. Choosing too small a font will make the title almost impossible to read when the book is displayed for sale.

The same goes for the subtitle. Even though it won't be as large as the title, it should still be readable on the thumbnail size images that appear on web sites. This is also the time to make certain that your subtitle conveys clearly the content of your book. This is especially critical for a how-to book.

Don't ignore the rest of the information on the front and rear cover. Notice on the cover of this book that it is easy to determine exactly what you will learn by reading the book. This is important on the cover of books appearing in bookstores where information that clearly explains the content will make a difference.

Adding text to your cover is a multiple step process. Each section of the text must be handled so it will be on an independent layer. This allows you to move it to any location easily if necessary. This first screen shot below shows how to start creating the text.

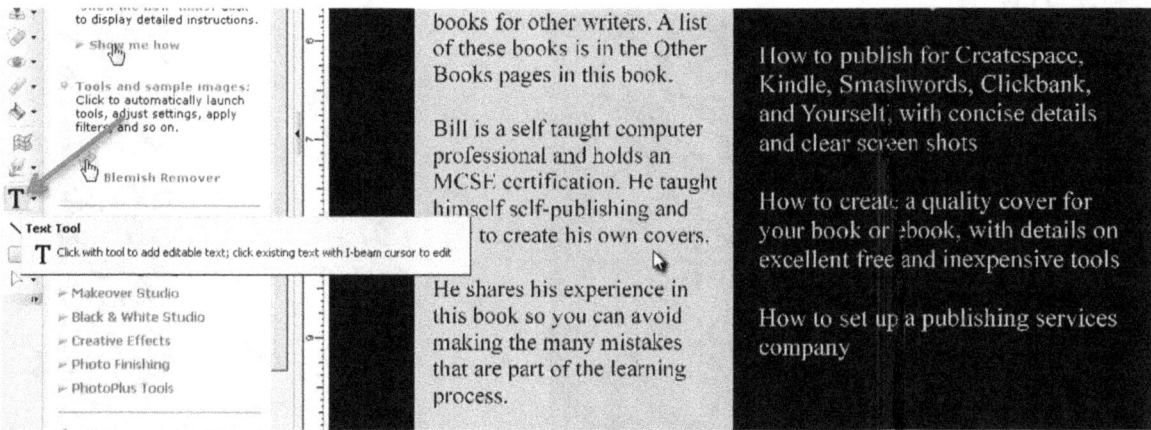

After clicking the text tool icon, you move the cursor to the location of the text, click the mouse and then begin typing. Don't worry if the text is placed correctly. Each time you begin to input text, a new layer is created. If your text is not exactly where you want it you simply click on the move tool and move the text to the correct location. You can always move the text around by simply selecting the layer and then using the move tool to make the move.

Above is the title text. Notice the large size of the font even in the reduced size of this screen shot. The subtitle goes right below it and is only slightly smaller than the title so it is also easy to read.

You can proceed to create all the different text sections for your cover. Not all covers require as much text as this one. It was important to me to convey as much information as possible about the book. That may not be helpful for other kinds of books but it is important with a how-to book.

Before showing you the final cover for this book, I still have one more shape and two photographs to add. I will describe the addition of those objects and then show you the final cover.

This is the final shape to be placed on the background. Notice that this object is the same color as the background. This is part of the design of my book cover. This shape is placed so that the left side and the bottom are the same size from the edge of the larger shape.

In addition to this spacing, a much larger spacing is left above the shape for a large line of text. On the right hand side of the shape there is room for more text about the book.

This is a design concept that I developed for two of my previous how-to books. Those two book were in the 8 inch by 10 inch size instead of 8.5 inches by 11 inches of this book but the design is basically the same.

This new shape will serve as the frame for a photograph that I had taken especially for this purpose. The photograph will be placed in this shape with even borders around it. The important thing to remember is that this shape is created exactly like the other two except for the size.

Placing photographs is handled a little differently but one thing remains the same, you want to add the photograph as a new layer so that it can be moved and controlled should changes arises. I repeat the caution about layers because it is the only easy way to create a cover. The cover for this book has more than 20 layers.

The next step is to place the images on the cover. To do that you must edit the images to make certain they are at least 300 dpi (dots per inch) in resolution and the correct size for the cover. It is not a good idea to increase or reduce the size of a photograph when placing it on a cover for printing. These changes tend to have an adverse effect on the quality of the image.

To make the image for this cover the correct size, I calculated the size of the blue shape where I was going to place the photograph and then deducted .25 inch from the top and the side and that gave me the correct size for the photograph. Once placed on the blue shape, there would be a .125 inch (1/8 inch) border of blue around the photograph. You can adjust the size for your photographs accordingly.

Once the image is the correct size and resolution for the cover, use the rectangle tool to capture a copy of the photograph. Then either select Edit and Copy or use the Ctrl, C keys on your keyboard to capture a copy of the photograph.

Now, return to the main cover workspace and select Edit again and this time select Paste. Make absolutely certain that you select Paste As a New Layer. This will paste the photograph at the upper left hand corner. Then select the move tool and move the photograph to the correct location. This will work perfectly for every photograph you need to place on your cover.

Should your photograph size be incorrect, simply select Edit, Undo and resize the photograph. Until you become proficient with PhotoPlus X4, it may take several tries. The photo below shows the capture lines and is not the final.

To copy and paste the photographs into the cover use the Menu icons as shown in the screen shots below.

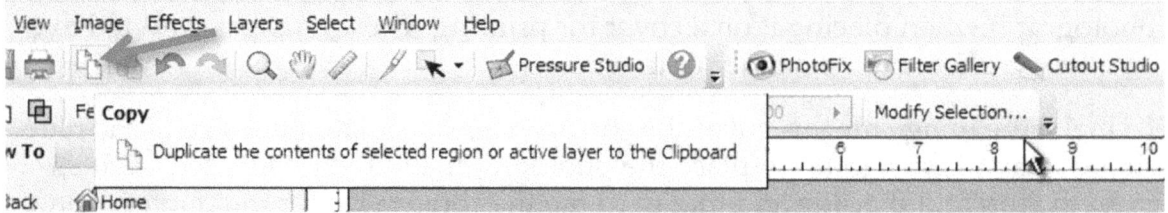

Remember, as shown below, always Paste As New Layer so you will have complete control over the positioning of the photograph, shape, or object. Once the layer is moved and the photo is placed in its correct location it will look as it does in the screen shot below.

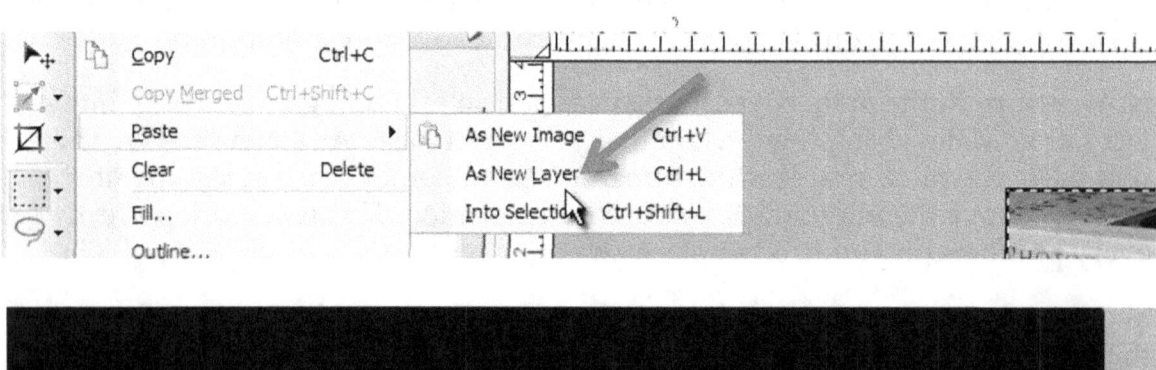

Creating Text For The Spine

The process of creating text for the spine can be difficult but using layers can simplify it. The first step is to create lines to identify the exact location of the spine so you will know where to type the text.

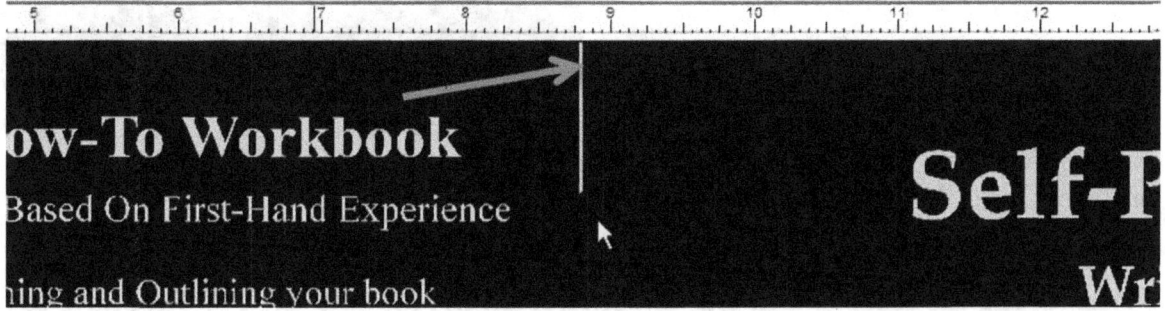

Each of the lines should be drawn from the top of the cover to the bottom. Use the ruler at the top to place the lines in the correct locations. The space between the lines must be the size that you determine by using the calculations from the Createspace web site. These lines will serve as a guide to type the spine content.

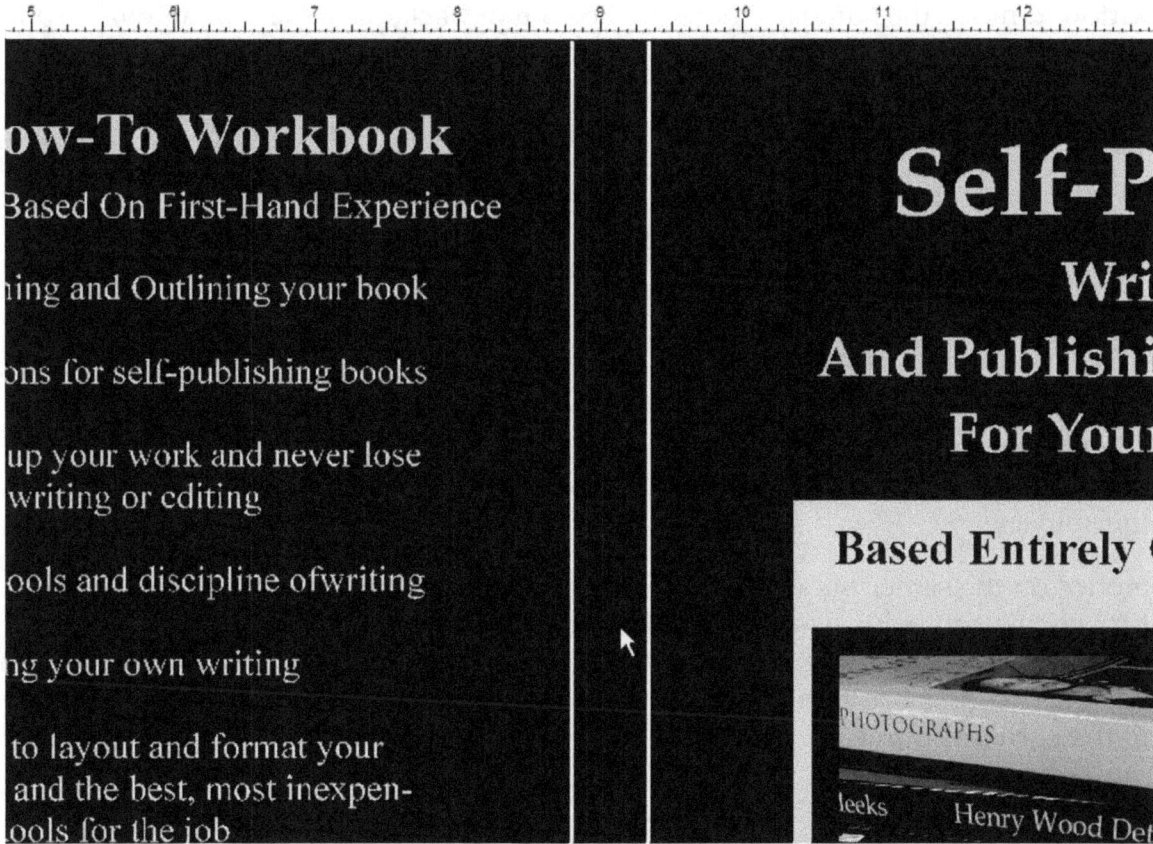

After drawing the two lines using the line tool, you must rotate the entire cover so that you can type the spine text. You must rotate it counter clockwise so the spine writing will be correctly oriented. The screen shots on the next page show how to rotate the cover and the rotated view blank and with the spine text typed

As shown in the screen shot above, rotating the image is a simple task. Just click on Image and then Rotate and then choose Image 90 Counter-clockwise. This will place the image in the correct position for typing in the spine text.

When typing the text leave at least .75 inch from the top and the bottom of the cover. Simply start typing at the left as you normally do and type the title of the book. Unless the subtitle is very short, only the title will fit in this space.

Next leave several spaces and type the last name of the author. You may type the full name but standard practice is to include only the last name in the spine. Once the name is typed, put the cursor in front of the name and either press the space button to move the name closer to the bottom or backspace to move it away from the bottom.

When you type the spine text, as with all the other text sections you created, a new layer is created allowing you to adjust the spine text to be perfectly centered in the spine.

Notice on the screen shot below that the spine text matches all the other text in font choice and color. This is part of my design for the covers of all my how-to books. You can add other things to the spine including a small logo or some other design. Just make certain that it isn't too large so that it overlaps or gets too close to the corner of spine.

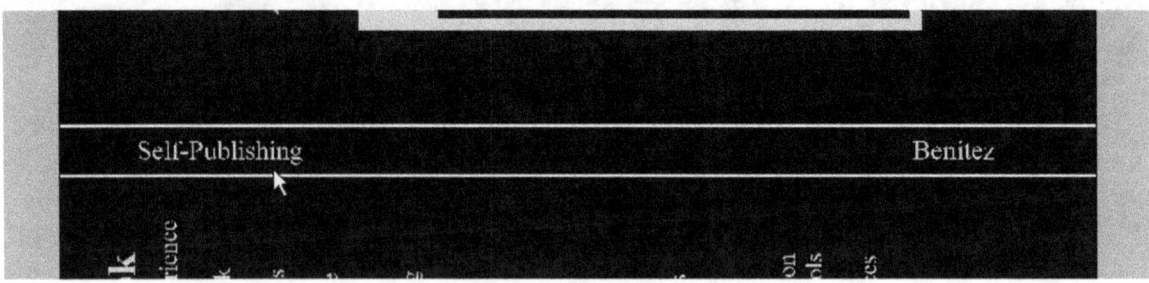

Creating A Cover For Your Book

After the image is rotated back to its correct position, the lines are still visible and must be removed from the image. This is easy to do by simply clicking on the small eye in each line layer. You can see on the screen shot below that one of the lines is gone and the arrow is pointing to where I click to get rid of the second line.

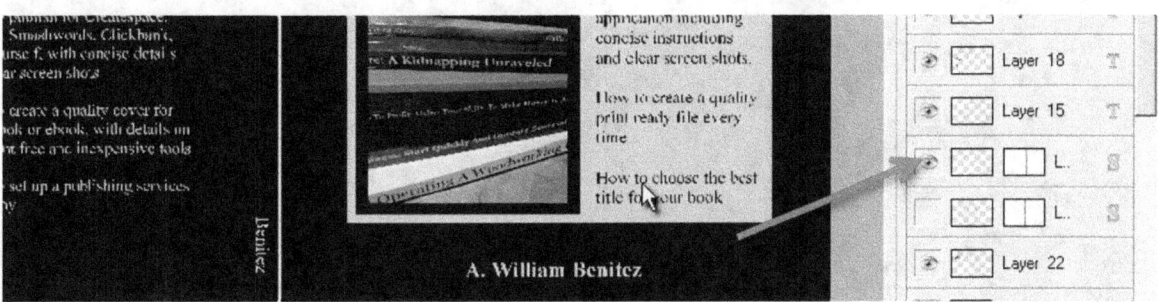

Clicking on the eye not only gives you control of the visibility of this line but this also works on every layer in the photo. So, you can turn off all the layers or leave them all on as you choose. Working with layers provides great flexibility when creating covers or any other photo projects.

On the next page I have included the entire cover and rotated it on the page so it is viewed in a larger format. In this chapter every step for creating a cover using PhotoPlus X4 has been covered. However, it is important to develop a familiarity with the software because this will help you to learn how to create better covers or other projects.

The same work can be done with Photoshop at a cost of $600.00 plus or with GIMP at no cost but I like working with PhotoPlus X4 and it is a bargain.

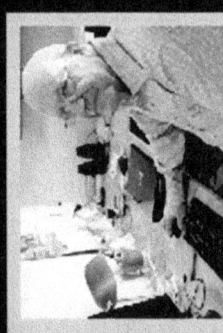

Using The Createspace Cover Creator

The simplest way to create a professional looking cover is to use the Createspace Cover Creator software available on the Createspace web site when you join as a publisher. It is an easy to use tool with excellent templates to help you produce a quality cover for your book.

In the next few pages I will take you through the entire process of creating a cover for your book using this valuable tool. The next two screen shots introduce you to the Cover Creator with some excellent and helpful articles and guides. These should help you to create your cover. Once ready, click on Launch Cover Creator.

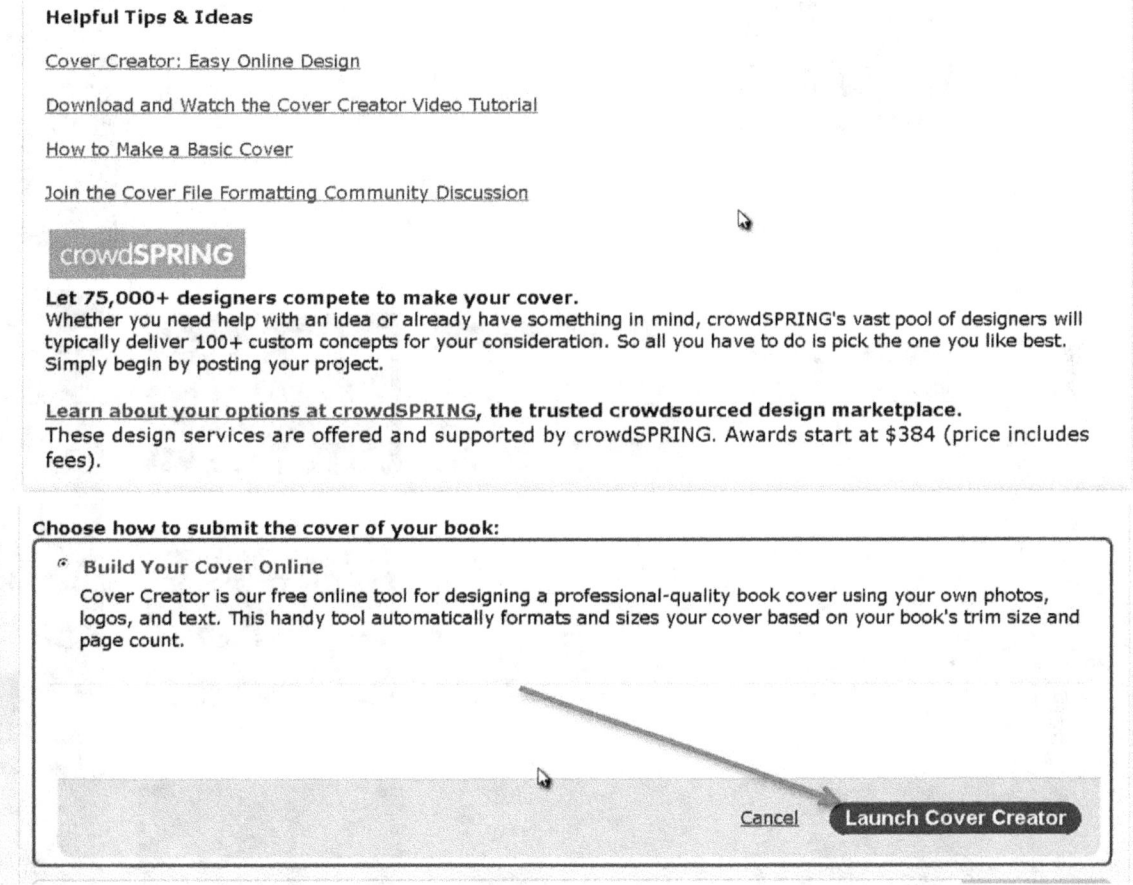

When you launch the Cover Creator there will be five pages of templates you can use to create your cover. Each template is geared to a different theme and you can go through all five pages and choose the one that looks best for your book.

Each of the templates has a great deal of flexibility and you can choose from a number of themes that may make the cover better suited to your particular niche. Take your time with this because there are many choices.

The templates also allow the choice of several background color and a large number of stock photographs to help you come up with a great design. You can also use your own photographs, as I did, to improve the quality of your cover. If you don't feel up to choosing, get some help before making a final decision.

On the next few pages there are screen shots showing the many options available with the templates in the Createspace Cover Creator with a few notes to help you choose the best one for your book.

Above are the first three pages of choices for the basic template which is just a starting point for the creation of your cover.

Creating A Cover For Your Book

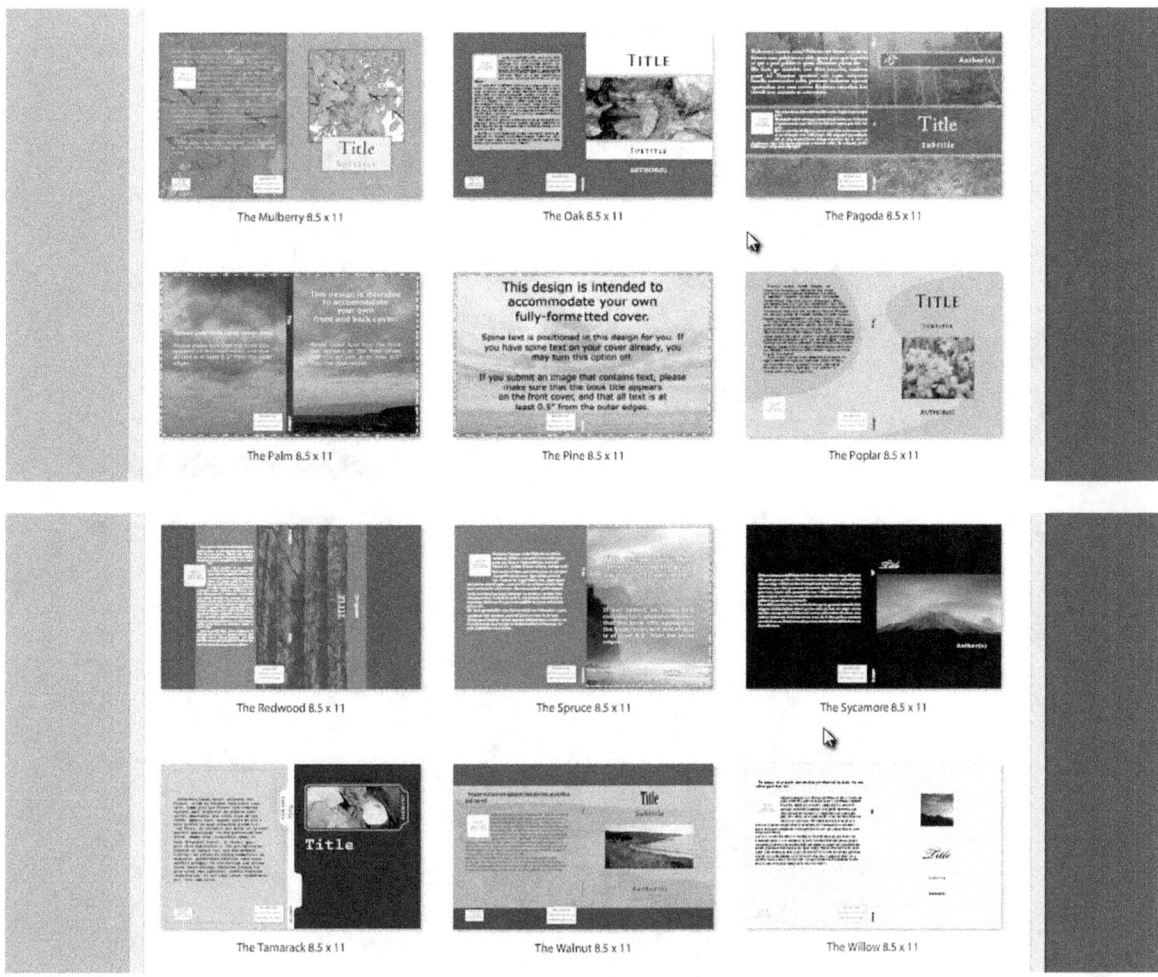

The screen shots above show the fourth and fifth page of templates from which to choose the one you prefer.

The screen shot below is the one that I chose as a test for the cover of this book. This was only for test purposes since I normally design my own book covers.

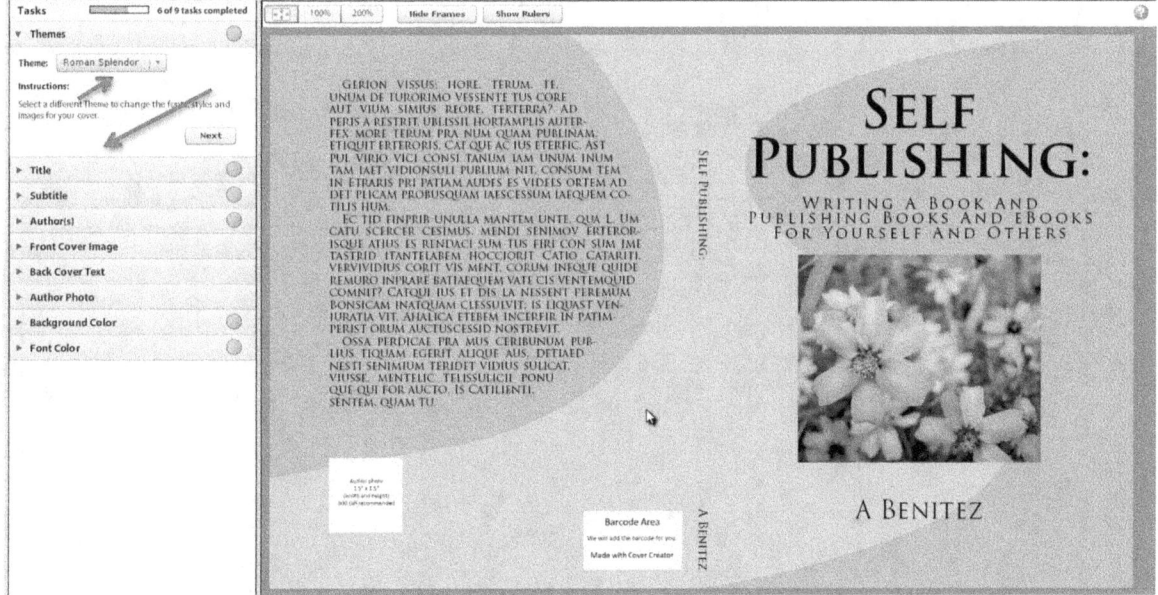

On the previous page there are three themes of many that are available for the template I selected for my cover. After you have selected the theme, the next step is to type in the title and subtitle as shown in the screen shots below.

Explore these templates and themes and you realize that the Createspace Cover Creator is easy to use and will help you come up with a professional cover for your book.

On the left column are the various sections that you can alter on the template you choose. These include the theme, title, subtitle, author name, front cover image, author image, the background color, and even the font color. This flexibility helps you even after your have selected your template.

For those who do not have their own photos, there is a nice collection of stock photos to choose from.

On the screen shot below you see how the author's name is added to the cover. Notice how placing the author's name, like the title, includes placing it properly on the spine of the book cover. Normally this can be a more difficult task but it is handled automatically in the Createspace Cover Creator.

The screen shot below shows the photograph on the cover of my book changed to my own photograph. On the left column there are tools that allow you to manipulate the photograph after you have placed it on the cover. This will help you make certain the photograph is placed exactly as you planned.

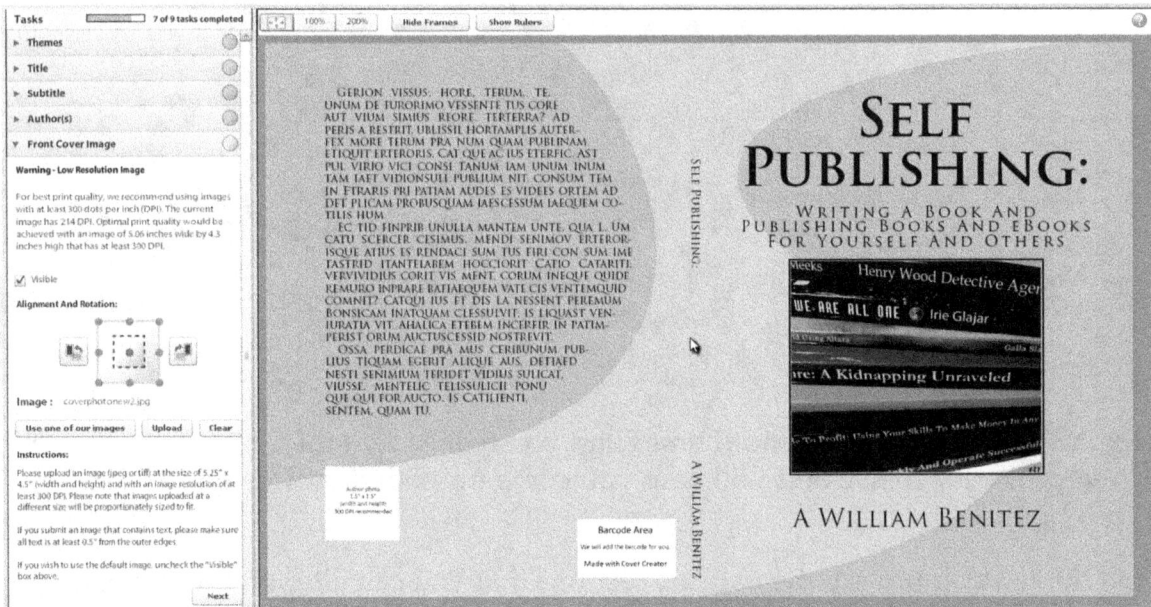

The first screen shot on the next page shows how I located the photograph for use on my cover. You can make use of any photograph on your cover. I suggest you size it as close as possible to the required size but the Cover Creator will manipulate it to fit the space and you can then do the final adjustments.

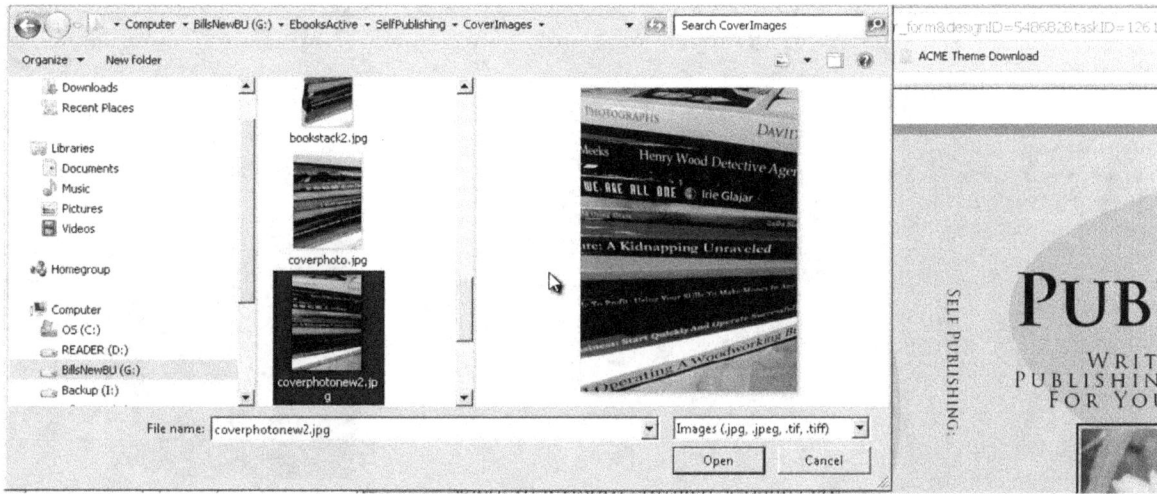

The next step is critically important to the display of your book. Everything on the cover of your book should be a message that helps it sell. So, the information on the back cover must convey information about your book that will peak the interest of any prospective buyers.

Even though this message may not normally be in plain view online, it can be read using the look inside feature and should be accurate and interesting. While you can say a little about the author, mostly it should be devoted to the benefits for the buyer. Everything about your cover should be giving the prospective buyer the motivation to make the purchase.

To create this message, type it as a text document and edit it carefully before you create your cover. When you are working online on the cover there is a tendency to rush a little. Take as much time for this as you do for creating the title of the book.

While the saying goes, "Don't judge a book by its cover," many people do exactly that. Be prepared for them by making the cover a full time sales person for your book.

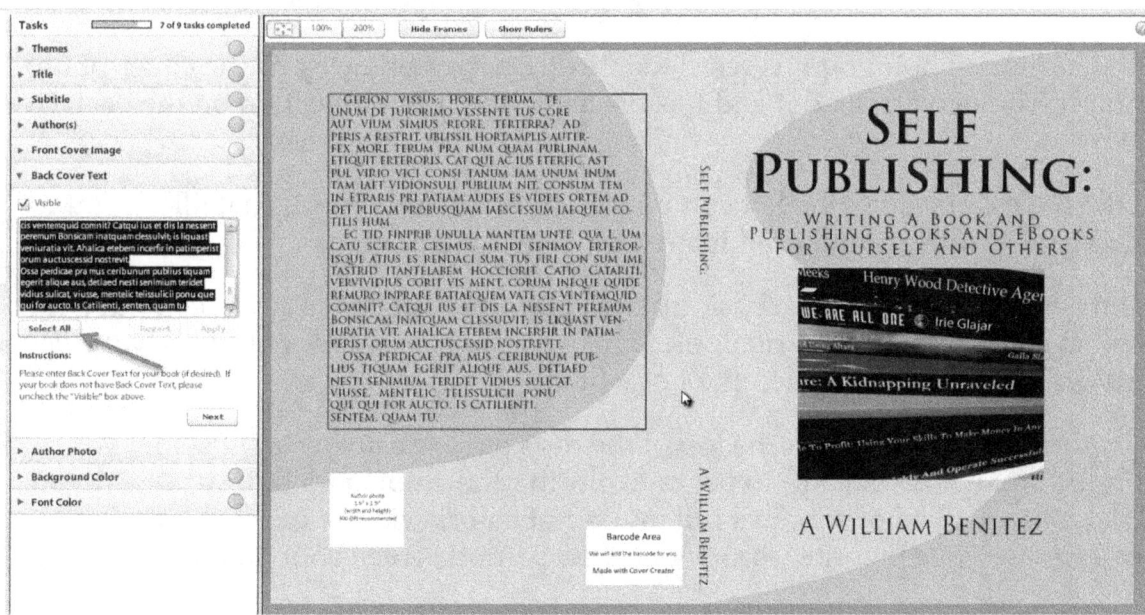

The author's photograph is selected in exactly the same way as the cover photograph. Then you upload it and it is placed in the proper location on the back cover.

Like the cover photo, the left column has the various controls that allow you to move the photo around until it appears as you planned.

The next step is to pick the background color for your cover. I checked out a few colors before making my final selection. You can easily check out how various colors will look before you accept one as final.

On the first screen shot at the top of the next page the arrow shows how you click on the small color square to begin exploring the color possibilities. When you click this small color square a full myriad of colors will appear from which you can choose your favorite, as shown on the second screen shot on the next page.

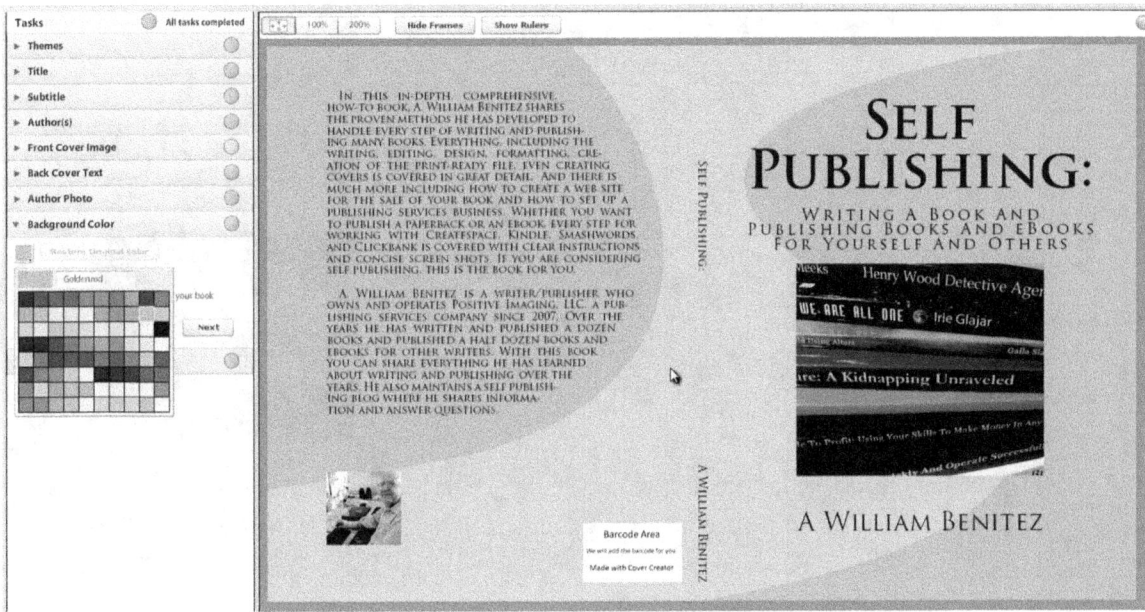

I tried several background colors. I suggest you copy and paste your favorites as I did the three screen shots on the next page. Then print the page to help you decide the best one for your book. You will be able to appreciate the different colors unlike the grayscale on these pages.

You can also do full landscape printouts of each color showing the full template. Even if it isn't the correct size of the full cover it will give you a good idea exactly how the final cover will appear even before you order your first proof.

Even though it has been mentioned several times, the importance of your book cover can't be overemphasized. Take as much time as necessary to create an attractive and professional cover for your book.

Self Publishing: How To Publish Your Print Book or eBook Step by Step

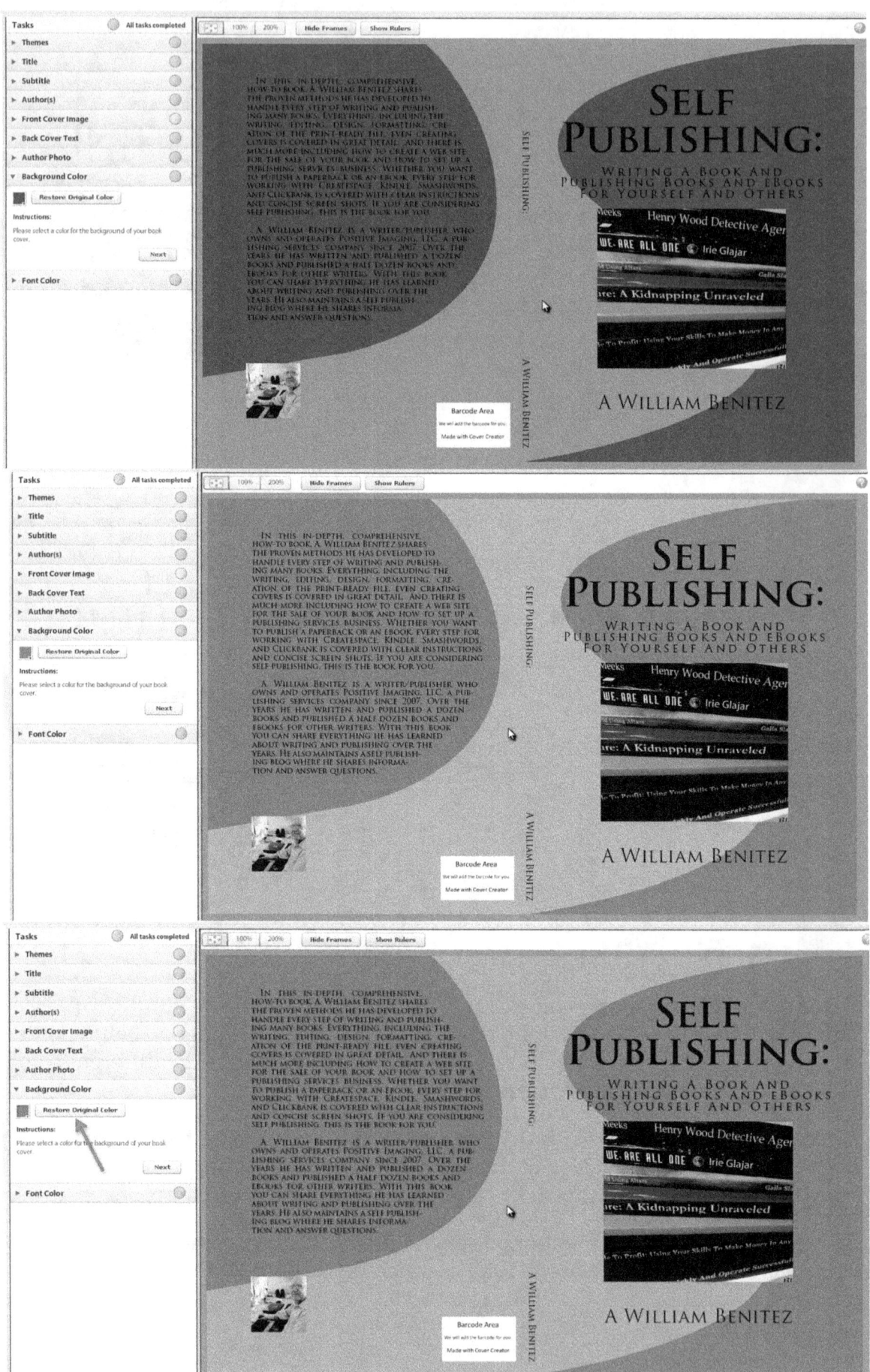

This is a screen shot of the final test cover of my book after all the various sections are completed. Unfortunately, you can't appreciate the great blue color.

The screen shot below shows the Submit Cover button used after you have completed making changes to your cover. Notice also the white square for the bar code. There is nothing you have to do to this section. Createspace handles the bar code for you.

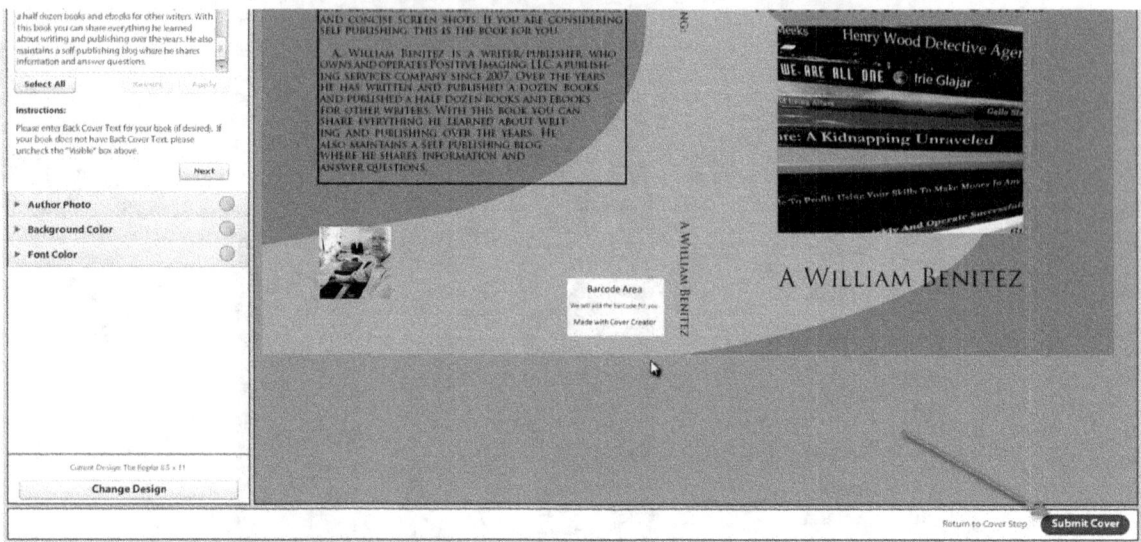

The screen shot below shows four selections. The two marked by the arrows are Full-Size Preview and Edit Cover. The Full-Size preview allows you to see the entire cover again and the Edit Cover button opens Cover Creator so you can make changes to the cover.

The final button is the Complete Cover button that you click once you are completely finished. And, the final link is Start a new cover from scratch. This is only to use if you are completely disappointed with your cover and decide to begin anew. Once you click the Complete Cover button your cover is finished.

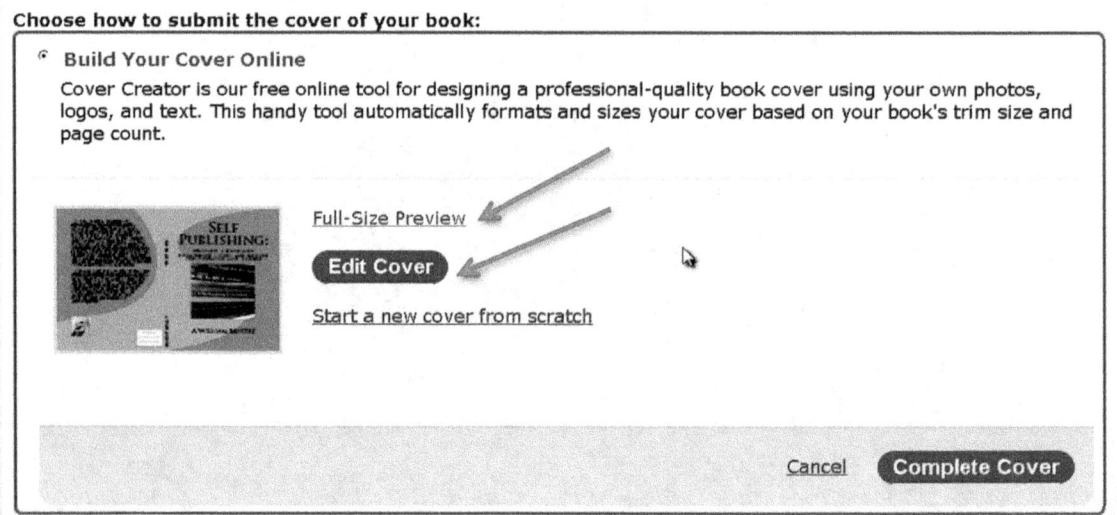

Nineteen

Creating A Web Site To Market Your Book

Creating a website for your book is a critical part of marketing. Even though this book does not deal with the many details of marketing books, it does cover the important preparations required to begin marketing any book.

Even if you have no interest in selling your book, you almost certainly would like others to read it. A good web site will allow it to be found and read by others.

In this chapter you will find illustrations of many web sites with some details of how the were made and how they impact the marketing of books.

Before beginning the illustrations it's important to have some idea of the many tools available to help you create your own web sites. Many of these tools perform quite well and are completely free. Others also perform well but must be purchased. Still others are quite easy to use but require a monthly financial commitment that can be difficult to cancel. Let's start with a brief list and then the details

WebPlus X4 or X5 - This is a fine product from Serif, the same company that created PagePlus and PhotoPlus.

NVU and Kompozer - These two WYSIWYG web site creation applications are both free and easy to use.

Website Tonight - Is available free from many web hosting companies when you sign up with them to host your web site. More on hosting later in this chapter.

Yahoo Small Business - This service and other similar ones provide a one stop location for domain names, web hosting, and web site creation tools, all online and easy to use at a reasonable cost.

> *There are other ways to get a web site created and hosted but these are the only ones that I have used personally. I prefer to handle all aspects of the process myself but Yahoo provides a good service.*

Let's begin this section with illustrations of web sites created for a specific book.

This web site was created for the children's adventure book my wife wrote back in 2007. It was one of my first experiences with POD. I shot the video of the granddaughter of a good friend talking about the book and it turned out well. This site was created with NVU.

The cover drawing was done by a local artist and then I did quite a bit of Photoshop work on it to get the exact look that we wanted. I designed the cover and then scanned it and just put a flat picture of the cover on the site.

Later, I found an artist who would take my flat drawing and make it into the book design that you see above for only twenty dollars. I had him do most of my web site covers after that.

The clock was something I found for free on the web and have used it on several web sites. The rest of the header is an animated file and the words Lottie's Adventure move slowly and continuously giving an scary effect.

The two black and white drawings were taken directly from the inside of the book which has a small drawing at the beginning of each chapter.

At first I hosted this web site with a popular hosting company and that worked fine but I found that I could save a lot of money by purchasing a hosting reseller arrangement with a company and then host all my sites for one small monthly payment. I have so many web sites now that my hosting cost me less than a dollar a month for each site.

Creating A Web Site To Market Your Book

The next two web sites were created for books that were published by Positive Imaging, LLC but I did not write them. The web sites were designed to serve as the press kit for this author.

These web sites include a page about the author, a press release page, and a direct link to the eStore where the book can be purchased. The We Are All One site has its own domain but the Teach For Life site is a sub-domain of the Positive Imaging web site. That is a way to save the cost of hosting a second or third site.

Below is another web site made for a book that Positive Imaging, LLC published for another individual

Introducing The New Book For World Peace
Peace and Healing For The World
Using Altars

Click Here For More

Written By
Lucretia and Gaila

.The three previously illustrated web sites and the one below were all created with Web Plus X4, another excellent software application from Serif, the same British company that makes PagePlus and PhotoPlus. The site below is for a book I wrote and my company, Positive Imaging, LLC, published.

Woodworking Business

Woodworking Business: Start Quickly And Operate Successfully

Woodworking skills are important to the success of a woodworking business but many other business skills are also required. After years in construction I started my woodworking business but it still took time to hone the skills needed to make the business profitable. Now I've decided to share the many proven techniques that were developed duing that time in my book "Woodworking Business: Start Quickly And Operate Successfully."

If you are already a competent woodworker wanting to start a woodworking business, or if you are already in the woodworking business but would like to increase your profit and simplify your work, **Woodworking Business: Start Quickly And Operate Successfully** is for you.

I started in construction at a young age but always enjoyed building cabinets. After leaving construction I spent over twenty years building cabinets and furniture for hundreds of customers. In spite of making many business mistakes while getting started I succeeded in the business. Now I have compiled all those years of lessons into my book **"Woodworking Business: Start Quickly And Operate Successfully."** It covers every step of how you can use your woodworking skills to make money.

Notice that all of the web sites are clean looking and easy to read and easy to create. In making the web sites the design of the book cover was considered. In most cases a small book cover photo, either flat or with a 3D appearance can be used. However, with some books, like the We Are All One book, the title and subtitle information is too small to read in a small size.

If go back two pages and check the screen shot of that web site you'll see that the cover of the book is quite large and is integrated into overall design of the page. This makes it much easier to read the title and subtitle of the book.

On the Peace and Healing book on the left hand page, the cover is quite busy with the title, subtitle and several small pictures of individuals. For this site there is an introduction or lead in page that allows for the name of the book in large letters and large pictures of two of the altars pictured inside the book.

These are decisions that you will need to make if you wish to create your own web sites for your book or books.

If you aren't sure about creating a design you can hire a graphic artist to help you with a drawing or two and design the web site around them. Most often you can start your web site design by making the book cover an integral part or perhaps even use parts of the cover.

It's not really necessary to put a lot of graphics into a web site to market your book. What is necessary is to make it easy to find and purchase your book. In the page to the left showing the web site for the Woodworking Business book you can see the simplicity. It does have a picture of the book but the rest is writing in various sizes in text boxes that add emphasis to certain messages.

Throughout the text the idea is for the information to be down-to-earth and obviously an honest description of the benefits of the book. The entire thrust of the web site should be to put across how the potential purchaser would benefit from buying your book.

While you should mention a little about yourself, it should only be enough to show that you are highly competent to speak on the subject of the book. Remember, the web site is not about you. It is about what is in it for the potential buyer.

Before writing the content of your web site, list the keywords that apply to your book. As was previously indicated, the title of your book should be developed based on the best possible key words and then those same keywords are used on your web site. Good keywords will encourage the search engines to place your site high in rankings and this will help book sales.

The name of the book advertised on the web site at the bottom of the previous page is Woodworking Business followed by the subtitle. The title is an excellent keyword and because it is, the book remains high in search results and most importantly it remains number one in Amazon.com searches for "woodworking business."

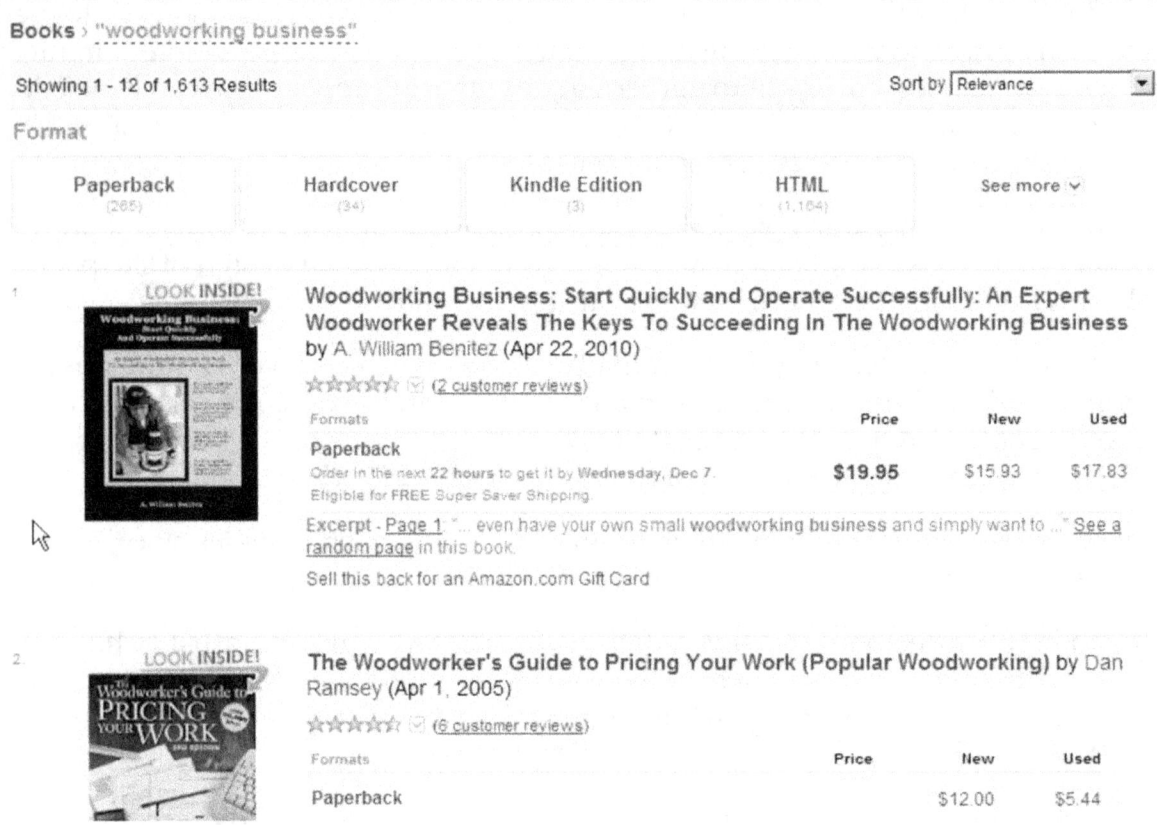

This is what appears when you search for "woodworking business" in the books category at Amazon.com. Notice that there are sixteen hundred results in this category so a mistake in selecting your title and your keywords can place your book completely out of sight and reduce sales. If sales are important to you, this has to be a major consideration because, at last report, Amazon sells sixty five percent of the books in the world. It's not a market to be ignored and neither is the importance of the search process.

The title of this woodworking business book is considered quite long and it is. However, it does convey exactly what you will find in the book before you ever turn the first page. If this is the kind of information you are looking for, the title quickly lets you know this is the place to look.

Just in case you have some doubts, the look inside feature provided by Amazon lets the prospective buyer open the book and check out important parts to make absolutely certain he or she will get the information for which they are searching.

At this point the potential buyer can either look inside the book or simply click on the link to go to the main sales page for the book. The screen shot on the next page illustrates the main sales page on Amazon.com. At this page you want to make certain that there are additional details about the book or even a review that includes some details.

This is also a good location for some information about the author of the book to indicate knowledge of the topic.

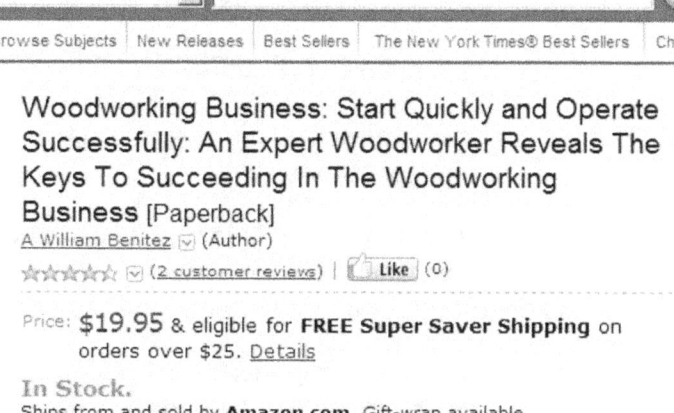

At this Amazon page the prospective buyer can scroll down and read additional details about the book in addition to looking inside. This is an important sales tool but the screen shot below illustrates another critical sales tool.

The web page below was the eStore formerly created for you by Createspace when you published your book through them. Unfortunately, they no longer provide this free service.

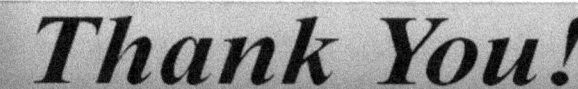

Woodworking Business: Start Quickly and Operate Successfully

About the author:
A. William Benitez has run one-person businesses for over thirty years. He owned woodworking businesses in Tampa, FL and Austin, TX for over twenty years and is now a writer and publisher of how-to information.

An Expert Woodworker Reveals The Keys To Succeeding In The Woodworking Business
Authored by A William Benitez

Praise for Woodworking Business: Start Quickly and Operate Successfully:

"Woodworking Business: Start Quickly and Operate Successfully is a must read with practical tips on every aspect of the woodworking trade. I would recommend this book to anyone in the woodworking profession. The insight within this book will do wonders for your business. It is one of the few books I have read more than once. This book is a remarkable tool that not only helped me in the beginning; it serves as a reference that I can look back on when I have questions about my business."

Chris Looney

"I would like to thank you for your latest book Woodworking Business:Start Quickly and Operate Successfully. It has been of immense
value to me while I start up my own woodworking business. I soon discovered that it is an entire business plan and that alone has saved me hundreds of hours of writing and research. I particularly liked your simplified woodworking chapter which I intend to adopt to improve my profitability."

The eStore is the direct sales page for your book and it is an important tool for making sales and handling every aspect of fulfilling your book orders. There are several important things to remember about your eStore:

> It helps you increase your profits because of the lower commission. Amazon charges a forty percent commission on all book sales. Your eStore only charges a twenty percent commission. This means you make twenty percent more on every book sold through the eStore.
>
> Like purchases made on Amazon.com, all the fulfillment is handled without your involvement. The eStore processes the credit card payment, has the book printed, and handles the shipping directly to your customer.
>
> The eStore sales are reported consistently through your Createspace account and your royalties are deposited in your bank account each month.
>
> You receive a direct link to your eStore so you can connect to it directly from your web site or an email sales message.
>
> You can customize your eStore and include whatever information you wish about your book or yourself.

All of this is available at no cost except for a commission so you only pay for your eStore if you make sales and even then at a lower commission.

> *Throughout this book you will read a lot about Createspace. After working with them for over four years, I am a fan. In addition to the eStore arrangement described above, publishing through Createspace gets you directly into Amazon.com with no additional effort. It allows you to connect at one location and do your entire book publishing and my experience with their customer service has been excellent.*
>
> *I have read some negative comments about them regarding the quality of the various publishing related services they offer. I can't comment directly on them because I handle every aspect myself and just have them handle the printing and fulfillment. However, I can comment on their generic covers because I sometimes use them for proofs before I actually complete my cover design and they have been flexible and quite good quality.*
>
> *As to their customer service, I have had several small issues that were resolved promptly. I also experienced a large issue with one of my customers for whom I published a book with color interior. I ordered forty books and my customer sold them at a presentation. A month or two later one of the book buyers informed the writer that one of the color pictures was completely missing.*
>
> *The writer checked with several of the other buyers and realized that it was a problem and informed me. I contacted Createspace and they immediately printed forty more and shipped them to me and never even took the time to request a copy as evidence. That is customer service that I appreciate.*

Amazon.com and your web site or blog are excellent ways to sell your books but there are other options.

Using Web Sites and Blogs for Free Content

Obviously you want to sell copies of your book and marketing activities are essential but don't lose sight of various ways to use web sites and blogs to get prospective buyers interested in your book or books.

Free content is a great tool to draw interested prospects. The main objective of such content is to establish your expertise in whatever your niche happens to be. Below is a woodworking based web site that has been online for several years and is consistently on the first page of Google when searches are made.

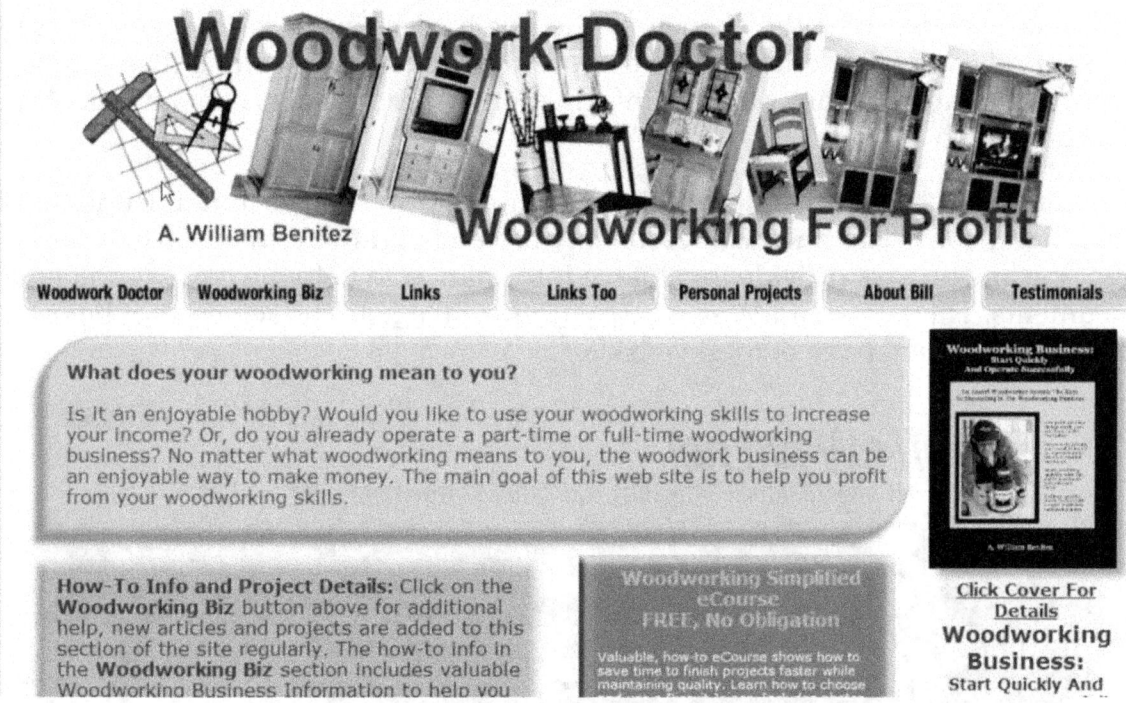

I created this web site over five years ago and it always has good traffic because it is on the first page of Google for "woodworking business" together with the sales page for my woodworking business book.

You can see that this web site has quite a bit on the first page. In addition to linking directly to many interesting articles on the woodworking business, it has an ad for the woodworking business book on the right side. That link takes you directly to the Woodworking Business sales web site.

Also, in the center of the page is a small box with information about a free course called Woodworking Simplified. This ecourse is distributed free by an autoresponder company that keeps track of information on anyone requesting the free ecourse. When someone fills in their first name and email address. The autoresponder sends out the ecourse in daily increments for a total of eight to ten days.

Email marketing can be a good tool but it can also get you in trouble if done incorrectly. Certainly you should inform all your friends and acquaintances about your new book by email, on FaceBook, Twitter, etc., but beyond that you don't want to be a spammer.

To avoid spamming with email you need a double opt in list. Double opt in requires that the individual request that you send them sales material and then also confirm that they made the request for the sales material. If you send emails to strangers who have not gone through this process you wind up accused of spamming and you could lose your Internet Service Provider.

Any autoresponder company facilitates the creation of a double opt in email list whom you can contact regularly. First you prepare a series of short articles on the subject. Make it informational and well organized so it comprises a six to ten part information course of sorts. Then you schedule the lessons in the course to be sent out every day or every other day to persons who request the course. The course information must contain valuable information but should also contain links to your book web site.

There are many autoresponder services at various price ranges but the one that I have found consistent and also reasonably priced is Trafficwave.net. They do a great job and always provide invaluable information to help me create good email documents. Their email address is http://trafficwave.net. The screen shot below illutrates the main page of their web site.

Try a thirty day free trail to find out if it will work for you. Check out their entire site to learn all the possibilities of using an autoresponder.

While autoresponders are good tools for email marketing, there are other good methods. Another method that also involves free content is to give away a complete ecourse on your web site. You can also work out arrangements with other writers or publishers to give away your ecourse as a bonus to their readers.

This free ecourse would have good solid content of value to the readers but also include links to your book's web site. With this method you shouldn't even ask for a name or email address. Make it a totally open, downloadable link and just count on the links within the course itself for potential customers to contact you. People are often more responsive to links that do not require any input.

> **FREE HANDYMAN BUSINESS EBOOK**
>
> Another FREE ebook? Sure, they are free except for name, email address, etc. and you wind up bombarded indefinitely. Not this time! This ebook is really FREE eCourse on how to start and operate a financially successful handyman business. Click the link, the ebook opens, you read it or save it to your PC and share it with friends. No name, no email, no obligation. Plus, got questions about the handyman business, just email bill@positive-imaging.com for free answers.
>
> Click HERE for eCourse NOW.

On the left is a small ad that appears on the Positive Imaging web site for a free Handyman Business eBook or eCourse. A brief course was created for this give away for those who are interested in starting their own handyman business.

The free content is a 23 page eBooklet that is a summary of the book **The Handyman's Guide to Profit: Using Your Skills to Make Money In Any Economy** which is a popular seller for Positive Imaging.

The eBooklet contains lots of information of real value to anyone interested in profiting from the handyman business and several links directly to the sales site for the handyman book

You can get a free sample of this eBooklet at the web site address below: http://billbenitez.com/HandymanQuickCourse.pdf.

A booklet like this can be most helpful with the marketing of non-fiction and how-to books but I believe there must be some way of taking advantage of such a booklet even for a fiction book. The important thing is that the booklet have real value and not simply be a sales pitch for your book.

There are many ways to create these booklets and the simplest one is to use a pdf file. Just create the booklet in any word processor or using PagePlus X4 and then convert the finished product to a pdf file for distribution.

The most common ebooklets are made in normal letter size. You can improve on this by creating your book in a size that better fits a standard monitor screen. This will ensure that the reader can see each page in full on the computer screen and then just move to the next page without scrolling.

To make it even better, you can use a pdf editing program to create bookmarks and navigation buttons on your booklet making it quite professional looking.

Does all that sounds like a lot of work for no money? In fact, everything you do to establish yourself as an expert in your field is time and money well spent. Experts can command higher payment for their work and people will more readily buy books from someone who is an acknowledged expert.

Blogs are another way to distribute content that exhibits your extensive knowledge of any topic and there are many ways to create them. If you have created a web site and have your own domain name and a hosting arrangement, you can easily host a blog using your own domain name.

To do this you simply follow the instructions in your hosting providers support page and create a sub-domain or a folder. For example, you previously saw the sales web site for the Woodworking Business book. I created a folder within that same domain and now have a woodworking business blog where woodworkers can read posts and comment on them and no additional hosting expense.

The blog address is: http://woodworking-business.com/woodworkbiz and the blog is shown below:

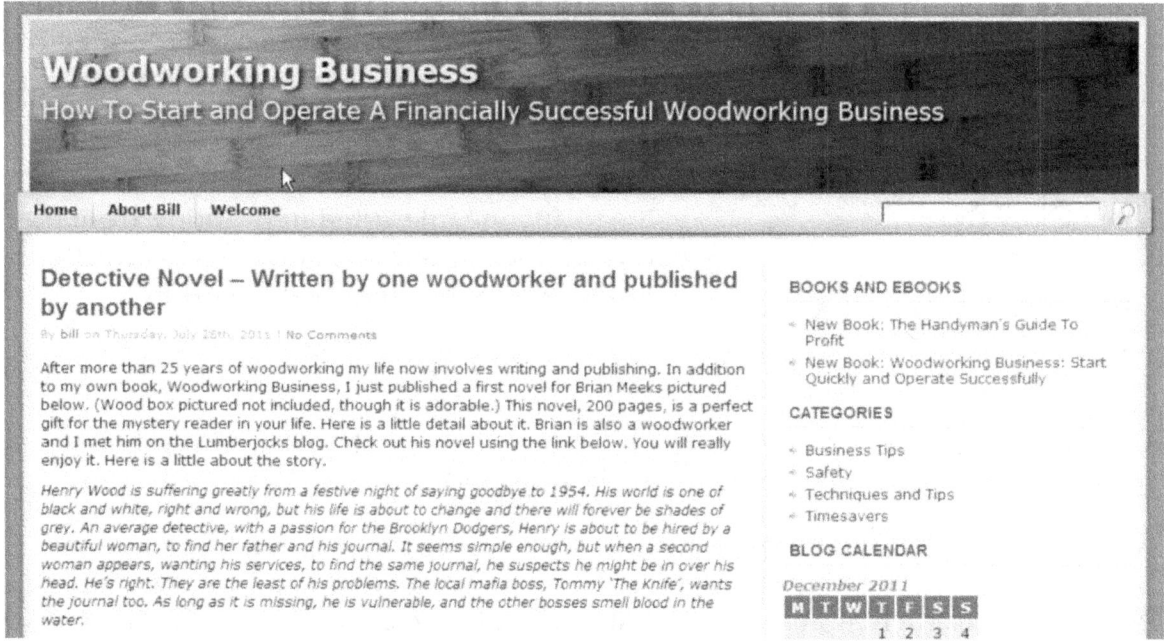

This blog has quite a lot of valuable information and links to free ebooklets. This particular post is about how one woodworker (me) had just published a book for another woodworker (Brian). The post is not really directly about woodworking or the woodworking business but it's still of interest to woodworkers.

Blogs can also be created directly in free blog sites like Wordpress, Blogspot, etc. I prefer to create blogs using the Wordpress software that's available within standard hosting programs.

For more information about web site hosting at the lowest prices and more details about creating your own web sites and blogs, email me at: bill@positive-imaging.com

Below are a couple more blogs on other topics.

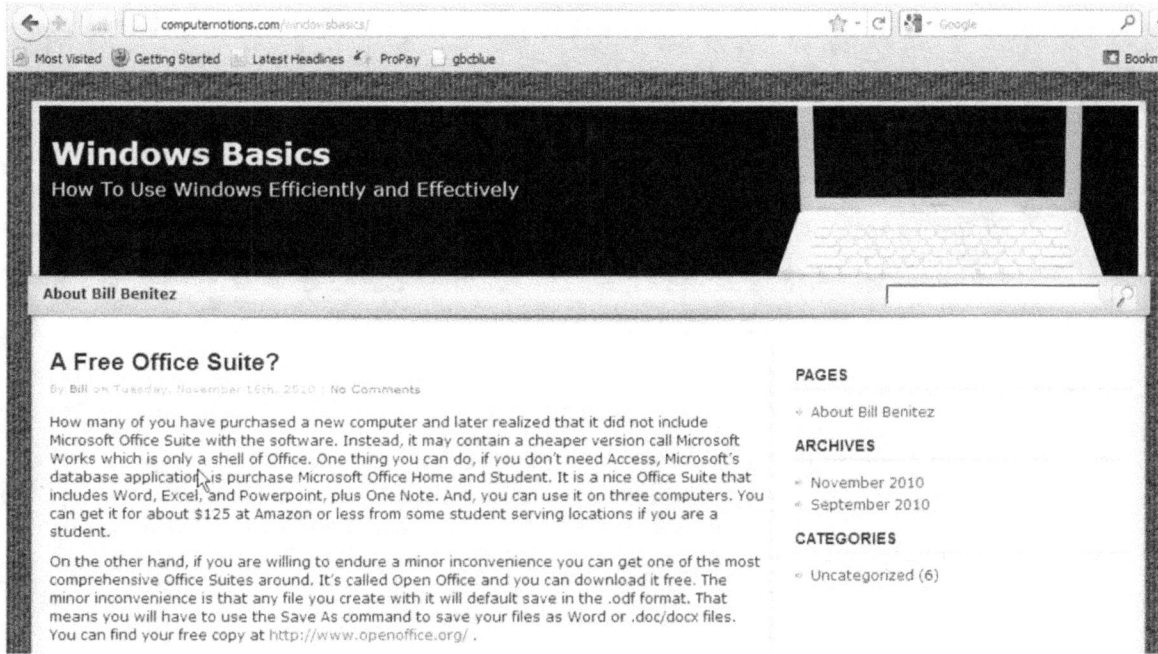

The blog above was created to help Windows users make better use of their computers by teaching some simple things they can easily learn to make their computers more effective tools.

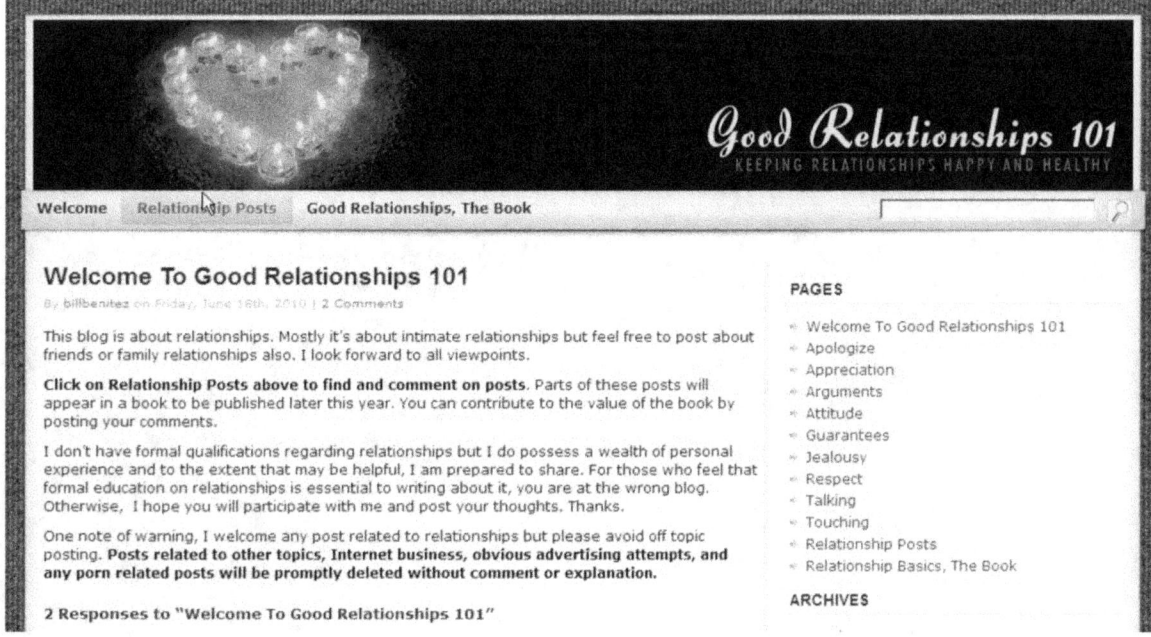

This blog is all about relationships and it also ties in with a book on the subject of happy and healthy relationships.

Below are more blog designs.

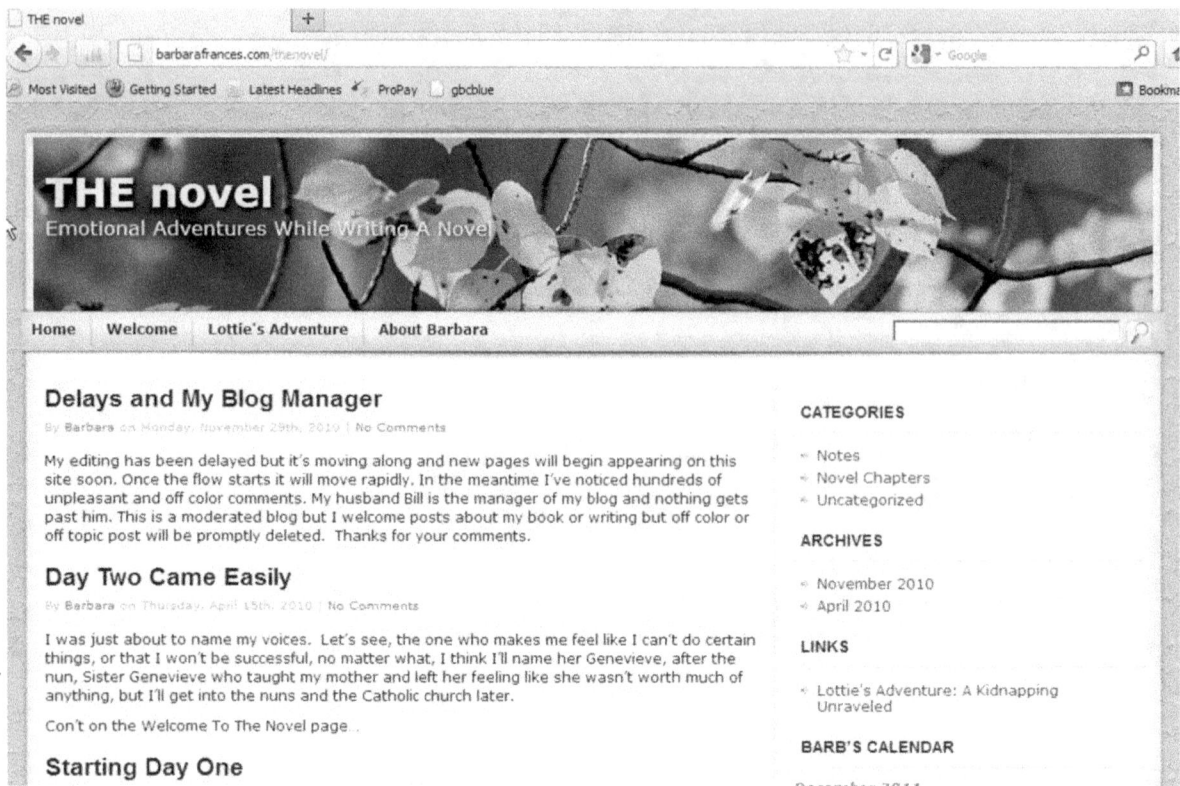

Notice the address on the blog above. This blog is set up as a sub-domain of the writer's web site. On the address of the blog below you can see that it is created on the Wordpress site. You can maintain a blog on this site absolutely free.

Creating free content does take time but I have definitely found it to be worth the effort. It clearly indicates that you value and want to serve your potential customers. Share your knowledge and you will encourage more purchases of your book.

Domain Names For Your Book Web Site

Some believe that getting a domain name should be the first step in creating a web site for a book or for content sharing. I prefer to create my web site and then use the content and design to lead me to a good domain name. Start by using your web site to develop good potential domain names. Don't just come up with one because it may be taken by someone else. You should have several options.

In creating potential domain names consider keywords that are related to your topic. Some topics are quite popular and you may find it difficult to get the domain name you choose. If that happens search for names that are close or for the same name with a descriptive word at the beginning or end. Strive to keep the important words in the domain name if possible.

Getting a good domain name for this book is a prime example. I checked for the domain name selfpublishing and self-publishing and neither was available at the regular domain registration prices. But the domain registration site I use came up with quite a few options including the list below:

    Self-publishingtoday.com
    Self-publishingshop.com
    Self-publishingblog.com
    Self-publishingnow.com
    Self-publishingstore.com
    Self-publishingsite.com
    Qualityselfpublishing.com
    Self-publishing-support.com
    Publishingsimplified.com
    Self-publish-your-writing.com

All of these were available and I now own the last three on the list. I believe that the last one on the list will be best for the web site that I create for my book. I am considering buying one or two of the others.

One way to get exactly the name you want is to use a sub-domain on a web site you already own. For example, I own the positive-imaging.com domain name. By going into my hosting site I can create a sub-domain name selfpublishing or self-publishing and then the name of my book's web site could be:

Selfpublishing.positive-imaging.com or self-publishing.positive-imaging.com

This may work well for me because it contains the exact name of my book and it has the further advantage that I don't need to buy a domain name or web hosting since I am using an existing domain name and web site hosting account.

Web Site Hosting

There are many web site hosting companies that you can use to host your web sites. Go Daddy is one that I have dealt with for many years and they have always done a good job. They have all the services you could ever need at reasonable prices. You can buy your domain names and the hosting for your web site at a single location and they have excellent support services if you have questions or need assistance. There is no need to pay more for either domain names or for web hosting services. Go Daddy services are available at: http://godaddy.com .

There are other options and since I have more than 25 web sites and blogs, web hosting could have become quite costly. Instead of hosting my sites with a regular hosting arrangement, I became a web site hosting reseller for Hostgator. This allows me to host all my web site for only $24.95 per month plus I can sell web hosting services to others. Not only do my 25 plus web sites and blogs cost me less than $1.00 per month each to host, I make extra money selling web hosting services.

Hostgator offers an excellent service and support and makes maintaining your web sites quite easy. If your business involves many web sites it is definitely wise to consider a hosting reseller account with Hostgator. You can learn about it at http://hostgator.com .

Whether you choose Go Daddy, Hostgator, or some other domain registrar or web hosting company, most of them have excellent tutorials and tech services available for their customers. You can learn a great deal from them that will help you make better use of your web sites.

Twenty

Creating Sharp and Clear Screen Shots

Throughout this book, and perhaps in your book, there are many graphics created using screen shots. Here they are intended to make each task in preparing a final print-ready file, and the many other aspects of publishing as clear as possible. The screen shots are critically important to ensure every step of the process is understood. Obtaining printer-ready screen shots can be problematic because screen shot software applications capture at either 72 or 96 dpi because of the limits of computer monitors. This resolution is fine for an ebook to be read on a monitor but totally inadequate for printing, whether in color or black and white.

All the screen shots in this book were captured using Snap 5, a good, solid application created and sold for only $19.95 by Ashampoo, a company that sells various kinds of software. Snap 5 does a good job of capturing screen shots but is still limited by monitor resolution and inadequate for quality printing which requires 300 dpi. I use Snap 5 because it has many great features that allow me to mark up screen shots with arrows, text, and other things to make them even more useful.

Because Snap 5 and other screen shot software are limited by monitor resolution, a photo manipulation software is needed to improve the quality of each screen shot so that it will look good and sharp when it is printed.

There are many good applications to manipulate graphics files including Photoshop, which is among the best but quite expensive. And there are many others costing much less including PhotoPlus X4 but both of these are only adequate. Depending on the size of a screen shot, even these applications can fail to produce the level of quality important to printing a book.

As graphics applications go, one of the best and certainly the biggest bargain, is Gimp. It is, in many ways, comparable to Photoshop and may be downloaded completely free. If you don't already own a quality graphic manipulation application, Gimp is an excellent choice and can be downloaded at:

http://download.cnet.com/GIMP/3000-2192_4-10073935.html.

You can also download Gimp from their own web site but CNET is the easiest and safest place to download free software.

The manipulation of the screen shots is the most important step and if not done properly will render the screen shots fuzzy. Attempting to simply change the dpi from 96 to 300 by resampling them will cause them to break down and lose sharpness.

Step one is to determine the actual size of the images needed for your book. For example, almost all the images for this book are 6 inches wide and varying heights except for two images that were placed vertically and were therefore 9.5 inches wide. When I resized the images I made them the exact width to fit the page. That way, when they were placed on the page they were not stretched or shrunk from their original size. This helps to maintain the critical sharpness.

It's best to first edit the color, levels, contrast, and brightness to their final settings. Then you are ready to increase the DPIs. The critical step in resizing screen shots is to turn resampling to **None**. The default is usually set to bicubic or cubic. Leaving this on could cause your images to blur. When you turn off resampling, the pixels per inch will simply be increased without any manipulation that would cause issues. You will notice that even though the screen shot will actually become a smaller size in inches, they will show up larger on your screen. This is because the number of pixels per inch are increasing drastically. Usually you go from 96 pixels per inch to 300.

The most significant problem arises when you attempt to resize the image after you have increased the pixels to 300 per inch. For example, if you begin with an image that is 9 inches wide at 96 pixels per inch, increasing it to 300 pixels per inch will reduce the size of the image to less than 3 inches wide. If you can use the image at that size, then the previously described method will work fine. If you need to increase the size of the image to 6 inches it will degrade the image and could cause it to soften or even blur.

I had some luck with the images when I did not have to enlarge them much but if, as was the case with some images, they became quite small, then going to 6 inches wide made them too soft. As I worked on the book it became obvious that simply avoiding the resampling was not enough to keep the images sharp once I enlarged them. I needed an application that would help me get the quality I wanted.

I did find an excellent application specifically designed to resize graphics without degrading the quality. Unfortunately it cost $99. They did give me a thirty day trial period. I tested it on several of my screen shots and it worked great so I did buy the software. I think it might be too much to spend if you are simply going to write and publish one book. In my case, my work often involves screen shots that I have to manipulate so it was a worthwhile investment.

The resizing application is appropriately called Perfect Resize 7 and is made by onOne Software Company. It only works with .jpg photographs but that poses no difficulty. The steps to resizing a photograph with Perfect Resize 7 are quite simple. Just open the photograph and then use the gauges on the right side column to adjust the photograph to the size and pixels per inch that you choose and then you click apply and save the file. You can either overwrite the original file or rename and save the file in a different location. Perfect Resize 7 is available at:

http://www.ononesoftware.com.

In Chapter Eleven there are complete instructions for placing screen shots and other images into your book. Once you have the images ready, you can use those instructions to place them properly in your book.

Notes and Ideas

Twenty-One

Final Notes

Doing It All Yourself

To anyone reading this book it will be obvious that I like to maintain complete control over my writing and publishing and do almost all the work myself. There are reasons for my actions and they have changed over time.

When I started I was doing everything myself because I didn't want to risk my personal funds investing in a new venture. I had much more time than money so I spent my time learning how to do everything myself. It wasn't easy but I did learn a lot and was able to do most everything alone.

Now I can afford to invest in the necessary steps but since I learned to do them myself I find that more comfortable. This is the fourth book where I have done everything including the writing, editing, typesetting, cover design, publishing, and marketing. Of all these, my weak area is marketing but I am working on learning much more.

Will you be doing it all yourself? This is an important decision. I wrote this book so it could be used as a guide for doing it all yourself. That is the reason for all the detail and instructions.

Using Createspace As A POD Printer

I have been using Createspace to print all my books and fulfill book orders since 2008 and have always been well satisfied with their work and their customer service. While I have had a couple of issues come up during those years, Createspace has always handled things with excellent and prompt customer service.

The way Createspace handles the printing and order fulfillment on Amazon and your eStore always works well so I never hesitate recommending them to anyone. I'm sure there are other services that can handle all the necessary steps but I like Createspace and appreciate how my books are automatically listed fully on Amazon.com with no additional effort on my part.

I strongly advise any self publisher with limited experience to use Createspace to print their book and fulfill book orders.

Besides fulfilling book orders for you in the US and Europe, they also do an excellent job of keeping records for you and depositing your royalties directly into your bank account.

Createspace Professional Services

Unlike their POD Printing and book order fulfillment, I can't recommend Createspace professional services. Not because they aren't good but because I won't recommend any service or company I haven't used. Their professional services might be excellent but I have no way of knowing for certain since I handle all aspects of preparing my print-ready files and create my own covers.

Because I know that Createspace is a reputable company I suggest that you visit the Createspace community, one or more self publishing blogs or lists, and just ask about their professional services. You will probably get plenty of input that may help you decide if you should use them. I also suggest that if some publishing services company is recommended to you by someone you trust, it might be a good idea to consider them for the services you need.

If you are going to use Createspace professional services or those of any other company, take the time for due diligence. Often a person may not get what he or she really wanted because of not making their desires clear. If you want a cover designed, you may not have the skills to do the job but you should know what you want and be able to explain it clearly to another person. If you don't make your desires clear for any publishing related services you will probably be disappointed by the results.

I spend time everyday visiting self publishing blogs and lists and often read posts by individuals planning to self publish a book asking questions that show no effort has been made to learn even the most basic things about self publishing. Whether you are going to do it yourself or pay others to do much of the work, it is critical that you have sufficient knowledge to recognize quality work even if you can't produce it yourself. If you haven't taken the time to acquire even the most basic details about self publishing, it's a good idea to do so before trying to self publish your book.

PagePlus X4

I have used PagePlus X4 for several years and find it to be a great tool for creating either paperback or ebooks. It has always worked well for me and I have often recommended it to other writers. Besides the quality of the software, the old versions are now available for an extraordinarily low price.

It is not the only desktop publishing software that may be used to produce your book but it is the only one that I can recommend from first-hand experience. I know you will find it an excellent publishing tool.

I believe that choosing to use Word or some other word processing application to create your final print-ready file makes the job more difficult. Even so, many writers still use them to create their files for the POD printer. As with so many things, that decision is entirely yours.

Book, Ebook, or Both

With the great popularity of ebooks they are becoming the self publishing route of choice. I have consistently created a paperback first and then followed that with an ebook version. Either way will work but with the present book buying market you definitely want to have both versions available for your prospective readers.

I think that my choice has always been paperbacks because I found that the readers of my woodworking and handyman books prefer to read paperbacks. That may be different for this book on self publishing but I still chose to do the paperback first.

Marketing Your Book or Ebook

If your goal is to sell copies of your book then marketing is of critical importance. There are many ways to market your book but good marketing information merits a book of its own. There are many books and other sources of marketing information that I have found of real value over the years in learning to market my books. The latest one that I feel comfortable recommending is a great resource by Patricia Fry the Executive Director of SPAWN (Small Publishers, Artists and Writers Network).

"Promote Your Book: Over 250 Proven Low-Cost Tips and Techniques For The Enterprising Author" contains a wealth of ways to promote and market your book and I consider it required reading for self publishers who do their own marketing.

I also encourage writer/publishers to join SPAWN because their monthly newsletter and many other services are invaluable to any self publisher. Membership is a small investment that will help you write, publish, and market your book.

Changes From Screen Shots

You may notice some differences between the screen shots created from the files of this book and the final book. This is evidence that changes are a continuing part of writing and publishing a book. My books continue changing right up to the last proof. I normally order at least three different proofs before I am comfortable with the final product.

Even though my relationship with Createspace has advanced to the point that they do not require me to purchase proofs before publishing, I always order proofs and I advise you to do the same. Seeing the complete book in your hands will motivate you to read it carefully and you will find mistakes which can be corrected before publishing.

Another Benefit Of POD

Ever considered what would happen if a couple of months after your book was published someone pointed out a serious error that you feel must be corrected. It seems so serious that you want to take the book off the market rather than have others see the error.

Without POD this would be a nightmare and it might even be a nightmare with some POD companies but not with Createspace. If this happens you can resolve the problem by correcting the error in your print-ready file and going back into your Createspace dashboard and changing the interior file. The minute you do this the book is taken off the market until your uploaded file is checked. Then you simply purchase a proof, check it and publish again and your corrected book is back on the market.

There are some conditions and they seem obvious. Since you have already purchased an ISBN and registered with the Library of Congress, you can't change the size of the book or the cover.

> *One of the writers for whom I published a book found himself in this situation. I had cautioned him about the editing even though it was not part of my contract but he believed his book to be well edited so I published. After the book was published, it looked great but it did need editing and since he was an academic it became a real problem for him. Because it was POD with Createspace we were able to have it edited again and bring it back on the market quickly.*

Glossary

Accounting: Detailed maintenance and reporting of the financial transactions and state of a business.

Acknowledgments: The section of a book containing recognition of persons who have influenced a book or made a difference in the life of the author.

Active Table of Contents: A section called "Contents," that appears in the book's front matter and lists the book's chapters, sections, or parts with active links leading to their opening pages.

Advertising: Calling public attention to a book or other product to increase sales.

Android: Operating system for smartphones and touchpad computers that also serve as ebook readers.

Appendix: A part of the book that comes after all the chapters and contains supplemental material which doesn't fit into a chapter.

Artist: A person engaged in some type of fine art including drawing, painting, designing, photographing, directing, writing, etc.

Author: A person who writes books and other works.

Autoresponder: A service used to respond automatically to requests for information from potential customers and distribute information in hopes of encouraging sales.

Back Matter: Opposite of front matter. The location of materials such as appendixes, notes, references, a glossary, or an index.

Background: The part of a cover upon which all objects and text appears.

Backup: A duplicate of valuable data created by using backup tools and maintained in a safe location for use in the event that the original is somehow lost or rendered useless.

Blackberry: A brand of smartphone for wireless email that can also be used as an ebook reader.

Bleed: A bleed extends outside the normal trim area of a book's page or cover.

Blogging: A blog is basically an online journal (Web log). Blogging is writing in a blog.

BookPlus: A built-in application that is part of PagePlus and is used to assemble parts or chapters of a book into a cohesive group for ease of writing, editing, and creating a .pdf file.

Book Spine: The part of a book which is visible when the book is stacked on a shelf. It is on the opposite end of the book opening.

Bowker, Inc.: The official source for ISBNs in the USA

Brick-and-Mortar Book Store: Describes retailers who sells books in a store as opposed to online.

Built-in Applications: Applications for various functions that come as part of a software program for no additional cost.

Bullet List: A text list where each item is separate with a bullet point or dot of some form.

Chapter: A division of a book with a title and\or number.

Clickbank: This is a leading retailer of digital products and an excellent place to sell ebooks.

Collecting: Obtaining payment for the work, products, and services of a business which is critical to its financial success.

Contract: An agreement between two or more parties regarding the performance of certain tasks. Contracts are intended to ensure the proper completion of the tasks and full payment upon completion.

Contributors: Persons whom contribute to the writing and creation of a book or other product.

Copy: A duplicate of a page or group of pages such as a book.

Copyright: Ownership of intellectual property, such as a book or ebook, protected by law.

Cover Creator: An online tool on the Createspace web site that facilitates the simple creation of book covers for books printed by them.

Editor: A Person who edits the content and the form of a book and recommends corrections to a manuscript.

Cover: The outside, protective surface of a book whether paper or hard material.

Cover Design: The layout on the cover of a book, usually intended to be attractive or alluring.

Createspace: One of the largest and most popular POD (print on demand) publisher/printer.

Credit Line: Line of text giving copyright credit to the owner of the copyright.

Data: Pieces of information stored and used for various purposes.

Design (Book and Cover): Layout, selection of font and font size and typesetting of a book and its cover.

Discipline: In writing, a regimen develop to improve skills and increase productivity.

Disclaimer: A statement disclaiming responsibility for the actions of others in relation to information you are providing with a book or some other source of information.

Distributor: One who sells products or services to retailers instead of to consumers.

Domain Name: The registered Web address or URL of an individual or company.

Download: The movement of files from a server, a network, or the Internet to a computer or other form of storage.

DPI (Dots per Inch): Expression of the graphic resolution of a graphic file (image) with 72 dpi being ideal for monitors and 300 dpi being ideal for printing.

Draft: A preliminary document subject to revision.

eBook: A book transmitted in digital form and read using a computer or some other digital device used especially for reading digital text in various forms.

Editing: The revision and correction of a manuscript.

Endorsement (Blurb): Complimentary comment by someone recommending a book, usually found near the front of the book.

eStore: A single book web site created by Createspace for the sale of each book they print.

Final Manuscript: A manuscript that is complete and has been fully edited making it ready to typeset for printing.

Footnote: A footnote is a reference that appears at the bottom of a book page.

Font: An assortment of type in various styles and sizes.

Formatting: The process of laying out a manuscript to create book pages including text effect applied to characters to make them appear bold, italic, etc.

Forum: A location on the Internet that is open for discussions of a specific or general topic by members.

Genre: A kind of book based on its subject matter and may include romance, sci-fi, self-help, true crime, and how-to.

Free Content: Interesting and valuable information made available on the Internet at no cost.

Free Software: Software applications available for download from the Internet at no cost.

Ghostwriter: A writer who writes a book for which some other person will receive credit when it is published.

GIMP: An image manipulation application similar to Photoshop but open source so it is free to anyone.

GoDaddy: A large web hosting and domain registering company with reasonable prices and good service.

Grammar: The correct use of language in speech or writing.

Grayscale: Images in black and white and gray shades.

Hardcover Book: Book with hard pasteboard material forming a durable cover and spine.

Hobby: Activity pursued for pleasure instead of as an occupation.

Home Office: An office, located in a home, that is used to run a small business.

HostGator: A web hosting provider who also allows the establishment of reseller accounts

Hyphenation: The joining of words with a hyphen.

Illustrator: An excellent but expensive graphic program perfect for covers, signs, and many other projects.

Images: A painted or photographed likeness of people, places, or things.

Index: A List of words at the end of a book to guides readers to specific pages on which subjects may be found.

Interior graphics: Pictures and other graphical images that appear within the contents of a book.

International Standard Book Number (ISBN): Unique 13-digit number (10 or 13 digits prior to 2007) that identifies a specific version of a book and issued only to Publishers.

Introduction: An early part of a book describing and leading up to the main contents of the book.

iPad: A tablet, touchscreen computer made by Apple Computer, Inc.

Justification: The spacing of words and letters in a column to ensure that there are even margins on the right and left side.

Keyword Tool: A Google tool that facilitates determining the popularity of certain keywords and finds useful related words that also make keywords.

Keyword: Important word or phrase are attractive to search engines and can bring increased Internet traffic for your book..

Kindle: A popular ebook reader created by Amazon.com and used to read Kindle books, a specialized version of ebooks.

Layers: Invisible sheets that are stacked to facilitate various elements in a photographic image.

Layout: The arrangement or plan for some design.

Manuscript: The complete version of a book as an electronic or paper file prepared by the writer or artist. Finalized manuscripts are used for book pages.

Marketing: Promotional and advertising efforts to sell books.

Master Page: A specialized page used to duplicate certain elements in a book on a large number of pages without having to repeated create the design.

MCSE: Microsoft Certified System Engineer, a certification issue by Microsoft after taking and passing at least seven difficult exams.

Microsoft Word: The word processor application that is a part of the Microsoft Office Suite.

Mobipocket: An excellent ebook reader and creator software that facilitates the creation of ebooks for the kindle and many other readers.

Multi-level List: A list of items in a book or manuscript that contains various levels separated by numbers, letters, and even bullets.

Networking: Meeting with others to expand your social network or influence by developing new relationships with people.

Niche: A specialized and targeted market of a particular interest, topic or subject that is potentially profitable.

Nook
An ebook reader created by Barnes and Noble for reading the ebooks sold in their stores and other ebooks.

Number List
A list of items in a book or manuscript that is separated by numbers.

NVU: An open source (free) web site creation tool with WYSIWYG and HTML modes plus site management features.

Objective: Something you choose to accomplish or attain.

Online Bookseller (Online Retailer): A bookstore selling books on the Internet to customers at retail or discounted prices.

Online Marketing: Advertising or selling books or other products over the Internet.

OpenOffice: An open source (free) office suite including applications for word processing, spreadsheets, presentations, graphics, and databases.

Outline: A written account of the main features of a book to facilitate organization of a draft.

PagePlus: An excellent desktop publishing application that is a main topic in this book.

PaperRater: An excellent and free editing web site that helps writers improve their manuscripts and their writing skills.

Paragraph: A portion of text in a book or manuscript dealing with a particular idea and beginning on a new line.

Part: A section of a book or manuscript.

Paypal: A fast, simple, and safe way to collect fees from your customers.

PC: The abbreviation for an IBM compatible personal computer.

PDF (Portable Document Format): An Adobe Systems file format that can be easily and precisely reproduced on different systems regardless of the computer manufacturer.

Permission: Obtaining agreement from a copyright holder to reproduce or publish copyrighted material.

Photocopy: A reproduction on copying equipment of any document or other image.

Photographer: A person who practices photography professionally.

PhotoPlus: An excellent imaging manipulation application created by Serif, the same company that created PagePlus.

Photoshop: A high end image manipulation software program created by Adobe and used by many professional photographers, designers, etc.

Planning: To arrange a method or scheme beforehand to perform any work or enterprise.

POD Publisher: A publisher who prints books only after receiving an order for them. Usually these are actually POD printers who handle the fulfillment for self publishers.

Preface: A beginning statement in a book setting forth its purpose and scope.

Print-on-Demand (POD): Publishing arrangement in which books are printed only as orders are placed.

Print-Ready
Final PDF files of a book that have been flight-checked and are ready to go to the printer. See also PDF (Portable Document File).

Professional Level Skills: Ability to perform tasks with outcomes equal to that of professionals in the same field.

Promote: To encourage the sale and acceptance of a book or other product.

Proof: Printing of a book completed before the book's official release date

Proofreading: Readthrough of typeset material to ensure that content matches the book's manuscript. Incorrect grammar, punctuation, spelling or usage, is queried to the editor.

Propay: A merchant account company that accepts small businesses and does not require a minimum monthly fee.

Publication Date: Official date when a book is to be released to the public.

Publishing Services Company: A company that provides services to publishers for a fee.

Publishing Services: The various services used by a publisher including, but not limited to, editing, proofreading, formatting, etc.

Publishing: Issuing or printed or other textual or graphic materials or software.

Review: Professional book reviewer's published opinion of a particular book in a periodical or online.

Royalty: Payment to a book's author that is usually a percentage of sales revenue.

San Serif Font: A typeface without the small features called serifs at the end of each stroke.

Screen Shot: A reproduction of all or a part of the display on a monitor saved as a graphics file.

Scribus: An open source (free) software application used for professional quality page layout.

Section: Similar to a part of chapter in a book or manuscript

Secure eBooks: An online company that facilitates securing ebooks using an activation process.

Self-Publishing: A book production method in which the writer assume the financial risk of publishing and usually either does or contracts most of the work normally handled by a traditional publisher including editing, distribution, and marketing.

Serif Font: A typeface with the small features called serifs at the end of each stroke.

Shopping Cart: Basically an online store with images and details about products for sale with links to complete information about the products and facilitating their purchase using credit cards.

Small Business: There are varying definition for what constitutes a small business ranging from the one-person business up to businesses with an annual income of less than five million dollars. For our purposes it is a home-based business with few, if any, employees that is independently owned and operated.

Small Press: Smaller publishing house that releases books often intended for specialized audiences.

Smashwords: The world's largest distributor of independent ebooks. A good place for ebook publishers.

Spine Width: The width of the edge of the book that connects the front and back covers and is visible on a bookshelf.

Style: The manner in which something is expressed apart from the actual content.

Subsidy Publisher: Unlike Vanity Publishers, subsidy publishers do pay part of the publishing cost and market the books through retailers. A writer will bear some of the cost for editing, typesetting, proofreading, and printing. Some of them also require a writer to purchase a minimum number of the books.

Table of Contents: This section, always called "Contents," appears in the book's front matter. It lists the book's chapters and their opening page numbers.

Target Audience: The individuals who would be interested in a specific book and upon whom marketing should be concentrated.

Template: Anything that serves as a pattern for the cutting or assembly of some item or page.

Termination Clause: Section in a contract or agreement describing the actions necessary to terminate the agreement.

Text: The actual wording of anything written or printed.

Title: The name of a book, poem, picture, painting, piece of music, etc.

Trade Paperback: A trade paperback is bound with a paper or heavy stock cover, usually with a larger trim size than that of a mass-market paperback. Compare Mass-Market Paperback.

Traditional Publisher: A company who publishes books selected from thousands submitted and then handle all aspects of editing, printing, marketing, and distribution.

Trim Size: The Final physical size of a book page after it is bound and trimmed.

Tutorials: Programmed instructions on a specific topic often provided online with the student at a computer.

Typesetting: Formatting a book on a computer so as to result in the desired layout, font and appearance on a printed page.

Upload: Move a file from a computer to a server, network, the Internet., or some external storage device.

Vanity Press (Vanity Publisher): A company who publishes books financed solely by the writer. Vanity publishes leave the entire responsibility of marketing to the writer of the book.

Virtual Book Tour (VBT): An Advertising method focusing on publicizing a book on the Internet and including the use of ads on Web sites.

Vocabulary: The collection of words in use and comprehended by a specific person.

Web Plus: An excellent, easy to use, web creation software from Serif, Inc.

Web Site Hosting: The placement of a web site on a server to make it visible to anyone surfing the Internet.

Web Site Tonight: A web creation online application available from many hosting retailer to facilitate the creation of your own web site.

Web Site: A group of pages on the World Wide Web considered a single entity.

Word Choice: Choosing the best words to make your writing clear and comprehensive to your readers.

Word of Mouth: Free advertising for a book by satisfied readers who recommend it to friends, family members, and other.

WorkBook: A manual of instructions intended to teach the reader how to perform certain tasks.

WritePlus: A word processor application built in to the PagePlus desktop publishing application.

Writing: To compose by setting down words by hand or with a computer or other device.

Yahoo Small Business: Yahoo's package for small businesses that includes domain name registration, web site hosting, web design templates, web creation online software, and ecommerce help.

Notes and Ideas

About A. William (Bill) Benitez

After spending much of my youth working in construction in Tampa, Florida, I went to work for local government managing federal assistance programs for several years and then as a consultant to government agencies. During those years the National Association of Housing and Redevelopment Officials asked me to write a book about housing rehabilitation. "Housing Rehabilitation: A Guidebook For Municipal Programs," sold thousands of copies and while I wasn't paid, I gained national publicity and parlayed that publicity into a one person business writing, publishing, and consulting for local governments across the country. In addition to the consulting, I wrote and published seven more books and a monthly newsletter on housing rehabilitation.

This was well before the advent of POD so publishing those books involved a significant investment. After the election in 1980, all federal financing for housing rehabilitation activities dried up and the consulting and publishing business diminished. Finally, I returned to construction and home repair and then to the woodworking business for over 20 years first in Tampa, Florida and then in Austin, Texas.

During those years in woodworking I wrote and published a small book called "Simplified Woodworking I: A Business Guide For Woodworkers" and it sold well for a couple of years. I also published a newsletter called "Simplified Woodworking" that never really took off but was a good writing and publishing experience.

In 1998, in response to poor technical support for my wife's computer, I managed to fix it and that peaked my interest in computers. That early interest led me to move into information technology obtaining both an A+ and MCSE certification (Microsoft Certified Systems Engineer). For years I've worked as the network administrator for a large national brand hotel.

In 2007 my wife wrote an excellent children's book but couldn't generate interest from a traditional publisher. Since I had published books years earlier, I decided to publish her book and began to learn all I could about POD Printing. Publishing her book was a real learning experience and it took several tries to get my files approved for printing. After that I published a book that I wrote on the woodworking business and decided to start my own publishing company. Since then my company Positive Imaging, LLC has published eight more paperbacks and several ebooks on Kindle, Smashwords, and Clickbank.

Everything described in this book is based on my first-hand experience writing, formatting, creating covers, and publishing the books and ebooks listed in the Other Books section at the end of this book. I've hired graphic artists to do some covers and other jobs but create the covers for my own books. I also hired someone to translate my handyman book into Spanish but for the most part I performed every task on my books. I use the software that I recommend and the related web sites to create books and I do business with the recommended companies regularly.

Note: *I make some specific recommendations regarding certain software applications. These recommendations are based solely on my experiences with the software. I have no interest in any of the companies that make the software nor do I profit in any way when these software applications are purchased by anyone.*

I enjoy sharing all kinds of information with others and spend a lot of time every day answering questions. I honestly believe that anyone willing to take the time to follow the steps described in this book can learn how to publish quality books.

Disclaimer

To handle all aspects of publishing books, including the final formatting, layout, and cover, there is a lengthy learning curve for those skills you don't already possess. Publishing a quality book is time consuming, hard work because there is much to learn and do. With a willingness to learn and the persistence to continue trying when you fail at any task, you have a good chance of success.

> *Over the years I've managed to learn a great deal about woodworking, home repair, computer technology, network technology, writing, web design, publishing, and operating home based businesses by home study and practical experience. My efforts at learning have helped me develop many skills and reasonable competence in business. I believe that anyone with as much or more education and training can successfully self-publish books and even operate a publishing business. That being said, I can't, nor can anyone, guarantee that you or anyone else will succeed in publishing or any other business and no such guarantees are expressed or implied regarding your own results using the information in this book.*

Some individuals are more apt to profit from self publishing than others due to the level of their skills, business acumen, and communication ability. Your interest in this book is an indication that you are among those individuals, but even so there is no guarantee that you will succeed.

Business of any kind involves the risk of loss, including, but not necessarily limited to: money, time, and energy. In addition to the financial and time considerations, every effort has been made to accurately describe all the publishing and business related experiences in precise detail but the author nor the publisher can be held liable for your failure to succeed financially or for any legal or financial difficulties your activities may encounter, even if you inform them prior to or after these situations occur.

The user of this information agrees that he or she is solely responsible for the consequences of such use. It is also the user's responsibility to conduct a reasonable level of due diligence prior to making any business or legal decisions. The information contained and distributed in this book is not intended as nor should it be considered professional, business, or legal advice.

For any questions please contact bill@positive-imaging.com

Other Books From Positive Imaging, LLC

Paperback

Woodworking Business:
Start Quickly And Operate Successfully
by A. William Benitez
http://woodworkingbusinessbook.com

The Handyman's Guide To Profit
Using Your Skills To Make Money In Any Economy
by A. William Benitez
http://handyman-business-guide.com

Lottie's Adventure:
Facing The Monster
by Barbara Frances
http://lottiesadventure.com

Peace And Healing For The World Using Altars
Lucretia Jones and Gaila Slaughter
http://peaceandhealingfortheworld.com

The End Of All Worries:
We Are All One
by Irie Glajar
http://the-end-of-all-worries.com/

Teach For Life
Essays On Modern Education For Teachers, Students, and Parents
by Irie Glajar
http://teachforlife.positive-imaging.com/

Deep Photographs
The Education of a Sociologist
by David Weiner
https://www.createspace.com/3723277

Digital Books (ebooks)

Starting and Operating A Woodworking Business
How To Make Money With Your Skills
by A. William Benitez
http://woodworking-business.com

Lottie's Adventure:
Facing The Monster
by Barbara Frances
https://www.smashwords.com/books/view/665238

The Handyman's Guide To Profit
Using Your Skills To Make Money In Any Economy
by A. William Benitez
https://www.smashwords.com/books/view/28293

Teach For Life
Essays On Modern Education For Teachers, Students, and Parents
by Irie Glajar
https://www.smashwords.com/books/view/42694

www.ingramcontent.com/pod-product-compliance
Lightning Source LLC
Chambersburg PA
CBHW081348080526
44588CB00016B/2416